REPORTING ISLAM

REPORTING ISLAM

Media Representations of British Muslims

Elizabeth Poole

I.B.Tauris *Publishers*

London • New York

Published in 2002 by I.B.Tauris & Co. Ltd
6 Salem Road, London W2 4BU
175 Fifth Avenue, New York NY 10010
www.ibtauris.com

In the United States of America and Canada distributed by
Palgrave Macmillan a division of St Martin's Press
175 Fifth Avenue, New York NY 10010

A full CIP record for this book is available from the British Library
A full CIP record for this book is available from the Library of Congress

ISBN 1–86064–686–7 hardback
ISBN 1–86064–687–5 paperback

Library of Congress Catalog card number available

Copy-edited and laser-set by Oxford Publishing Services, Oxford
Printed and bound in Great Britain by MPG Books Ltd, Bodmin

Contents

List of Tables

List of Figures

Acronyms and Abbreviations

BMMS	*British Muslims Monthly Survey*
CERD	United Nations Committee on the Elimination of Racial Discrimination
CMCR	Centre for Mass Communications Research
CRE	Commission for Racial Equality
FBI	Federal Bureau of Investigation
G8	Group of Eight (leading industrial nations)
GCSE	General Certificate of Secondary Education
ID	identity
MoD	Ministry of Defence
NUJ	National Union of Journalists
OFSTED	Office for Standards in Education
RE	religious education
UKACIA	UK Action Committee on Islamic Affairs
WTC	World Trade Center

Acknowledgements

Here, I have the opportunity to thank those people who have been important in helping me, intellectually and emotionally, to complete this book. First, I would like to mention staff at the Centre for Mass Communication Research, University of Leicester, in particular my supervisor, Professor Annabelle Sreberny; but also Ralph Negrine, Roger Dickinson, Chris Newbold, Margaret Crawford, Corin Flint and Cathy Melia for all their support and advice; Elaine Styles for her help with the audience research and of course, those of you who participated in it; and special thanks to Rebecca Eynon and Jenny Allsopp for their heartfelt encouragement; you made this time easier for me and a lot more fun! Thanks also to staff at Staffordshire University and other friends for the after-care and interest in my work. I am grateful for all the postgraduate friends I have gathered along the way. Go for it guys! Thanks also to Philippa Brewster for her interest in this project and Susan Lawson, who has shared a long (not so hot) summer with me striving to work in days and months that were never quite long enough. Can we have a proper holiday yet?

Thank you especially to my loving family, Richard, Mum and Dad, and David for your consistent support and inspiration. I owe these special people more than I can say. And to Katrina and David, thank you for the happiness that is Isabella. The efforts and sacrifices involved in making this book mean that I dedicate its soul to you.

Preface:
after 11 September 2001

This book was due to go to press in September 2001. Given my argument in the introduction that we can only analyse media coverage in relation to the political conditions within which it is produced, it seemed important following 11 September to try and determine if the framework established in this research was still relevant.

In this preface I attempt to explore the complex relationship between coverage and the current political context before going on to make some general observations about coverage in its early stages. However, to avoid presenting the kind of anecdotal evidence I criticize in the main body of this book, I have examined a week's coverage on British Muslims from Wednesday 25 September to Tuesday 6 October 2001 in both the *Guardian* and *The Times*. This was further contextualized through a search of both newspapers' Internet sites to try and identify wider patterns of coverage (from the period from 12 September to 25 October). It is important to stress that I am attempting to hit a moving target. New material appears daily, shifting the boundaries of representation. The discursive meanings of current events will continue to be contested and are therefore better analysed with some temporal distance to them. I can only at this stage provide an indication of patterns that will need revisiting at a later date.

In describing the coverage analysed here I am leaving a lot unsaid because the framework elaborated in this book illustrates in detail the application of the discourses I use. This preface therefore should be understood with reference to the relevant chapters.

Context

Commentators — politicians, journalists and others — continue to argue that the events of 11 September signal a kind of rupture, that the world has changed irrevocably and that a new world order must be established in the aftermath. At a global level, the media have played a role in constructing this idea in the psychic imagination. As the live feed projected into our spaces of consumption and people's scripts of previous events informed their interpretation of this one, new boundaries were being formed, allegiances solidified, people excluded, and 'us' and 'them' created in varying forms across the globe. We witnessed this almost immediately at a political level with President Bush's statement that you are either with us (the democratic world) or with them (the terrorists). The reductionism in attempting to force countries to choose sides (which are strongly signified as good versus evil) obscures the political/cultural frameworks that inform definitions of 'terrorism' and the balance of power that enables particular groups to signify the world's ins and outs.

Yet, in this instance, both President Bush and British Prime Minister Tony Blair have made it clear that this is not a war against Islam. It clearly is not. Nor has it been the primary target in previous conflicts, but Islam has been mobilized to demonize enemies when politically it has been strategic to do so. The distancing here then also has a political function: on an international level to maintain support for the US-led coalition's actions against terrorism and, on the domestic front, to appease the Muslim community to avoid dissent within it. However, this shift in rhetoric does not guarantee that the meanings and values that have been attached to Islam in the past are not in operation. This becomes particularly problematic when 'the enemy' itself appears to be confirming the 'Islamic' motivations behind its actions. Whether these events are about Islam or not, it is through sporadic coverage of conflicts like the Iranian Revolution and the Gulf War that Islam enters the public consciousness and becomes known.

The rhetoric surrounding the events of 11 September suggests we have a new enemy that requires a different kind of war. Yet the coverage we have seen so far parallels that of the Gulf War, not only through television images but also in the dominance of a military register and the focus on tactics over and above an emotional or moral reaction. Coverage of previous events has shown that in a war situation it is difficult for journalists to get access to anything other than official sources and that the news is tightly managed on all sides. In this case, there have been even fewer press conferences or MoD briefings, and journalists are further constrained by being denied access to hostile territory. Though the extent to which propaganda is playing a part in this campaign will most likely only be revealed in years to come, we know from recent history how often policy can be driven by the need to create a 'media performance' – so that the public can be gratified by seeing 'the threat' dealt with.[1]

If this is then a new era and these highly 'unusual' times involving different circumstances, can we still apply the same frameworks to the reporting of Islam? If our understanding of the world has substantially shifted and physical and imaginary borders been reconfigured, can previous norms still be applied? In a situation of heightened vulnerability in which the internal serves to remind us of the external threat, will normative identities be destabilized? One thing is clear. Islam is now a salient issue. Previously at the margins of coverage in the British news media and a distant object in the consciousness of the majority of British people, as this book demonstrates, it now has an uncomfortable familiarity. Islam is suddenly 'recognizable' but it is the form in which Islam is known that is of concern here. That people are suddenly more interested in Islam could be a positive development, but if the knowledge that is produced only reinforces an Orientalist perspective then this will be an opportunity lost.

Observations

Generally, the media play a significant part in the sequence of events. Their central role in the reproduction of political power ensures that it is a key factor in the considerations of actors on all sides of the war.

In their initial coverage, by emphasizing a build up to military action rather than exploring alternative solutions, the newspapers provided support for, even helped create a context in which, armed intervention was both expected and accepted. By defining the solution to the initial attack as a 'war on terrorism', policymakers provided the moral mandate for and legitimated the course of action taken;[2] to have conceived of it as a crime would have required a different, and for the USA, a politically less satisfying approach.

Yet the ambiguity and lack of attempt to define the enemy over and above this statement again had political motivations. It allowed the actors to name the terrorist enemy as and when it became necessary. Currently, terrorism appears to exclude acts perpetrated by states, allowing some, such as Israel, to exploit the situation.

Reporting on the international situation appears to operate within a framework of foreign news coverage with which we are already familiar (Dahlgren and Chakrapani 1982). The dehumanization associated with representing the tribes of Afghanistan as warring factions of primitive barbarians is clear, while every possible strategy is used to personalize the victims of the terrorist attacks and provoke an emotional response that encourages us to identify them as 'one of us'.

Only one individual on the other side is subject to the same attention to detail: Osama bin Laden. But the characterization of bin Laden that is constructed in the acres of newsprint tells us little about him and rather more about the cultural-political context in which the coverage was formulated. The vast amount of space that is given over to this event and that needs to be filled has led to speculation from all spheres and disciplines. The desire and process of knowing about the Other results in his demonization and, consequently, he is elevated to a mythical status. He is the rich Arab manipulating 'Western technology' for his own ends. He has also become the personification of evil, which makes the battle against him more reassuring and easier to digest than acknowledging the situation's complexity. So where does religion sit within this reductive discourse? It is clearly used in contradictory ways. On the one hand, bin Laden and his followers are perceived as manipulating Islam to mobilize the ignorant masses for political gain. For example, the specific focus on the Muslim victims of the World Trade Center attacks highlights this perfidiousness. In this construction, the perpetrators are often conceptualized as 'mindless' and are assigned an irrationality that closes down any other potential solutions. Yet, on the other hand, by continuing to refer to 'Muslim and Islamic terrorists', the perpetrators are seen as products of a fanatical strain of Islam. As a result, the associated negative behaviour is seen to evolve out of something inherent in the religion, rendering any Muslim a potential terrorist. While the *Guardian*, in this case, has mainly shifted its lexicalization to describe groups as 'Islamists', and differentiates between Muslims and 'tyrants', it also suggests that 'Muslims have to look at why their religion breeds so many violent militant strains' (6 October 2001).

Findings

In the first instance then, the *Guardian* appeared to have improved its coverage by giving voice to a range of commentators such as Edward

Said, Samuel Huntington, Ziauddin Sardar, Umberto Eco, Faisal Bodi, Salman Rushdie, Tariq Modood and Hugo Young. It printed articles such as Young's, which asserted that 'It may not be PC [politically correct] to say it but Islam is at the heart of this' (9 October 2001) to Modood's 'Muslims in the West', which challenged the 'clash of civilizations' thesis (30 September 2001).

The *Guardian* also included a series of positive features that attempted to grapple with some key questions about Islam that fascinate secular society, such as women's desire to wear *hijab* (5 November) and reflective articles in which it communicated to its readers its heightened sensitivity to issues of language use and spelt out its editorial policy (Mayes, reader's editor, 29 September).

A search for *all* articles on Muslims and Islam appearing between 12 September and 25 October found that there were 700 in *The Times* and 1058 in the *Guardian*, equivalent to each paper's annual coverage previously. It is clear then that already we are seeing a huge increase in the volume of coverage in both papers, a growth illustrated by the amount of daily coverage on Islam after 11 September, for example, 20 articles on the 13th and 19 on the 12th, compared with just four articles appearing on the 11th.

The subject of *British* Muslims accounted for 108 of the *Guardian*'s 1058 articles, continuing its annual growth from previous years, then, while the surges of global coverage correlate directly with periods of conflict (around the time of the Gulf War, for example). It should also be remembered that these figures included only articles in which Muslims were clearly marked as Muslim and it should be expected that the actual volume of articles about Muslims (but not identified as such) was significantly higher.

The *Guardian*'s coverage of British Muslims so far can be split into two main types. The first of these report Muslim fears, focus on dis-crimination towards Muslims and cite Muslims' (generally supportive) responses to the events of 11 September (32 articles). The second is terrorism and counter-terrorism legislation, about which there were 27 reports (17 and 10 respectively). Little falls outside this framework. The *Guardian* covered a further, related,[3] debate on a proposed religious discrimination law, on which there were 12 reports, all opposing the law. Other coverage reflected the framework described above. For example, following the attacks ten articles on education either criticized segregation or fundamentalism in universities or highlighted efforts to promote anti-discrimination in schools. Nine reports on protests against the war referred to the Muslim community's support for them. Baroness Thatcher's comments about British Muslims not doing enough to condemn the attacks on America received some attention (six reports), but this was partly to discredit her and like-minded members of the Conservative Party.

Other coverage was slight but included three articles on the church's response and two on the unrest in Oldham over the summer, focusing on segregation and racism in the community, which was firmly located as a Muslim problem (12 September, 2 October). From this cursory review we can see how a bipolar system of representation has developed between what Bodi calls 'the loyal citizens and fifth columnists' (22 October). The distinction is initially made between *British* Muslims and non-British Muslims who reside in Britain and may be involved in covert activities.

A qualitative examination of one week's coverage supported these initial suppositions. In the week analysed, 17 articles in the *Guardian* explicitly referred to British Muslims, 18 in *The Times*, while eight others covered the activities of potential terrorists within without referring to Muslims or Islam (17 in *The Times*). Because of the frequency with which articles on bin Laden and al-Qaida have referred to Islam since 11 September, it is probable that people will assume that those under suspicion of terrorism are Muslim, even when this is not the case or when their religion is not clearly signalled, hence the need to study all these articles. This is almost a reversal of the situation prior to 11 September, particularly in the *Sun*, where Muslims were caught up and their specific religious identity lost in coverage of the Other. It now seems that there is a greater chance of a range of Others getting caught up in the conceptualization of Muslims. This has become evident in attacks on Sikhs and Arabs in both Britain and the USA. For example, a report on the arrest of an Algerian pilot, Lotfi Raissi, in London, on suspicion of training the hijackers did not mention Islam but followed an article on the previous page with a headline that screamed, 'Straighten out your clothes, open your chest and welcome death for the sake of Allah'. And it continued with details of instructions found among one of the hijacker's belongings that highlighted the religious motivations for the attack, juxtaposed against a colour photograph of one of the planes hitting the WTC (*Guardian*, 29 September 2001, pp. 3–4)

Since 11 September, the news reported in the two papers has been almost identical, but with less diversity in the topics covered by *The Times*. Both focused mainly on terrorist activities in Britain, seven articles in the *Guardian* and 11 in *The Times*, and on legislation needed to counter these (seven and 13 respectively). Both included a few articles on race relations and voiced Muslim concerns (four and three); other than this, occasional articles echoed the approach established before 11 September, with the *Guardian* emphasizing freedom of speech and segregation and *The Times* a Christian perspective and focus on royalty. Each paper also included one article on the following topics:

Guardian	*The Times*
Rushdie	Rushdie (restrictions now upon him)
Nation of Islam	Nation of Islam (extremism)
30 September Education	Blasphemy (against Christians)
'faith schools spark fears of apartheid'	Prince Charles
Freedom of speech	Politics (Tories appoint Asian to key post)

The last article in this list from the *Guardian* defended the right of Julie Burchill to publish her Islamophobic opinions on Muslims earlier on in the year, in the light of support from the Press Complaints Commission whose code only protects individuals from attack. In referring to the complaints received, Muslims were positioned as censorious. There had been little change so far then.

Several themes were addressed in its coverage.

First, the 'threat within' continued to be covered within a dominant hegemonic framework as with previous coverage of fundamentalism. In particular, articles focused on the movements of the hijackers in London prior to the attacks; hence Britain was once again constructed as a safe haven, a base for terrorism. At that stage, this was an investigation, as yet unsubstantiated, but strong assertions using a rhetorical style and authority-giving sources enhanced its factuality. Articles focused on individuals who previously appeared to be ordinary chaps constructed through witness accounts and pictures of residential neighbourhoods as with 'From suburbia to martyrs' (*Guardian*, 29 October) and were now suspected of aiding terrorism. A further example arose in the middle of October in reports of a Muslim cleric's fight against deportation after he was deemed a security risk.

These articles used the kind of linguistic register that demanded tough action, a 'crackdown' on 'terror suspects', previously mobilized in the fallout of Luxor, and nearly all articles on this topic made readers regard the events of 11 September as top-level information. Evidence of terrorist networks spanning the globe and earlier events involving 'Islamic groups' worked to spread fear, act as a warning of more terrorist acts to follow, and accrued evidence to justify measures taken against them. Little alternative information, such as defence statements made by suspects, was supplied. There was also coverage on the harmful economic, social and psychological after effects for Britain.

Yet Sir John Stevens, commissioner of the Metropolitan Police, was quoted in the *Guardian* of 25 September as saying that there was no evidence of any attack on Britain, no history of Islamic terror plots in Britain and 'home-grown extremists' were dismissed as 'irrelevant'. Also, an article on 23 October, which reported that an FBI investigation had found no evidence of al-Qaida cells in the UK, shifted its attention to British Muslims taking up arms to fight for Islam. Hence, its macro-proposition was first rejected and then reinforced. By comparison, this information was not included in *The Times*.

This initial coverage was followed by reports on what legislation was needed to counter terrorism. The *Guardian* gave qualified support to such measures, thus raising the potential for a curtailment of civil liber-ties. This was illustrated by the importance the Liberal-Democrat Party assigned to this question at its conference held that week — 'counter-terrorism measures which affect liberty should be seen as a last resort says Hughes' (29 September, p. 5). Young (2 October, p. 18) held that changes to the laws on extradition, asylum and increased intelligence were necessary, whereas a reduction in the discussion of domestic policy and ID cards were not. In these articles, acceptable authoritative liberal sources were employed, such as Liberty, a human rights organiz-ation, in addition to the authority-giving sources used above.

The main difference in coverage in *The Times* was its greater atten-tion to these issues to the exclusion of others and the detail awarded to the more sensationalist aspects of the events. It was also more likely to link the activities of terrorists living in Britain to British Muslims and to be less sensitive to language use, frequently employing terms like 'Muslim rebels' alongside words such as 'gangsters' (26 September) and referred to Muslims as 'the Islamic community' (27 September). For example, two articles about the 'twentieth hijacker', Zacarias

Moussaoui, used his mother as a source to provide a profile of an 'ordinary' person (namely irreligious, ambitious and a model immigrant) who was converted to 'a strict form of religion through contacts with Islamic organizations while living and studying in Britain' (26 and 28 September). This suggested that anyone who had associated with these extremist groups in Britain had been indoctrinated and was therefore a 'would-be bomber'. Again, the interpretation of the subject's desire to convert was based on deficiency (loneliness) and a reversal strategy operated in which he became 'a black racist'. Although the newspaper differentiated between fanatics and mainstream Muslims, it was also made explicit in *The Times* that they all subscribed to Islam, the terrorists 'a branch of Islam that condoned violence' even 'a pure form of Islam' (30 September). Islam was also implicated in the identification of Islamic groups that funded terror, such as 'the Islamic Media Observation Centre' (30 September, p. 2). While there is a clear difficulty here for journalists given that the actors do claim religious motives for their actions, failing to make a distinction between Islam and Islamists has negative implications for all Muslims because it implies that the problem resides in the religion and in the people who follow it, rather than in alternative factors.

The Times was therefore not only explicit about locating the hijackers' activities in Britain, which it saw as providing them with a secure base for their operations, but it also, at this early stage, introduced and gave much more space to British Muslims fighting for the Taliban. An initial article suggesting that 'at least 500 young British Muslims have been trained at terrorist camps in Afghanistan' was confirmed by reports of 'Britons in Kabul' working for 'bin Laden's al-Qaida' (26 September). Five further articles on 26 September demonstrated the global links between Muslims in the terrorist network. These suspicions were strengthened the following day by raids 'from the Costa del Sol to Leicester', the photographs of police in Leicester amplifying the macro-assertion of the terrorist threat within. This, a 'suspected master bomb-maker in the European wing of Osama bin Laden's worldwide army of radical Muslims' was then linked to 'anarchist' protesters at the G8 summit further delegitimizing anti-globalization activists.

The paper's overarching narrative, encapsulated in its daily header 'war on terror' followed by varying subheadings applied to specific events such as 'the Hunt', 'Islam in Britain', and 'British Muslims', firmly located Islam and British Muslims within the framework of terrorism, and the hunt within the Muslim community.

For *The Times* this was very much a Muslim problem, 'Young British Muslims are arriving in increasing numbers at mosques and asking how they can fight *in what they describe* as an imminent holy war. ... Muslim leaders admitted it was a growing problem' (29 September, emphasis added). Here 'the youth' are not incorporated within a minority, 'Britain is regarded as a popular recruiting station for al-Qaida because of its sizeable Muslim population', and hence the community appears to be out of control. A number of rhetorical strategies and stylistic approaches were used such as listing the various wars in which British Muslims have fought and thus cementing the idea of a global force, and by quoting members of al-Muhajiroun who affirmed the necessity of these actions for Muslims because 'the Koran permits it'. This became more menacing when it was suggested that those trained abroad returned to the UK to act as 'sleepers'. Violence was even portrayed as a pastime when 'Love of guns led Briton to fight for the Taliban' (2 October). Any sympathy we may have had for this prisoner of the Northern Alliance (invoked through an emphasis on his foolishness) was removed by the claim that he 'shed no tears over suicide attacks in America'.

This kind of tension was raised throughout the week, with warnings of more attacks and 'dozens of terrorists on the run in Britain' (28 September). These articles dominated the first few pages of daily reporting and police sources were used to confirm the allegations. This, and a shift in focus to the failings of British intelligence and police so far, culminated in explicit calls for quick action in *The Times* leaders from the 29th, 'Tough on camera but weak on what causes Britain to be the world's terrorist haven' (p. 19). The emphasis in this article on 'desperate confusion at home' and on the 'Dickensian pace of British justice' put pressure on the government to take immediate action.[4] The extradition process came under particular focus and was widened to include those who incited 'racial hatred' (namely Muslim extremists) and suggested that the police were constrained by fear of 'resentment in Muslim communities'. Moderate Muslims were not seen to be doing enough to denounce the activities of extremists, implying that Muslims supported each other whatever the circumstances. The paper moved firmly towards focusing on the need for anti-terrorist measures on the 30th. The leader 'Who defends Britain?' adopted arguments against the laws and reformulated them so that, for example, increased security was interpreted as liberating. It also supported a further 'crackdown' on illegal immigrants who saw Britain as a 'soft touch'. On 1 October this was emphatic, 'Blair's robust words now need to become rigorous legalisation' (p. 17). Its editorial position on this matter was much stronger and clearer than the *Guardian*'s in all but a few letters that raised potential problems with the laws.[5]

Second, freedom of speech continued to be a significant issue for the *Guardian* and resulted in a number of negative articles about Muslims. While debates about the pros and cons of ID cards was on the agenda for both papers, unlike articles on related legislation, these in the main did not tend to refer to Muslims. The *Guardian*'s secularism was most explicit in its coverage of the proposed religious discrimination laws whereby it exaggerated their potential to discredit them, for example, the censoring of comedians (which David Blunkett had already refuted). The debate was partly triggered by the publication of a letter from a British comedian, Rowan Atkinson, in *The Times* (17 October), which provoked further letters using mainly negative arguments to reject the law. These included the restriction on freedom of speech, its unworkability, the secular nature of Britain, and even the draconian nature of the laws. These types of arguments were more usual in the *Guardian*, and were in sharp contrast with *The Times*' response to the new laws on extradition (24 October). However, the argument was even stronger and more frequent in the *Guardian*. Catherine Bennett described the move on 23 October as 'Blunkett's bold repudiation of the Enlightenment', in a commentary that equated religious hatred with 'saying horrid things' and was most powerfully debunked, along with religion itself, in Nick Cohen's 'Damn them all' (7 October). For the *Guardian*, Islamophobia itself was already operating as a form of censorship. *The Times*, on the other hand, used a reversal strategy, suggesting that in demanding these laws, those Muslims who 'preach hate' may find themselves censored (30 October, p. 2).

Third, there was also evidence, in both papers, of a seemingly genuine effort to support Muslims, with more space devoted to Muslim voices. In those articles there was an attempt to differentiate the moderate and Islam, from extremists. The *Guardian*, for example, had, in the main, replaced the more extreme sources like al-Muhajiroun with more acceptable 'representatives' such as the Muslim Council of Britain. 'Extremists', such as Sheikh Abu Hamza al-Masri, were treated with a similar absurdity, as was previously evident (22 September, p. 18). I have already suggested that this polarization is problematic and may result in another form of monopolization that is equally unrepresentative of the diversity of Muslim voices. The polarization was also reinforced through the layout of reports that placed articles such as 'Blair condemns racist attacks' next to 'Egypt protests at Islamist refugee' (28 September, p. 6). Equally, these articles tended to remain at the level of commentary, particularly as features and letters, and could frequently be found, therefore, in the *Observer*, which allocated more space for this kind of material.

Muslim voices (Choudry, 30 September; Khan, 2 October) were also used to locate the problem within the 'Muslim world', arguing that Muslims must accept responsibility for their own failures (effective in avoiding charges of racism), while articles such as 'Muslims refuse to be victims of racism' (30 September), which assumed a conflictual relationship between American Airlines and Saudi Arabian staff at Heathrow airport, succeeded in reinforcing a mentality of Islam versus the West.

This pattern of focusing on negative aspects of the Muslim community while giving a voice to Muslim concerns is more evident in *The Times*, for example, in its emphasis on the community's opposition to the bombing of Afghanistan (28th), in snubbing Prince Charles (29th) and in its continued use of extreme sources such as al-Muhajiroun and Sheikh Abu Hamza al-Masri (29th).

I want to draw attention, for example, to the reporting of government attempts to build social cohesion by promoting unity among British people regardless of race or religion, 'Prescott forsakes banter to call for common purpose' (*Guardian*, 1 October), 'Offer Muslims the hand of friendship, says Prescott' (*The Times*, 27 September). Although coverage of this in both papers had mainly positive intentions, *The Times* shifted the blame from wider structural problems to individual discrimination as 'racists exploiting the war on terror'. Hence 'the solution was in the hands of individual people', reducing support for affirmative action. Even the *Guardian* article, with its call for unity against the 'evil of terrorism', and by specifically marking out the Muslim community for attention, meant that any dissension to this aim, including an antiwar position, could be located as antisocial behaviour within the community while the government was constructed as a peacemaker promoting tolerance and dialogue.

Despite efforts to improve coverage and feature 'a Muslim perspective' then, the weight of evidence still supported an anti-Muslim stance.

The sequence of events in both papers followed a similar pattern. Initially, in the aftermath of 11 September, the press attempted to maintain order and show sensitivity in a nervous climate. This was followed by a focus on the 'threat within' and legislation that needed to be exacted to counter this threat. However, in later days, coverage veered much more towards a greater focus, in both papers, on British Muslims who may pose a security threat to the UK. While this was already evident in *The Times*, it became more of a focus for the *Guardian* following the death of three British Muslims in Kabul who had been fighting for the Taliban. This generated numerous articles 'investigating' British Muslims who might have taken a similar course of action and more extreme voices were once again allowed to enter the framework of reporting. While the *Guardian* was the only paper consistently to hold that 'The majority of Muslims reject violence', this one statement against the weight of evidence was unconvincing and appeared to justify focusing on the sensational. This appeared to the exclusion of more positive activities by Muslims, for example in covering pro-bin Laden marches (12 November) but not peace rallies (20 October).

This type of coverage has created the conditions for the reform of the asylum laws, already a major issue in Britain before 11 September. On the 29/30 October, proposals for tighter measures in this area included citizenship classes, restrictions on the right of appeal, increased space to detain those facing removal, loss of benefits for those who refused to stay in proposed new centres or who failed to report to networking centres, and ID cards. A particular offensive element of the *Guardian*'s coverage appeared on its front page on 30 October. A cartoon showing an ID card featured a woman wearing a *hijab* on one side and a fingerprint on the other while the owner declares, 'the thumbprint is the one on the left' (Austin). Perhaps the worst is yet to come.

Conclusion

In the electronic journal *Ctheory*, Dennis (2001) writes that as the symbols of 'spatial deterritorialization and globalization slammed into icons of information, commodification', the end of the 'utopian belief

in market society' was signalled. In conclusion then I want to return to
the question of continuity or discontinuity. Has this attack on 'Western
values' led to a rupture in the political world order and how is this
played out in the media?

The coalition against a common enemy is based on a coincidence of
interests of major superpowers fighting regional conflicts and is not a
fixed stable entity. In fact we have already witnessed dissent and irri-
tation brought on by its coercive construction. Although it would now
appear that we have entered a time of disorder, it is expedient to
emphasize this to secure the kind of New World Order that has been
emerging since the end of the cold war. If the events of 11 September
and their reporting have made all kinds of political projects possible,
both globally and on the domestic front, with the maintenance of political and economic hegemony a key priority for a number of countries,
this needs careful examination. For example, is the ethical humanitarian
mission to save ordinary Afghans from their tyrant rulers a convenient
by-product of other strategic aims? Or is this an example of the use of
liberal discourse concealing imperialist practices illustrated by the kind
of politics that places little value on the lives of the Afghan people?
Equally, has the emphasis on security at home, by the allied governments and magnified in the press, allowed for a greater regulation of
boundaries and tightened control? This emphasis is evident in statements such as that of the US House of Representatives minority leader
Richard Gephardt that 'We are in a new world. We have to rebalance
freedom and security. We can't take away people's civil liberties. But
we're not going to have all the openness and freedom we have had'
(Kroker and Kroker 2001).

The British Anti-Terrorism, Crime and Security Bill introduced to
Parliament on 12 November emerged in a context of similar rhetoric. It
has particular implications for minority groups because of the increased
police powers it gives to stop and search and, in the wording of the Bill,
'require the removal of disguises'. The only part of this legislation that
potentially favours minority groups, the religious discrimination laws,
now looks set to be withdrawn (25 November 2001).

I seek here to illustrate the centrality of the media in economic,
cultural and political power, for the media are significant social actors
in the process of reinforcing boundaries by amplifying the danger. In a
climate in which Islam is a central focus for the news media, its
reporting appears to be converging on the sensational. Current affairs

programmes that purport to be balanced offer inflammatory tabloid material, as with the BBC Panorama's, 'Koran and Country' (14 October) and Channel 4's Dispatches 'Bin Laden's Plan of Terror' (1 November) about which the *Guardian* stated that 'as this investigation of Osama bin Laden's al-Qaida is in the competent hands of Dispatches, it should avoid gratuitous scare-mongering.' It did the opposite; both programmes magnified the notion of a 'threat within', focusing on the role of a couple of extremist groups in Britain in transforming 'ordinary young men' into fanatics. There appears to be little interest in the Muslim community outside this framework.

We cannot, then, divorce 'events' from their reporting, for this is how they acquire their meanings. The consequence of these processes for British Muslims currently bears a resemblance to the situation in which they found themselves in the wake and at the height of the Rushdie affair, with their loyalty under question and a loyalty to both Islam and the UK deemed to be incompatible. Hugo Young's statement in the *Guardian*, for example, that 'any Muslim who insists that his religio-cultural priorities, including the defence against jihad against America, overrides his civic duties of loyalty, tolerance, justice and respect for democracy' locates Muslimness as the antithesis of all these things. Again raising questions about the failure of multiculturalism, the *Guardian* continues to promote a view of British society that is integrationist. This has significant implications for Muslims given the paper's construction of them as separatist (see editorial, 1 November and Hugo Young, 6 November).

Will the current climate allow for a more extreme situation to develop? It appears to have provided a context in which previous media scripts about Muslims can be revisited and reinforced, for example in the backlash against faith schools. In this context, attacks on Muslims and mosques have also occurred. Or will a greater interest in the news, and politics generally (with newspaper sales in the UK up since 11 September, Presswise.org.uk), along with a surge of interest in Islam and the volume of material now available on the subject, which allows for a greater diversity of opinion, lead to better understandings? This obviously depends on what type of material is made available to the public and how it then circulates and is reproduced within the public consciousness. The changing political situation ensures discursive fluidity with uncertain outcomes. However, it would appear, both in the deeds of political actors involved and in the coverage analysed here that there are currently attempts to maintain the structure of normativity, reinforcing old certainties. An Orientalist discourse is continually transformed to fit the developing circumstances. The current situation may not be about Islam, but the meanings and values attached to Islam in recent times are reproduced to demonize the enemy, even where the signifier 'Islam' remains unused. My argument is that rather than representative of a significant change in the world order, there is greater public awareness of it (with a clearer idea of who the enemy is), which is useful in mobilizing support for measures that maintain and even accelerate geo-political hegemony.

How, in this situation, can the current hegemony be challenged? Said recently argued that 'We need to step back from the imaginary thresholds that separate people from each other and re-examine the labels' (*Observer*, 16 September). The ethics of responsibility the previous foreign secretary Robin Cook once advocated have suddenly gained popularity with the government. But is this, as Kampfne argues (*New Statesman*, 15 October 2001), just rhetorical when the apparent justification for the current war is whether the objectives are achieved? Similarly, the present government's engagement with Britain's Muslim communities needs to go beyond appeasement. It needs to retreat from establishing a new stereotype, an acceptable Other, a liberal Muslim that can be manipulated and domesticated, and from defining any Muslim falling outside this framework as extreme.

The struggle to define the conflict and the people involved is ongoing. This book is significant in its detailed documentation of the representations of British Muslims in sections of the British press over a significant period of time, almost a decade. It therefore provides a framework for understanding and comparing past, present and future coverage and for the circumstances in which they arose. We can only make significant progress towards avoiding future conflict if we take such responsibility and challenge current formulations.

Introduction

At the time of writing this introduction, tensions in the Middle East were being discussed daily in the British press. Israel had once again collapsed into crisis; there was renewed interest in Saddam Hussein as a new Bush administration entered the White House; four Muslim men went on trial in the USA for bombing the American embassies in Kenya and Tanzania in 1998; and a British Muslim was named as the Christmas day suicide bomber in Kashmir. As Ramadan drew to a close, my morning newspaper (28 December 2000) carried no less than nine reports with the underlying themes of Islam and conflict.

Media coverage of Islam has been of concern to Muslims worldwide and academic interest in the last decade has seen a body of theoretical work develop that attempts to explain its negative image in the Western media. It is argued that as a result of contemporary political, economic and social processes Islam is increasingly a globally salient issue. Shifts in the global power equation, due to the collapse of communism, have led to anxieties and attempts by 'the West'[1] to maintain its hegemony.[2] Political Islam, which has emerged out of different experiences of colonialism and oppression, its initial signifier being the Iranian Revolution (1979), has allowed 'the West' to construct Islam as the new enemy (a global force that represents an ideological and physical threat) based on an historically polarized relationship. This has been necessary for 'the West' in order to reassert its power over an economically rich area and, in doing so, to defend its supreme Western identity. Consequently, the media as an instrument of public ideology demonizes Islam, portraying it as a threat to Western interests, thus reproducing, producing and sustaining the ideology necessary to subjugate Muslims both internationally and domestically.[3] The portrayal of extremist images within a framework that advances an historical 'myth of confrontation', Halliday (1996) suggests, absolves 'the West' of any need to justify its hostility.

17

Crucial to these arguments is the concept of Orientalism (Said 1978). Orientalism, according to Said, is the historical construction of Eastern cultures as alien, the Other, by the West. The ideological assumptions held and perpetuated by Western writers who see 'them' and 'us' constructed as naturalized, binary oppositions has allowed 'the West' to dominate Oriental cultures. The discourse, therefore, has a function.

Writing before contemporary manifestations of political Islam, Said's theory has been 'reworked and reinvested' in the present (Sardar 1999: 1). The Orientalist discourse has been strengthened to manage these new phenomena. Hence, the theory has it that an ethnocentric vision dominates current representations of Islam, which are reductive and predominantly negative. Only a few stereotypes[4] are offered. Muslims are homogenized as backward, irrational, unchanging, fundamentalist, misogynist, threatening, manipulative in the use of their faith for political and personal gain, and yet with politically unstable governments and movements.

However, postmodern conditions brought about by globalization clearly incorporate a fragmentary principle whereby destabilization and uncertainty have resulted in defensive constructions of identity of which Islamist movements and nationalist projects are a part. This process is of interest here. While scholars have been quick to describe the hybridity and diversity of Islamic groups, these have been discussed with reference to anecdotal, selective claims about bias within the context of a monolithic Western media. Valuable attempts to describe the heterogeneity of these movements have resulted in the homogenization of 'the West'. I take issue with this homogenization. Different countries have different political circumstances and motivations, which are reproduced and reconstructed in their ideological institutions, including the media. Equally, the 'media' incorporate a range of communication modes and within these there are numerous genres, different affiliations, priorities and constraints. The image of 'Islam' will differ according to these and cannot be a unified global discourse as it is imagined. Earlier global, theoretical approaches are now being followed by a more localized, systematic approach (Karim 2000; Männistö 1997; Richardson 2001). Although patterns of representation are evident, Hafez (2000) draws our attention to the importance of this approach by citing a number of studies that demonstrate regionalism in foreign news reporting through domesticating the meaning of events. Foreign news (about Islam) is interpreted through national frameworks. But how are

Muslims born in 'the West' understood? In this book I intend to deal with some of these issues, moving beyond other writing in this area. Based on a systematic and extensive research project, I examine the representation of *British* Muslims in sections of the British national press, thus contextualizing content and taking account of the conditions of production. On undertaking this project, I expected that, given the need for political stability and the integration of minority groups,[5] news frameworks depicting British Muslims would be more diverse than those of their global counterparts. Proximity creates an obstacle to representations based solely on violent conflict.

The proliferation of literature on the representation of Muslims has not included audience interpretations. However, I do not intend to make judgements about portrayals without taking into account audience reception. In this book I deal with the problems of trying to fix meaning within texts by including a substantial audience section.

In this introduction I seek to establish a theoretical framework for studying representations of Islam by describing the context of production, provide an account of the structure of the research and its aims and, for ease of reference, outline how the book is organized.

Islam in Britain

Processes of globalization and migration have resulted in a considerable Muslim presence in the UK. Here, I detail the nature of that presence and its consequences that have contributed to a particular image of Islam in Britain.

The number of Muslims in Britain is generally estimated, in available statistics, at around 1.5 million (Anwar 1993; Peach 1990). According to sources,[6] Muslims have been present in the UK for at least 300 years, the first settlers being Arab traders from Lebanon and seamen from Yemen and Somalia who settled in ports in the UK. Following the Second World War, many South Asian Muslims who had served in the merchant navy stayed in Britain. The biggest influx, however, came in the 1950s through economic migration, mainly South Asian men for whom early settlers were a point of contact. These Muslims came mainly from rural areas, the Mirpur district or North West Frontier of Pakistan and from the Sylhet area of eastern Bangladesh. They settled mainly in the industrial North, working in the steel and textile industries (although approximately 60 per cent of

Muslims today are now thought to reside in London). In 1951 the approximate number of Muslims in the UK was 23,000, which rose to 369,000 by 1971 as families began to join the male workers. Migrant workers also came from the mainly Gujarat district of India and were joined in the 1970s by people from the Middle East and from East and North Africa. More recently, Somali, Bosnian, and Kosovan peoples have been displaced. There are also about 5000 converts to Islam in Britain, of whom about half have African-Caribbean origins (Lewis 1994; Nielsen 1991b; Runnymede Trust 1997). The Immigration Acts of 1962 and 1971 first slowed down and then virtually stopped immigration, bar dependants; hence an increasing number of Muslims are now British born. The Muslim community has a larger proportion of young people and fewer old people than other communities, 60 per cent are under 25 compared with 32 per cent of the white population.[7] Predictions estimate that there will be about two million Muslims in the UK by 2020 (Anwar 1996; Runnymede Trust 1997).

Current statistics show that Muslims in Britain are severely disadvantaged in relation to other groups. It is important to note, however, that many of these statistics have been compiled through the last census (1991), which, having no question on religious affiliation, have been calculated through the conflation of ethnic groups and countries of origin. This usually includes mainly Bangladeshis and Pakistanis, approximately 95 per cent of whom are Muslim (Anwar 1996; Brown 2000) along with a percentage of people with Middle Eastern, North African and Indian origins.[8] Other statistics, such as those provided by the Prison Chaplaincy Service, which show an increase in Muslim prisoners in England and Wales of 40 per cent between 1991 and 1995, may be distorted by changes in self-definition (Runnymede Trust 1997).

Those statistics that are available do, however, show the extent of Muslim disadvantage. At the time of the Gulf War, there was evidence of an increase in racially motivated crime towards South Asians in Britain. For example, statistics from the British Crime Survey (1996) show that nearly one-third of Pakistani respondents who had been crime victims recorded their attacks as racially motivated compared with slightly less than one-fifth of Indians and 14 per cent of Afro-Caribbean people. For Pakistanis this rose to 70 per cent in relation to threats, yet they are less likely than other groups to report these crimes to the police (self-reporting survey results) (FitzGerald and Hale 1996). Given the probability that perpetrators of racial violence are unaware of the religious affiliation of their victims, the reproduction of an anti-Muslim discourse subjects all South Asians to becoming the potential victims of anti-Muslim hostility.[9] Evidence provided by the Runnymede Trust (1997: 41) bears witness to the convergence of these hostilities. One such example is the nine Muslim names present in the list of 13 racist and religious murders that took place between 1992 and 1993.

In education, a recent OFSTED survey shows that both Bangladeshi and Pakistani children are underachieving. Although having improved on previous years, they continue to lag well behind their Indian counter-parts. In 1998, an average of 31 per cent achieved grade A–C in their GCSEs compared with 47 per cent of white and 54 per cent of Indian pupils. Bangladeshi and Pakistani groups combined accounted for only 2.8 per cent of entrants to higher education in 1998 (with Bangladeshi children faring worse, accounting for only 0.6 per cent) compared with 89.8 per cent of whites and 4 per cent of Indians. The education system is still, however, failing the black Caribbean community, whose chil-dren continue to underachieve, an experience exacerbated by the high-est exclusion rates ('How ethnic groups fare', *The Times*, 11 March 1999, p. 6).

Muslims also experience 'employment disadvantage' (Modood et al. 1997: 143). An average of 39 per cent of Pakistani and Bangladeshi men are unemployment compared with 31 per cent of Caribbean, 20 per cent of Indian and 13 per cent of white men, and these differentials are greater for women. Those in work tend to occupy low income, low status positions but are under-represented (if at all) at every level of employment. Discrimination at work is also mostly directed at South Asians, who believe that most of the hostilities are aimed at Muslim workers. They continue to be discriminated against in the allocation of facilities such as housing. Their overall standards of living and health are therefore lower than they are for other groups (all data are from Modood et al. 1997). These statistics provide evidence for the severe social exclusion of Muslims in Britain. This type of exclusion from society often leads to feelings of alienation and disempowerment, which can exacerbate racial hostility and boundary making. The media contribute to the material practices of discrimination through their discursive practices, which normalize attitudes towards problematized groups and then legitimate and prefer negative constraining actions above other fairer solutions.

The Oriental constructions of the Other in Britain have come to be known as 'Islamophobia'.[10] A recent report by the Runnymede Trust gathered data on examples of 'Islamophobia' in the UK.[11] It argued that several events beginning in the early 1980s, such as the Rushdie affair, the Honeyford affair, and issues such as *halal* meat in schools and the Gulf War pushed Islam into the national arena. These events raised questions among dominant groups about the ability of Muslims to assimilate peacefully. Attempts, by Muslims, to preserve their culture have been interpreted as separatism, a threat to 'traditional British' values.[12] These responses have increased the desire for cultural autonomy by Muslims and resulted in their politicization. According to Silverman and Yuval-Davis (1998: 8), these processes have strengthened 'cultural racism' in which religion and culture (rather than colour or origins) 'constitute the most significant signifiers of racialization' (quoting Asad 1990).[13] Muslims have therefore entered the frame as the central racialized Other in Britain. In their own research, Silverman and Yuval-Davis (1998) found that anti-Muslim racism was more prevalent in 1998 than in 1984.

The processes of fragmentation and globalization that led to the Muslim presence in the UK have and are continuing to strengthen minority identities and affiliations. This in turn has resulted in a crisis of national identity and a defensive construction of a common national culture to provide stability and certainty that excludes Muslims from Britishness. The increasing visibility of Muslims to non-Muslims in the UK in a global mediated world, within which Muslims are homogenized, has resulted in their construction as a threat to non-Muslims. This ideological threat (in the UK) allows Muslims to be suppressed, the practical consequences of which have been described above.

Since the majority of Muslims in Britain are South Asians, it is essential to look at theories that examine the representation of ethnic minorities. Again, it is important that this analysis is located. National distinctions exist in approaches to minority groups. For America, questions of race have been crucial since its inception. For Britain, the establishment of diasporic communities since the 1950s has raised questions about national identity (Barker 1999). The press construction of Muslims should therefore be considered in the light of these wider processes and contexts. Extensive empirical work has been implemented on representations of minorities in the UK (detailed in Chapter 1). Findings have shown them to be marginalized, problematized and represented within a negative conflictual framework dominated by crime, violence and immigration. Increasingly, minorities are subject to 'modern racism', which, it is argued, has replaced unacceptable traditional racial sentiments in the media as broadcasters attempt to attract black audiences. Entman (1990: 332) describes this as an 'anti-black affect combined with resentment at the continuing claims of blacks on white resources and sympathies'. Hostility is fostered in three ways: through the type of news stories associated with blacks, through coverage that encourages opposition to any action that aims to increase equality and through a belief in the end of racism supported by the use of black reporters to illustrate this. This new framework, which reinforces resistance and denial, is equally applicable to coverage of Muslims and the consumption of news about them, as will become increasingly evident throughout this book.

Conceptual approach

I use the term 'representation' to mean the social process of combining signs to produce meanings.[14] While it is evident that the media do reproduce the dominant ideologies of the society of which they are a part, I would argue that they also construct their own 'meanings' (norms and values) through signifying practices. Representation is not then a transparent process of re-presenting an objective reality. There is always a mediating effect whereby an event is filtered through inter-pretive frameworks and acquires ideological significance. News, then, provides its audiences with interpretive frameworks, ways of seeing the world and defining reality. For this reason, I do not intend to question the viability of 'representations' of Islam or provide examples of an alternative, more probable 'reality', but rather to extract the discursive constructions within the texts that are related to wider social processes. These processes of ideological construction are imbued with power relations, since those who own the structures have the power to repre-sent society according to their own norms and values. Central to my theoretical framework then are theories of news production.

Studies show that, due to the processes involved in its production, news tends to be a limited, conservative and consensual product. Journalistic practices of gathering and selecting news are situated activities; they are subject to the organizational constraints their institu-tional context shapes by being embedded in a capitalist system. This has implications for the product we consume in that continually to attract large audiences (for profit) requires maintaining the status quo (conservative output). However, although it is argued that these conditions will inevitably lead to reduction, it is the consistency of the direction this issue takes that is in question here. The theoretical approaches that frame this project are examined further in Chapter 1.

Methods and structure

The aims of this research are to provide empirical evidence to substantiate claims relating to the image of Islam in the media, to establish the system of representation of Islam, and more specifically to ensure that this is situated, namely takes place, within a given medium in a given context. After exploring what is expected to be a limited framework in relation to Islam, I intend to show how this places restrictions on audience understandings of it.

To meet these objectives, I have used three methodologies. The book is structured so that an examination of theory explaining the current construction of Muslims is followed by three long chapters, each of which correspond to one of these research methods. In these chapters, after working through the data, I summarize the findings and return to the theory.

In Chapter 2 I detail the results of a quantitative content analysis of three years, 1994–96, of daily coverage in two broadsheet newspapers. Quantification employs a formal coding instrument and applies predefined categories to the units of analysis (newspaper articles). Articles are then coded according to these categories.[15] Through this process it is possible to measure 'frequencies' of coverage, which provide an indication of the importance newspapers accord to a subject area. Through content analysis we can identify both the quantity and prominence of the material (by measuring the 'type of article', the form in which coverage appears). However, we can also analyse how this material is presented or 'framed' by examining the type of topics covered and how they appear together, which allows the underlying meanings associated with topics to be developed. Developing categories of analysis is problematic in that it is always subject to interpretation. Decisions made about these should be informed by familiarity with the object under study; however, the topic categories chosen here proved to be fairly exhaustive in providing a relevant framework for analysis. Particular attention is given, in the analysis and interpretation of results, to dominant, recurring topics such as relationships, education, Rushdie, fundamentalism in the UK and politics. Other frequent patterns of coverage are also examined — prominent actors, sources and locations in the reporting of British Islam. Local coverage is compared with global coverage.

To ensure that the sample was representative, *all* articles from January 1994 to December 1996 in the papers chosen, including the lexical items Muslim(s) or Islam, were selected for analysis. Given that the hypothesis relates to current newspaper representation, the study has required annual monitoring to examine any shifts in the framework of reporting. From this sample, the 'typical' nature of coverage regarding Muslims and Islam (that is patterns and core themes) was established.

This basis for selecting an article, namely that it refers directly to the religion or its people, ensured that only content that explicitly mentioned Muslims or Islam was coded. Articles including people with Muslim names, from which ideas about Muslims could be inferred, were not, therefore, included. Only articles that could clearly be identified as depicting Muslims were selected, for people's interpretations of who Muslims are, if they are not referred to as such, will differ widely. In this way, only articles in which 'Muslim' was interpreted as an important category in the definition of an event were analysed. If the objective is to establish how Muslims are framed in the press, what associations are made with this category, and how Muslims in Britain come to be understood through these associations, only those articles that directly make these inferences could be included.

To some extent, these sampling decisions provide for a richer impression of the content, although quantitative analysis is restricted in its ability to do this. Attention to a limited number of variables was intended to provide the context for the qualitative data, explored in Chapter 3, through which a more detailed analysis could take place. The sample includes a year of coverage, 1997, in four newspapers, two broadsheets and two tabloids; the aim, in examining a wider range of positions, is to identify any competing discourses in coverage.

I chose stories for their prominence and development, but also felt that they should be consistent with the recurring topics found by the quantitative analysis because the main themes and perceptions of Islam in its different forms would probably be expressed through these subject areas. It is these that are likely to have some impact on the public's understanding of Islam.

Continuing stories were prioritized for analysis because they illustrate how issues are conceptualized and then problematized, and what
solutions each paper prefers, along with how they resolve and close in
around an issue (given that all these decisions have an ideological
basis). All items that ran on a story were therefore selected. Removing
just one of these articles could have had an impact on the overall
meaning because items often follow on or draw on each other in subsequent reports. The following stories, based on how much they
correspond to coverage in previous years, are analysed in detail: the
marriage of British teenager, Sarah Cook, to a Turkish Muslim; debates
on the content of religious education and on the funding of Muslim
schools; proposed legislation on religious discrimination; the activities
of dissidents in Britain and the UK government's reactions to them
following incidents of terrorism abroad; and the fraud allegations that
resulted in the trial of Mohammed Sarwar, MP. Most of these events
did not reach a final conclusion in 1997 and it was therefore necessary
to continue monitoring the papers for updates.

While a selective construction can inscribe a 'preferred reading' into
a text, making it more difficult to derive alternative interpretations (van
Dijk 1991), meanings can only be inferred through people's interactions
with the texts. Not only do images have differing degrees of impact but
a struggle over their meaning also exists at the reception level.

Content analysis, therefore, should be supported by qualitative
research to ascertain audience interpretations of coverage. The aims in
Chapter 4 are to establish the social meanings of Islam constituted
within differentially situated social groups and the degree of correspondence between press content and public conceptions of British
Islam, illustrating how far the limited representation prevents understanding and results in divisiveness and ignorance.

While one objective is to explore what factors result in differential
decoding, the main variable is cultural proximity. It is hypothesized that
the greater the cultural distance between sets of peoples, the greater the
reliance on media information for interpreting Islam. It is anticipated
then that, for the majority of non-Muslims, it is through the media that
Muslims are known.

The differentially situated reader (focus) groups were organized on
this basis, keeping other variables within the group as homogenous as
possible. They included Muslims, non-Muslims who interact with Muslims on a daily basis, and non-Muslims living in a monocultural

environment.[16] Because of their in-depth and socially oriented nature, focus groups are a particularly appropriate method for analysing the production of meaning. Given that theory shows that audiences actively negotiate and construct meanings through social interaction, focus groups operate as a 'simulation' of 'natural social networks' by which meaning is constructed through everyday talk (Livingstone 1990; Lunt 1996: 85). This, according to Lunt (1996: 85), occurs 'partly through the discursive interrogation of texts'. By examining how groups respond to newspaper texts and negotiate their ideas within pre-existing groups, one can gain some understanding of how the social processes that lead to attitude formation operate within a cultural context. Although the method contributes positively to the research goal, then, the limitations of what is actually an artificial, simplified, context should be considered for their effects on group dynamics. In the interests of reflexivity and validity then, the groups' transcripts were subjected to discourse analysis. By examining the interactional functions of language in such a way, it is possible to measure both the effects of the research and the group context (Gill 1996; Potter 1997).

In analysing the construction of British Muslims in British newspaper texts, and readings of these by differentially situated audience groups, I am incorporating two 'moments' of the communication process essential in examining 'meanings'. This study, therefore, provides current and dominant meanings circulating in British society around one of its minority communities. It is hoped that in making this evidence publicly available, it can be used to further the political process for improvement in which many are now engaged.

1. Representing Islam: in theory and practice

To develop a framework in which to understand representations of Islam in the British news media, I intend to examine not only what type of representations are said to be available, a subject about which little has been written in a specifically British context, but also the sociopolitical circumstances driving the negativization of Islam, for which an extensive literature exists. This analysis is located in the context of race reporting and religious representation with some attention to the news production processes that impinge on these. An assessment of the global and local context is also necessary for making sense of the results of the British findings that are mapped out in this book.

Representing the Other: Orientalism

Orientalism has emerged as a significant theory for understanding the historical production of knowledge about, in particular, the Islamic Other in the Western world. In a period of scholarly engagement with the study and negation of imperialist cultural products (Sardar 1999), Said's *Orientalism* (1978) is recognized as having unified these different strands. His text shifted the debate and marked the beginning of a period that has seen a wealth of interest on the subject of the image of Islam in 'the West'. It is therefore an important starting point for examining arguments relating to this subject.

Said defined Orientalism as a 'style of thought based upon an ontological and epistemological distinction made between the Orient and, most of the time, the Occident' in which Western culture and societies are essentially and inherently superior to Eastern ones (Said 1978: 2), and as a 'corporate institution for dealing with the Orient' (Said 1978: 3). The significant distinction in Said's work was his use of Foucault's notion of *discourse*, which placed the key aspects of knowledge and power at the centre of the analysis. Orientalism is thus an instrumental system of ideas that has allowed European culture to 'manage and produce the Orient politically, sociologically, militarily, ideologically, scientifically and imaginatively' (Said 1978: 2). It is this institutionalism, Said argues, that gives the myths employed in relation to Islam 'the authority of a nation' and that has ensured their success in maintaining hegemony (Said 1978: 307).

In *Orientalism*, Said analyses mainly academic texts, ranging from post-Enlightenment British and French texts to modern day Anglo–American social science studies that claim to know something about the Orient and its people. Orientalism, according to Said, has its origins in, and has been maintained by, such scholarly work, which has produced a specific Western ethnocentric discourse surrounding the Orient, developed within unequal relations of power. Naturalized to the point of scientific knowledge, this essentialist and reductive discourse, which allows for cultural generalizations, consists of an Orient comprised of despotism, sensuality, irrationality, backwardness, degeneracy, deviancy and barbarism, and is unchanging and incapable of describing itself. These traits are characteristics of a 'Muslim mentality' or 'Arab mind'. A key aspect in the critique of Orientalism is the notion of identity, that the West *needed* to constitute the Orient as its Other in order to constitute itself and its own subject position. For the West then, it has been an instrument of policy, providing the conditions for imperial exploitation to take place, including current forms of economic and media imperialism. In turn, colonial expansion reinforced and secured the discourse, reasserting the supremacy of the West. Oriental society thus became the object of a colonial discourse of knowledge and power, the basis of which, Said argues, is fear and the need to control the Other.

Said's Orientalist discourse is based on a cultural, temporal and geographical distance from the subject that has produced specific ideas about the Orient 'out there'. Recent processes of globalization and migration are creating new connections and with them new sensibilities requiring a reassessment of how the Orientalist discourse may have changed and adapted to this.

The publication of *Orientalism* provoked a controversial debate about its arguments, methods and conclusions, including a range of criticisms from across many disciplines. Most of these could be said to be textual, emerging from the spaces and ambiguities in Said's text. This makes some of them questionable or at least rectifiable. An examination of these prepares a researcher seeking to apply the thesis to representations of the Other for some of its shortcomings.

While some Orientalists who sought to justify and defend the integrity of their scholarship rejected the thesis and its 'positive' outcomes (Lewis 1982), others criticized specific omissions and selectivity within the text. This included, for example, the presentation of a monolithic discourse that omitted space for oppositional work from within the Orientalist tradition, any positive elements, and practical resistance from without (Ahmad 1992; Turner 1989). The role of the 'native' in the development of the discipline was also excluded along with any adaptations to Western culture in its colonial encounters (Mani and Frankenberg 1985). While it could be argued that these omissions are crucial in providing for the unifying feature of the Orientalist discourse, they raise issues relating to the methodological assumption about the relation between the genesis of ideas and their validity. As Halliday (1996) puts it, if they are produced in a context of domination are they invalid? This allows for the dismissal of an entire civilization, the 'West', and therefore has parallels with the Orientalist discourse being criticized. Sayyid (1997: 35) claims that Said's limited attention to the consequences for Islam after the dissolution of Orientalism is caused by the ambiguities in his text: 'If Islam is constituted by Orientalism, what happens when Orientalism dissolves?' Is the negation of Orientalism the negation of Islam? This has resulted in the alternative system of the 'anti-orientalists', which Sayyid (1997: 37–40) argues is equally reductionist.

For the purpose of this research, I consider some of the criticisms relating to Said's methodology. Though Bhatnagar (1986), Jalal al-'Azm (1981) Kerr (1980) and Turner (1989) have criticized Said's anti-foundationalism in the identification of a discourse, Mani and Frankenberg (1985) point out that the purpose of Said's thesis was not to assess the accuracy of Orientalist representations in relation to a 'real' Orient but to elaborate Orientalism in the context in which a Western discourse about the Orient arose. However, Said is caught between a position of seeing Orientalism as a misrepresentation of Islam (Mani and Frankenberg 1985: 272) and one that sees all 'reality' as 'representations of representations' (Ahmad 1992; Irwin 1981; Mani and Frankenberg 1985: 273).[1] Mani and Frankenberg (1985), have argued that some of these criticisms failed to understand that the three key aspects of Orientalism — historical specificity, knowledge and power — cannot be divorced for the purpose of analysis. For example, to suggest that all cultures have a tendency to create self/other dichotomies (Turner 1989) is, they argue, to assess the production of knowledge without considering differential locations within global relations of power. My own position on 'representation' is that 'the media' construct their own reality. It is not, therefore, helpful to try and measure the content of the media against some kind of actuality but rather to examine representational frameworks produced and therefore knowledge produced about Islam.

By locating and describing the context within which research takes place, one can avoid the contradiction in criticizing the 'Western' representation of a monolithic, undifferentiated, reductionist discourse on the Orient that then produces a unified and hostile discourse of 'the West' in the same way. By projecting an idea of imperial culture as stable and unbroken, any mutuality in the relationship is ignored. By attending to the temporal, spatial, historical and generic specificities of representations, I hope to avoid unwarranted generalizations. My methodology is purposeful in revealing modifications to the ethnocentric discourse as it attempts to incorporate the Other through the hegemonic process. A further aim of this research is to assess the usefulness of the Orientalism thesis in the face of criticisms that the debate is outdated because globalization has pushed traditional forms of 'society-centred' analysis off the agenda (Turner 1989: 635).

Other criticisms of the contradictions and even hypocrisies of Said's text exist. However, as these are well rehearsed, the aim here has been to show an awareness of the crucial criticisms that raise issues for the approaches I take in my own research. It is recognized, however, that a researcher cannot cover all aspects involved in the communication process and so is always open to criticism.

Any weaknesses in the argument do not, however, totally invalidate the thesis as being applicable to patterns of representation prevalent in Western contexts. The significance and value of *Orientalism* is that it describes the complex historical and cultural circumstances by which a set of institutions progressively developed a 'suitable ideological superstructure with an apparatus of complicated assumptions, beliefs, images, literary productions, and rationalisations' providing the 'underlying foundation' of 'strategic vital interests' about the Orient and Islam

(Jalal al-'Azm 1981: 5). The theory has, therefore, opened up an important debate that has had productive and beneficial results. I would argue that the discourse of Orientalism has a continuing actuality, which finds differing forms of expression according to its location. However, these together contribute to a relatively consistent discursive formation of a type of Orientalism. It is the contribution of the British press to this that is of interest here. What Sardar (1999) has termed 'neo-Orientalism' has remained persistent as its common features are transferred across time, place and history. However, this does not presume homogeneity, rather the discourse reinvents itself according to circumstances. The following section examines the historical situations that, it has been argued, have brought Islam and the West into conflict. These arguments have both emerged from and strengthened the Orientalist discourse.

Development of the Islamic Other: historical context

An Orientalist discourse sustains the belief that Islam as a coherent, transnational monolithic force has been engaged in a unilinear confrontational relationship with the West throughout history. This essentialist reading of history allows the myth of an inherent hostility between two polarized sides to be maintained. This is mobilized as a rationale for justifying negative perceptions of Islam and associated exclusionary practices. An example from contemporary theory is Huntington's (1996) 'clash of civilizations', where Islam is considered to constitute a real threat in military, demographic and socio-religious terms.

Many scholars reject the myth of a timeless essential truth about the West's relationship with Islam. Halliday (1996), in his thesis on 'the myth of confrontation', argues that the discourses currently circulating have their basis in contemporary needs and forces and are sustained on both sides for political purposes. 'Early encounters and confrontations, theological and political, provide the images and folklore which sustain mutual stereotypes, images and suspicions that continue to fuel fears and biases and perpetuate a vision of Islam against the West, of the West against Islam' (Esposito 1992: 24).

I turn now to explore some of those encounters cited in order to formulate an Oriental discourse of an historically conflictual relationship, including current political circumstances and their role in the latest manifestation of the demonization of Islam.

Though Orientalism can be located in the Western response to Islam and its expansion, this is problematic because it negates the existence of an Orient previous to this (Sardar 1999). Historically, the first encounter between the West and Islam was based on religious scrutiny from the Christian West. Turner (1989) argues that the clash of religions led to global theories of Otherness, the Other constructed as the morally and ontologically corrupt. Daniel (1993), in particular, shows how medieval Christian texts contained deliberately manipulative anti-Islamic polemic with the specific function of limiting the growth of Islam in its threat to Christian orthodoxy. The progression from scrutiny to actual contact was seen as a product of the universalistic missionary nature of the religions with the aim to expand and conquer (Huntington 1996).

While ancient Grecian and Roman knowledge and Christian thought provided the foundations for modern Orientalism in its defining phase, the Enlightenment's secularizing and modernizing elements then reconstituted it and represented it as rational knowledge. Comparisons of Europe with the Middle East were based on European definitions of modernity and religion as personal belief, and this allowed ideas of superiority to circulate. To distance itself from medieval thought, an image of the anti-Enlightenment developed in the form of 'despotism', and Islam became incomprehensible and extreme (Kappert 1995).

It was at the point of contact that a textual religious Orientalism was transformed into a geographical political Orientalism, and brought fully into a dominant relation constituting a 'will-to-power' (Said 1978: 222). Historical events based on military expansion, such as the Crusades (1095–1270), in part a response to the defeat of the Byzantine Empire, the expulsion of the Moors from Spain (thirteenth century), the invasion of Egypt by Napoleon (1798), the spread and defeat of the Ottoman Empire (sixteenth to nineteenth centuries), which saw the creation of Turkey, a Western ally, are cited as early conflictual encounters between Islam and the West that have resulted in an atavistic memory of these events (Ahmed 1992).

European colonial expansion, followed by neo-colonialism (post-1945); the creation of the state of Israel (1948); the oil crisis of the 1970s, for which the Middle East was blamed, and the Iranian Revolution (1979) constitute the modern political factors that are used to explain the rise of Islamism[2] and consequently of Western antagonism towards Islam.

The development of political Islam (Bishara 1995) has been located in post-colonial studies examining imperial processes in colonial and neo-colonial societies and the strategies used to subvert 'the actual material and discursive effects of that process' (Ashcroft 1995: 117). Sayyid (1997: 18) estimated that in the mid-1980s around 200 books a year were written with a view to explaining the rise of 'Islamic fundamentalism' as a response to the secularizing, universalist politics of the West. According to these theorists, departing colonial powers left artificial nation states and secular regimes that were based on Western models of power and modernity, that maintained ruling elites and that lacked popular participation.[3] Intrinsically unstable, the rapid but uneven economic development of oil wealth, which generated unrealizable expectations, further undermined them. Subsequent stagnation, unemployment and population pressures added to the general disillusionment caused by oppression and resulted in social and political crisis (Abu-Rabi 1997; Esposito 1992; Halliday 1996; Huntington 1996).

Western economic and cultural imperialism, then, resulted in experiences of dislocation, fragmented identities and the erosion of culture in Muslim societies. This led to the negotiation and translation of local traditional identities and values, and the rise of Islamism offering a solution to disfranchisement and instability and a way of resisting dominant forms of exploitation (Rodinson 1979). For Sayyid (1997), however, the conditions these states experienced explain their failure but not the emergence of Islamism above other forms of protest. He suggests that while 'Islam offered a common set of symbols, historic identity and value systems' (Esposito 1992: 109), a straightforward atavism did not occur. By associating the West with the corrupt regimes, the Islamists provided an ethical vocabulary that allowed the rejection and opposition of all that 'the West' stands for. Islamism then positioned itself through the deconstruction of the relation between modernity and the West. According to Sayyid (1997: 120), it is this that made it a politically significant discourse.[4]

Halliday (1996) argues that these processes have resulted in an equally essentialist discourse by Islamists in relation to a monolithic view of Islam and its ontological difference to the West. This 'Islamic' rhetoric then works to confirm ideas in the West about Islam (Sayyid, 1997).

The threat to the West then is in what appears to be a homogenous resurgent global Islamic force with its claims for political independence, denunciations of the West and challenges to Western supremacy. Islamists also appear to be resistant to change in rejecting Western modernism. However, it is not modernism that Islamists are rejecting, but the West (and its interpretation of modernity). It is the tendency to judge by Western standards that draws this conclusion. Esposito (1992), Halliday (1996) and Said (1981) have an alternative vision of Islamism that views the movements as based on specific political forces that constitute claims for autonomy and independence. According to Cohen (1997), these movements are based on ethnic, territorial or economic disputes for which Islam is used to increase support, but is interpreted as the main criterion by the West given that it is religion that is 'the most visible symbol of group differences to the outsider' (Levinson 1983: 51). For Esposito (1992), the variety of responses by differing groups to the colonial experience is testimony to the flexibility of Islam, the diversity of which, according to Bulliet (1997), will only intensify in the current (postmodern) climate.[5]

Sayyid (1997: 40) rejects both the essentialist notion of Islam by the 'Orientalists' and what he argues is an equally reductive argument, that of the 'little Islams'. In this, the role of Islam is displaced to various economic, ethnic and social factors of Muslim countries by what Sayyid calls the 'anti-Orientalists', becoming nothing more than a label providing 'symbolic authority and validation'. For Sayyid, however, Islam is privileged in Islamism, with Islam conceived of here in its broadest sense as 'goodness'. Sayyid suggests that manifestations of Islamism represent multiple (re) articulations of this 'foundation of Islam', and it is this 'master signifier' that Islamists attempt to centre within the political order (Sayyid 1997: 48). It is the (nodal) point of reference for all other 'signifiers', providing meaning, identity and unity (Sayyid 1997: 45). In this way Islam can be used to articulate a multiplicity of positions while maintaining its specificity (Sayyid 1997: 44).

The proliferation of material attempting to explain the rise of Islam continues and so the debate endures. Although disagreement exists on the nature of Islamism, there is agreement that the global events that are associated with it have been formulated as a threat in current Western discourse.

The perceived resurgence of Islam coincided with the collapse of the communist bloc (Nonnemann 1996). During the cold war, threats to Western interests came from the Soviet Union. Islam was not seen to be threatening because it was also anti-Soviet (Hippler 1995). This softened its hostile image. To quote Anderson and Rashidian (1991: 127), Iran acted as 'a fundamentalist curtain', so that 'any Soviet moves beyond its borders would be likely to encounter the full wrath of Islam'.

Following the Gulf War, 'Orientalists' such as Bernard Lewis reinvigorated the threat in the idea of Islam (cited in Bresheeth and Yuval-Davis 1991). According to Huntington's (1996) thesis, the New World Order is based on patterns of conflict and cooperation founded on cultural distinctions and identifications, 'the clash of civilizations'. Huntington himself talks of 'the indigestibility of Muslims' (Huntington 1996: 264) and their 'propensity towards violent conflict', which makes them threatening (Huntington 1996: 258). The notion of such polar models is argued equally from within Islam as with Bishara's (1995: 87) 'cultural anomie' where two new global orders made up of 'opposing cultural ecologies', the information society paradigm and Islamic community paradigm, struggle for power (Mowlana 1993). For both Huntington (1996) and Mowlana (1993), the former has dominance but the latter constitutes a significant force. Its strength and therefore threat is seen to lie in Muslims being contained by neither nation states nor any other geographical or political treaty boundaries in a time when nation states are no longer the only sole political and economic influences on the international system. For Sayyid (1997) and Ahmed (1993), this amounts to a total shift in the global order, what Ahmed calls a 'new phase in human history', a decentring of the West. According to this thesis, Islam is a challenge to the Western world, which is caused to question its identity. On this basis, it is necessary for the West to reaffirm its identity to preserve itself from dissolution (Kramer 1997).

However, this 'green peril', according to Halliday (1996) constitutes a second myth about Islam. It is not the religious or cultural character of Islam that is a threat, but the fear of loss of power and of anti-Western sentiments. In the current situation, Islam would be seen as most threatening if it endangered Western interests in the Middle East. The loss of control over oil prices would lead to a loss of control and power for, in particular, the USA, and would threaten its image as the number one superpower. Western activities against Islamic countries are defended under the guise that Islamic militancy threatens Western security (Djerejian 1997). An example of the contradictions in this ideology can be seen in the support the USA has given to Islamic countries and groups — Saudi Arabia, Pakistan, General Zia's Islamic fundamentalist programme, when it has *served their interests*. This has often been against secular countries such as Iraq. It is also a threat that allows the West to maintain and build its arms industry. According to Hippler (1995), the religious element is convenient to the West, allowing it to avoid having to examine and deal with the real problems, the socio-economic causes. The link with religion in Western perceptions allows only one response: that of irrationality, which makes dialogue and policy-making difficult. For Hassan (1997) and Halliday (1992), the apparent global phenomenon of Islam with a mission to take over the world is made all the more questionable by the actuality of Islamist movements. Given their relative weakness, both economically and militarily, and that conflicts tend to be regionally based, these groups pose little threat to 'the West'.

Islam has therefore been rediscovered and interpreted as a counter-alternative to the West. Halliday (1996) suggests that Islam fulfils the Western need for a menacing but subordinated Other, and thus fills Esposito's 'threat vacuum' (Halliday 1992: 3). This conceptualization is supported by the *image* of Islam, the global aggressor, as Muslims are seen to constitute a problem to many countries including India, Israel, Russia, the USA and Europe. While at the current time, Hippler (1995) argues, Western foreign policy does not match the ideology of Islam as a threat in the Western media; these images of 'the enemy' have created the politico-psychological prerequisites to justify military action if necessary.

Whether one believes the threat is cultural, political, significant or a myth, these scholars are in no doubt that Islam's challenge to 'Eurocentrism' has resulted in attempts by the West to recentre itself, re-establishing Western supremacy. This project seeks to sustain Western global power by creating an invisible empire through cultural domination.[6] According to Sayyid (1997), in conditions that make this unachievable, Islamism acts as a reminder in its failure to recognize the universalism of the Western project. Hence Islam is interpreted as 'the Other the West cannot embrace, even at its most tolerant' (Sayyid 1997: 160).

Some of these arguments result in an Occidentalism that allows the West to be unified and denies the diversity and conflicts within its own past and present. I would suggest that, in 'the West', these writers are primarily referring to the USA, followed by Europe. It is perhaps US foreign policy that primarily defines itself in relation to Islam in the ways described here. Does Europe, in particular Britain, follow this example and fall into US foreign policy speak? Yet these countries have had different historic relationships with Islam and the Middle East. Winter (1999), for example, has recently argued that Britain has lacked a history of self-construction against a specifically Islamic Other. From these arguments, it would appear that the media ignore this and follow the US ideological construction of Islam. This is something that will be examined within the demographic context of the UK. Is globalization partly responsible for an overarching discourse on Islam?

Globalization and Islam

Globalization 'refers to those processes, operating on a global scale, which cut across national boundaries, integrating and connecting communities and organizations in new space–time combinations, making the world in reality and in experience more interconnected' (Giddens 1990: 64). Shifts in the global order have resulted in turmoil and fragmentation in Europe, for the ambiguity of boundaries in eastern Europe has resulted in a lack of political certainties and alliances. This has led to a need to identify a common cultural heritage with a criterion for Europe's limits. The revitalized concern with Islam is an additional source of xenophobic hostility by Western European countries, according to Husband (1994). He argues that countries, becoming more 'fragile and neurotic' (Husband 1994: 6) due to varying economic and cultural assaults, have been experiencing 'a highly sensitized self-conscious negotiation of their concept of the nation' (Husband 1994: 8). Attempts to maintain the status quo have seen the emergence of 'Fortress Europe' as countries build bigger barriers to protect themselves from invasion from 'outsiders' (Bunyan 1991). Global instability has resulted in an increase in the movement of peoples. According to Lueg (1995: 25), the Third World with its poverty, disorganization and disease is seen to be migrating west and combines with other destabilizing trends to create a 'fear of the future'. For Sardar (1999), 'Islam' creates a further problem for the Western universalistic project of globalization (which does not exclude reverse flows) in not wanting to be subsumed within Western networks of politics and culture.

In a climate of rapid change and uncertainty, the negativization of the Islamic world is functional, fulfilling a 'psycho-political need'; 'Europe's efforts to reassure itself have been traditionally directed towards the East, until today it continues to find its antithesis there' (Lueg 1995: 41). As the site for the projection of negative aspects of Western culture, the Orient has been more about Western self-construction, for any points of criticism are removed to the Other (Sardar 1999). The lack of tolerance and freedom of speech the West shows in relation to Islam, for example, is hidden in its transference onto Islam where these characteristics are exaggerated, problematized and essentialized.

Processes of globalization, according to Robins (1991) are both eroding national identities and strengthening 'local' ones. This post-modern 'crisis of identity', seen globally, is reflected locally as resistance by host nations to the strengthening of minority identities and the loss of their own has led to an increase in ethnic absolutism in the form of 'national culture' (Gellner 1983). Halliday (1996) argues that this is a process by which groups make selective use of the past, rein-venting it to justify aspects of the present. Thus, the aim becomes to 'rebuild an identity that coheres, is unified and filters out threats in social experiences' (Sennett 1971: 15). It also constitutes a defensive strategy by minorities experiencing 'cultural racism'. [7]

The experience of migration adds to the dislocation of identity through exposure to new values. Alienation, responses to controls on immigration, unemployment and discrimination all add to feelings of loss. Islam has offered a sense of identity and values to offset the psychological disaffection (Esposito 1992).

Hence, negative projections onto minority groups are inverted. Mutually antagonistic perspectives and misunderstandings are fuelled by the construction of the cultural clash in the media that renders the 'problem' unsolvable. These processes have been evident in the British national context because specific events have raised Muslim conscious-ness and public awareness of their presence. Ahmed (1992) suggests that the Rushdie affair was the catalyst for the British demonization of Muslims, exposing the vast gaps in understandings of each other. This, and some Muslim support for Saddam Hussein in the Gulf War, has been interpreted as Muslim separatism and has led to a questioning of the loyalty of 'Muslims within' Britain's boundaries (Werbner 1994). The response for Ahmed (1992: 113) was based on an undervalued powerless community's 'cry of identity', which in turn sharpened the sense of a Muslim identity (or identities) and led to the politicization of Muslims in the UK.

Global coverage of world events through the media, along with feelings of isolation and cultural threat from the host community, allow feelings of empathy and solidarity across space and time, promoting the idea of the worldwide eternal 'Muslim community' (Cohen 1997). This has resulted, according to Vertovec (1996), in a transference of the anti-Western threatening stance of global 'fundamentalist' groups to British Muslims, who have increasing prominence in the public sphere due to improved organization and political articulation.[8] However, Vertovec (1996) suggests that migrant groups should interpret this as an attempt to exercise their liberal rights, often representing panic about how to maintain control in the community and responses to their exclusionary treatment, rather than extremism. Halliday (1996) also argues that the appearance of solidarity with other countries is usually for secular reasons like the need for funding, rather than solidarity based on faith.

Ethnic majority fears of a supposed Islamic threat have strengthened the politics of assimilation. The contemporary manifestation of this Orientalist discourse has been defined as 'Islamophobia' (Runnymede Trust 1997). In Britain then, as elsewhere, Islam has come to be represented as a homogenous threat, despite representing differing sects, ethnicities and language groups that have been further fragmented through emigration. The ideology of a fundamentalist threat allows the British government to suppress the activities of Muslims at home. One example of this is the suppression of 'terrorist' dissidents in London, amid fears of US embassy attacks following the retaliatory American air strikes on Afghanistan and Sudan, aimed at Osama bin Laden who was thought to be the prime instigator of the terrorist attacks on US embassies in Kenya and Tanzania (August 1998). However, I will show that, despite this largely negativizing process, the political necessity of maintaining harmonious social relations has meant, especially in recent years, that in the UK the government has encouraged minority voices in the public sphere to avoid the effects of dislocation and extremism. Hence, I expect the image of British Islam to be less extreme than that of its global Other.

To summarize, it has been argued that Islam is currently defined as a worldwide homogenous threat to 'the West' both physically and ideologically. The counter argument maintains that the rise of Islamism, in actuality, comprises heterogeneous movements that arise from specific political, economic and social contexts and thus Islam cannot be an explanatory factor for the behaviour of all Muslims.

Rather than having a unilinear history, the relationship between 'Islam' and 'the West' can be seen to have been constructed at historical moments when crises led to popular discourses that reflected the needs of the time. The current resurgence in the demonization of Islam, then, is due to specific political conditions. As Said (1978: 273) has already identified, an Orientalist discourse is a product of certain 'cultural, professional, national, political, and economic requirements of the epoch'. In current times, opposing sides use an essentialist discourse and historical relation of confrontation to justify specific actions, to 'legitimize, mislead, silence and mobilize' (Halliday 1996: 7). Despite shifts in the reasons for demonization, however, some discursive consistency towards Islam remains from early Christian constructions to the present day and this is evident in contemporary social structures. Academic subjects such as political science, for example, often serve powerful political and economic interests. However, these common features should not be interpreted as evidence of a fixed, unchanging Oriental discourse. Rather, new formulations reinforce the old to meet the requirements of the time. The aim here, as Halliday (1996) recommends, has been to reveal the myth and consequently the agenda behind it, usually concealed by the media production processes that render the product seemingly neutral. I will now examine arguments relating to the specific form that current images are said to take.

Representation of Islam: Islam the media villain

The bulk of literature on Islam and the West looks at media representations within a wider examination of the international context of power relations. The latter takes precedence while the set of images receives less attention. The media have become the primary focus of attention as they have superseded other institutions in the cultural production of knowledge. Though consensual, these theories on the *global* image of Islam are based on observations rather than systematic empirical evidence and tend to be measured in relation to some kind of 'truth' about Islam, be that Islamic belief or Muslims' lived experience. This belies a tendency to see coverage of Islam as 'misrepresentation', implying that there is a 'reality' that could be represented accurately (albeit a diverse and changing *reality* as opposed to an essential Islam). Once again, Said (1981), in work succeeding *Orientalism*, draws our attention to the problems of (cross-cultural) representation. He maintains that while he is not suggesting that there is a real Islam out there to be represented (as the religion itself will always be subject to interpretation) there are gradations of knowledge — good, bad, accurate and indifferent. It is then possible under certain conditions to know or represent the Other fairly. Mir (1998), however, questions the idea of a simple choice between self-representation and representation by a hegemonic or unsympathetic Other. She argues that due to processes of globalization and the increasing plurality of societies, identities are not so distinctly aligned. This is a debate that will be raised again but for now the aim here is to describe the 'Islam(s)' that is 'the result of agreed-upon convention, historical processes, assigned identity' (Said 1981: 42).

The starting point for this focus is again Said (1981). In his text, *Covering Islam*, he examines '*how the media and experts determine how we see the rest of the world*' by attending to US media coverage of the siege of their embassy in Iran in 1981. For Said, this was a significant moment both in cementing current manifestations of the Orientalist discourse through which Islam has become 'known' and the point from which media coverage of Islam increased dramatically. In particular, Said identifies the 1979 Iranian Revolution as being the initial signifier to the West of the resurgence of Islam and its problematization, with the result that Iran has come to symbolize relations with the Islamic world. Thus, Muslims are associated with militancy, danger and anti-Western sentiment. He argues that the eradication of any social/historical context involved in reporting the siege resulted in perceptions of Muslim terrorists holding the US to hostage. In fact, Said argues that, through ignorance, cultural hostility and racial hatred, Islam is not allowed to be known; it is 'covered up'. Yet, it is the media that form the 'cultural apparatus' through which Europeans and Americans derive their consciousness of Islam (Said 1981: 43). The media images received are informed by official definitions of Islam that serve the interests of government and business. The success of the images then is not in their accuracy but in the power of the people who produce them, the triumph of which is hardly challenged; 'labels have survived many experiences and have been capable of adapting to new events, information and realities' (Said 1981: 9). This type of reporting was equally evident in coverage of the Gulf War. Kellner (1992) has shown how the Western governments involved managed the media, providing little access to battle zones and resulting in depictions that were distorted but coherent with government ideologies.

Texts written after Said's work have a discursive consistency in identifying the same derogatory themes and topics associated with Islam. In a global context, this would appear mainly to be with regard to fundamentalism, political instability and the portrayal of women (Ahmed 1992). The application of a Western ideological framework, or alternatively ethnocentric 'ways of seeing' (Dahlgren and Chakrapani 1982: 45), has resulted in the 'domesticated Islamic world or those aspects considered to be newsworthy' (Said 1981: 26). The creation of a dichotomy between Islam and the West is a consequence of this, presented in the press along a series of binary oppositions in which the West stands for rational, humane, developed and superior, and Islam for aberrant, undeveloped and inferior. Opposition tends to be defined within these conceptual categories rather than, for example, Islam against Christianity or East against West. This is partly due to conceptualizations of the different civilizations that fix the (Middle) East as Islamic and therefore primitive, but also make it harder to find commonalities between them. While 'Islam' as a collectivity is used unproblematically, representing Christianity as 'the West' is deemed problematic. The concentration on cultural dualities as opposed to political processes contributes to this confrontational dichotomy and, according to Dahlgren and Chakrapani (1982), acts as a form of cultural reassurance. However, as we have seen before, the coherence of an Orientalist discourse does not negate change. One example of how prevalent themes are adapted to suit the political purposes of the time is the image of the oil-rich Sheikh with his harem, which dominated the 1970s following the oil crisis but has diminished in recent press constructions of Muslims.

After consultation with a number of Islamic groups and its own review of the literature, the Commission on British Muslims and Islamophobia (Runnymede Trust 1997) developed its own framework of representation for contemporary times in terms of 'closed' as opposed to 'open' views of Islam. It suggests, however, that while on some occasions closed views of Islam may be applicable to the policies and programmes of some Islamist groups, an undifferentiated image of Islam is entirely inappropriate, particularly in relation to Muslims living in the UK. It places the discourse relating to Islam into eight main categories. These are as follows:

- Muslim cultures are seen to be unchanging and monolithic;

- Muslim cultures are wholly different from other cultures;
- Islam is inferior, different, barbaric, irrational, primitive and sexist;
- Islam is threatening;
- Islam's adherents use their faith for political advantage;
- Muslims' criticisms of the West are rejected out of hand;
- hostility towards Islam is used to justify discriminatory practices;
- Islamophobia is assumed to be unproblematic (Runnymede Trust 1997).

What evidence has been provided to support these points? While these themes are interconnected, they are explored separately here for ease of analysis. It is common in discourses about Islam to ignore the diversity and differences between Muslims. For Said (1981), the homogenization of Muslims works as an 'ideological cover', which contributes significantly to ignorance about the Other. Thus, each Muslim bears the burden of responsibility required to represent Islam, with the result that the limited framework of representations is applied to all Muslims with little distinction. Homogenization based on ethnicity has also been found in wider research on minorities and the media (Sreberny-Mohammadi and Ross 1995).

This 'universal cover' has been used as a key to understanding how Muslim groups behave in social and political arenas, yet evidence of various practices and differences shows how Islam cannot be used as a sole explanation for the behaviour of Muslim groups. Other factors need to be invoked (Halliday 1995). Muslims are fragmented in terms of their varying nationalities, regions, politics, sects and languages. Demographic factors such as age, gender, class and education should also be taken into account. According to Halliday (1995), disunion has been further compounded, in Britain, by the absence of a central leadership and by the process of immigration. Werbner (1991) suggests that this diversity is reflected by internal divisions within the community on who represents it, for example, when bidding for council funding. This process, which promotes a 'divide and rule' ethos in competition for funding, has caused friction between the communities, fragmenting them in an environment in which collectivity is needed for strength. Westwood's (1991) research into the black youth group, Red Star, shows how groups can be more successful politically when they stress their commonality above their differences.

One method, which media producers use and which adds to this unified effect, is the repeated selection of more extreme individuals and sources (who claim) to represent the community. This is something to which Muslims and other minority groups strongly object (Gunter and Viney 1993).

The static nature of Muslim cultures is represented in the form of despotism linked to social stagnation. The Western ideology of modernization and the Islamicization of Muslim politics have provided a way of seeing Islam as anti-modern when, in fact, it is doctrinally blameless (Said 1981). Western states therefore appear to be models of progress, leaving Muslims in a situation where they are compelled to keep up.

Schulze (1995) refutes the medieval nature of Muslim societies. He argues that Islamic societies have their own versions of modernity that share many aspects of the 'universal kind' but have also been shaped by Islamic cultural traditions. Islam as the antithesis of modernity disguises the multitude of political positions and worldviews present in the discourse of heterogeneous civil Islamic society. 'The West's' hypocrisy in the fight for democracy versus turmoil and terrorism is illustrated by its support for authoritarian states like Saudi Arabia.

It is this aspect of Orientalist discourse that results in Muslims being subject to 'rituals of degradation' (Hall 1992a). Thus, they are represented as uncivilized and barbaric. Focusing on stories of inhumane punishments in the Muslim world and ignoring stories about their victimization create a distorted picture of Muslims created for a public that has few alternative images (Hassan 1997).

Misogyny and the myth of Muslim women are images also used to reinforce the idea of oppression at the 'hands of an ancient religion', particularly accentuated by Muslim women's 'medieval' dress (Lueg 1995). This demonization of Islam occurs from within both patriarchal and feminist cultures, hence from the right and the left, encompassing a wide political spectrum (Nazlee 1996).

Furthermore, the supposed conflictual *nature* of Islam, further strengthened by images of extremism, fanaticism and irrationality, compounds the discourse of backwardness (Ahmed 1992). This extremism is attributed to all Muslims by linking every conflict to the concept of *jihad* and Islam (Hassan 1997) and contributes to a cumulative conception of Islam as threatening. According to Lueg (1995: 15), this is based on images of 'oriental irrationality and the fanatical masses', allowing Muslims to be kept at a distance and impersonalized. Hansen and Murdock (1985: 231) used Le Bon's concept of 'the crowd' to show how it invoked primitiveness and irrationality in the populist discourse of newspaper coverage of the 1981 Toxteth riots. The crowd was shown as 'an illegitimate form of expression' based on 'violence and extremism' as opposed to the legitimate form of democracy based on 'orderliness and moderation'. Media use of unfavourable terminology in relation to Muslims is another aspect of their dehumanization (Hassan 1997). These discursive practices accord texts their credibility and the appearance of truth in their 'scientific expertise' (Said 1981: 39).

As an example of this practice, the 'fundamentalist' is by far the most prevalent image that is used to constitute a threat (Lueg 1995). By omitting to associate it with a larger resurgence of political religious movements, such as the Christian Coalition, and paying little attention to, for example, Jewish religious fanaticism, Sayyid (1997) argues that Islamic fundamentalism has become a metaphor for fundamentalism in general. All Muslim acts interpreted as extreme are then constituted as fundamentalism, which is then linked to terrorism. Yet, as Bishara (1995) maintains, there is a huge difference between fundamentalism, which Bishara calls 'political religion', and the popular religion to which most Muslims, particularly those living in Britain, adhere. Bishara goes further to say that the activities of the radical movements under the banner of Islam have actually distanced them from the majority of 'ordinary' Muslims.

Islam is also perceived as threatening through being depicted as an alien culture. This is not a new phenomenon. Ethnic minority groups have long been portrayed as the alien Other and threatening because of mass immigration, with the use of the rhetorical device of 'them' and 'us' in popular discourse suggesting that 'we' are under attack. This was practised during the influx of economic migrants in the 1950s and more recently in response to political asylum seekers. Because the discourse is normalized, its links with particular power structures and interests are concealed. The recurring theme of immigration as a problem has now shifted to Muslims (van Dijk 1991), which Lueg (1995) suggests is due to the population explosion in the Middle East and Third World, but more recently has been reinforced by conflicts in Europe. British Muslims in their uniformity to other Muslims become the 'fifth column' within and their loyalty is constantly in question (Runnymede Trust 1997). The portrayal in numbers of people moving across borders further provokes ideas about desires to take over the world. These images of invasion and infiltration further contribute to the new enemy conceptualization. The combination of the hostile threat and movement of Islam promotes the idea that it needs to be managed in a way that allows varied prejudicial practices to continue.

Esposito (1992) suggests that, as we have seen, such images blind us to a reality in which Islam is far from a threat. Most Muslims live in the underdeveloped world, which, with its poverty and illiteracy combined with the geo-politics of the West, is far removed from global power (Hassan 1997).

Despite the consistency of this regime of representation, contra-dictory images abound. Islam is monolithic but sectarian. It is fixed and an excuse to adapt what is outside Islam, which allows Muslims to be seen as manipulative. Islam is a threat but inferior. This 'dual vision' reveals the functional aspect of the discourse, which positions Islam according to desired needs (Dahlgren and Chakrapani 1982: 55).

These constitute the representations of Muslims on a global scale, a limited range of stereotypes lacking in positive and apolitical images, a representation that appears to tell us more about the representers than the represented. This system of representation seems typical of report-ing on the Third World in general, with its lack of political explanations and historical context and the routinization of violence within a frame-work of instability (Dahlgren and Chakrapani 1982). Given the determining factor, however, the political context of the discourse, could we expect to find a wider range of representations on a local scale in a British national context? Some coverage in the UK has had positive intentions, such as the BBC's programmes *Living Islam* and *Mahabarat* (One World Broadcasting Trust 1993). Ahmed (1992) pays tribute to Channel 4's engagement with these issues. However, these are one-off programmes and are unrepresentative of coverage overall. Represen-tations of the war in Bosnia constitute one example of the image of 'victimhood', which has developed as a counter image in recent years (Männistö 1997). However, this image still associates Muslims with conflict and as posing a problem to other sets of people. The categoriz-ation of Kosovo's Albanians as Muslim has been minimal within the vast coverage on the war with Serbia (1999). However, Wiegand (1999) argues that there has been a greater tendency to focus on this aspect of their identity than with the Serbs, evidence of wider patterns of representation in which the role of religion in conflicts involving Muslims is misperceived.

The Commission on British Muslims and Islamophobia (Runnymede

Trust 1997) focuses solely on the image of Islam in the content of the British media and its findings are similar. It pays particular attention to imagery in cartoons for their explicit simplification of ideologies, drawing on 'stock images', and it is their repetition that gives these stereotypes about Islam 'greater currency and credibility such that they become part of common-sense, something to be taken completely for granted' (Runnymede Trust 1997: 21). However, it fails to differentiate between representations of British and non-British Muslims. Critical of all sectors of the British media, including the liberal press, which, it argues, is guilty of an exclusionary liberalism, it barely differentiates between the different sectors of the British media and does not present a systematic analysis of the representations. The purpose of my research is to examine 'local' representations of local people. Does it match theories relating to global images of Islam and, if not, what are the local factors impinging on these representations?

The sort of coverage that has been described here results in an 'identikit' Muslim, chosen for his or her ability to fit into the above pre-conceived categories (One World Broadcasting Trust 1993: 32). These arguments correspond with theories and research on ethnic minorities and the media in Britain and other European countries (van Dijk 1991). Findings show that ethnic minorities are critical of their negative portrayal; of their marginalization to specific issues; of the lack of provision and poor scheduling of minority programming on television; and of the undifferentiated, peripheral, rarely 'realistic' and one-sided portrayals of themselves in the media (Halloran et al. 1995; Sreberny-Mohammadi and Ross 1995). A dislike of Islam cannot be seen as the defining feature of hostility towards Muslims; it includes a complex mixture of xenophobia and racism. The supposed shift from skin colour to cultural practices as 'the ethnic signifier' has increased Muslims' visibility, given that being a Muslim often comprises an explicit projection of both (Hall 1977). What understandings have race research provided that can aid an analysis of Muslim representations?

Representation of ethnic minorities

Race research has developed in a wider context of mass media research with early approaches focusing on the ideological role of the mainstream media in securing social consent. Attention to the text as a site of hegemonic struggle, differentiation within and between cultural products in the expression of racial discourse, developed along with semiotic and structural analysis in the 1980s.

These ongoing and overlapping phases also occurred with changing significations of race. The history of race reporting is rooted in a specific colonial past in the UK, according to Hall (1992a), who argues that early expansion led to an over-simplified 'system of representation' based on a dichotomy of the 'West and the rest' through which difference became the standard by which the West's achievements were measured (see Said 1978 on *Orientalism*). This, according to Silverman and Yuval-Davis (1998) has developed in the post-colonial period into a conceptual framework based on a race relations paradigm that assumes that racism affects races in terms of commonwealth countries, thus excluding others from this discourse. Institutional categorization based on race has defined social relations and determined both mediations of the Other and research on this basis.

Early studies found that coverage was limited to the criminalization of minorities, with an emphasis on black youth and on their immigration being the site and source of problems 'within' (Chibnall 1977; Hall et al. 1978; Solomos 1988). News reports were found to pursue confrontational frameworks with the negativized Other contrasted with the tolerant host society. This was particularly evident in research on inner city disturbances in the 1980s (Joshua et al. 1983; Murdock 1984). Cottle (1992) suggests that this law and order discourse displaces attention from institutional inequalities and racism derived from a policy framework based on colonial criteria. Although these discourses are applicable to all minorities, it should be noted that the press problematizes minority groups in different ways and assigns stereotypical roles to them, so that, for example, the breakdown of the family may be a problem for Afro-Caribbean representation but not for Asians.

As definitions of race are politically and historically contested, resulting in their continual transformation, research has reflected dissatisfaction with the narrow basis on which race has previously been perceived. The marginalization of some groups within the black/white paradigm and the 'racialized boundaries' this reproduces, as well as changing social and political realities have led to a rethinking of black cultural politics along the lines of the politics of ethnicity (Anthias and Yuval-Davis 1992; Gilroy 1988; Hall 1988). Increasingly, questions are being asked about definitions of ethnicity and ethnic identity based on processes of globalization and postmodernism that have created a fluidity of cultural identities. Research has shifted to focus on minority media and on the creative reworking of cultural forms, experiences and expressions of fragmentation and displacement (Mercer 1988). Popular cultural forms such as rap music and hip-hop are examples of how boundaries of form and genre are being challenged in order to explore issues around identity, structures and conventions. Acknowledgement of these processes and their effects has resulted in a wider context of debate in which 'different histories, traditions and ethnic identities' are recognized. Through these acknowledgements, a space has opened up to include Muslims (both in terms of identification and dis-crimination).[9]

It is generally considered that a 'struggle around the image' has resulted in some broadening of the regime of representation of 'black' people (Hall 1997b: 257). Yasmin Alibhai-Brown, at a conference on Islam and the media organized by the One World Broadcasting Trust (1993: 5), suggested that on this basis there are possibilities for the improvement of the representation of Muslims *provided there is some awareness, in the public arena, of the representations and their conse-quences*. However, Entman (1990: 332) suggests that the result of this is 'modern racism', a more implicit protection of white interests. This concept has emerged from research in the USA, which shows that while people freely espouse abstract notions of equality, they continue to oppose policies that appear to 'favour' minorities (Katz and Taylor 1988). Entman (1990: 332) argues that TV news plays a significant role here in a climate in which 'old-fashioned racism', described as 'beliefs that blacks are inferior and should be segregated', is no longer accep-table and in which there is an economic imperative to appeal to black audiences. Journalists' efforts to portray blacks and their interests have, however, caused antagonism over what appears as blacks receiving 'special treatment' when this is no longer required. The portrayal of black politicians as emotional and conflictual in an attempt to boost ratings, juxtaposed with a continuing focus on criminal behaviour, has exacerbated the problem. Romer et al. (1998) have criticized this model for emphasizing the role of individual prejudice and suggesting that in ensuring that journalists were non-racists, ethnocentric biases would be eliminated. This is unlikely given the continuing dominance of market forces within the context of the wider capitalist system. In a climate that deems racism unacceptable, have the more explicit discourses applied to former groups shifted to an acceptable enemy: Muslims? Said (1981:

149) has argued that this discourse has now entered the 'cultural canon' and, consequently, will be very difficult to change.

Have 'repertoires of representation' around difference (in Hall's words 1997b) simply been transferred to Muslims, or has there been a shift to a more complex recognition of the politics of ethnicity in the press? Though Muslims are considered to be a minority group, this is based on a religious rather than an ethnic collectivity. This representational dimension therefore should also be included in this analysis to enable a comparison with a representational paradigm on Islam.

Representing religion

Research into the representation of religion reveals a general concern about the derision of religion and of religious people in popular television forms. Gunter and Viney (1993), in their research on religious broadcasting in Britain among multi-religious audiences, found that there was a general concern (80 per cent of respondents) that the media compounded negative images and inaccurate stereotypes, distorting ideas about religion. Other research in this area has been completed mainly in America around Christian traditions, concentrating on religious groups and their encounters with the media rather than religious representation and the general population. For example, studies have shown that people are attracted to content that is most congruent with their own needs and values (Roberts 1983), that the religious are regular newspaper readers, particularly of local papers (Stamm and Weis 1986) and that negative news is more persuasive in reducing support for particular religions than positive news is in generating support. This was the case for a drop in support for televangelists among religious audiences in America who received more exposure to the secular media's highly critical coverage of the Praise The Lord (PTL) television network's financial and sexual scandal (Abelman 1991). The recurring problem with studies on mass media and religious groups has been the measurement of religiosity, which has been defined, on the whole, as attendance at a place of worship.

A central issue of concern to this project is whether 'the media' can ever 'capture' any religion effectively given their secular nature and attention to 'surface appearance', situated, as they are, in a commercial environment (Shayon and Cox 1994). Secularization theory has it that as society becomes more secular, religion will be increasingly seen as a more primitive way of life (Merton 1957). The media, as a modern institution in a secular society, will reflect this. Religion, therefore, is also an Other that becomes more problematic when it involves non-Christian religions, entailing all the difficulties of cross-cultural representation. It is essential then to examine the context within which representations are produced in order to understand the nature of the output. In the case of this study, what are the conditions of news production and the consequences for representations of Islam?

The manufacture of news

It is widely recognized that one cannot make judgements about portrayals without considering the wider context within which they are produced. This has been the basis for a number of studies on news practices from within a political economy approach. Such studies have found news to be a conservative phenomenon, limited and maintained by constraining factors such as organizational routines and journalistic values and practices. Early studies showed news to be a reproduction of the dominant ideology of leading groups in society (Glasgow University Media Group 1976). More recently, this theory has developed to see it as a contested space among the definers of news, within institutions and for audiences, but ultimately limited by the hegemonic discourse of the ruling elites (Hall 1980).

At a micro level, production studies have concentrated on examining media institutional arrangements and professional practices (Tuchman 1978; Tunstall 1971). Factors involved in the news-making process include the predominance of elite media personnel, the news selection/gathering process, the continued persistence of news values, and the privileging of elite and institutional news sources, which work to marginalize alternative voices.[10] Structure and routine combine with the dominant interpretative frameworks of journalists, resulting in consensual output based on preconceptions and assumptions rather than on wilful manipulation (Bell 1991; Chibnall 1981; Epstein 1973; Galtung and Ruge 1965; Gans 1979; Kushnick 1970). In relation to race reporting, studies have emphasized the lack of specialist ethnic reporters and understanding as well as processes of integration and constraint on ethnic reporters (Corner 1986; Cottle 1993; Entman 1992).

News practices are inscribed by relations of power (and therefore the power to represent) with degrees of power in the hands of different groups within and outside the industry. At a macro-level, structures of ownership are key to this and can only be understood within the wider social and economic context. Market driven media must maximize profitability by attracting large, well-defined audiences for their sponsors — hence the tendency to promote a conservative consensual ideology, reinforcing the status quo (Curran and Seaton 1992; Murdock 1982). For the media to develop in a more democratic way would take regulation and subsidy, internal and external reform. This is not something that looks imminent as an increasingly freed-up global market, with its growing commercial pressures, moves towards conglomeration, furthering the closure of the communication process. The growth of populist commercialism is one outcome of these processes. In addition, we are witnessing greater attempts at manipulation of the political agenda by political parties and powerful lobbies. Ironically, one of these strategies includes reducing political intervention as politicians try to win over the powerful media moguls, aware of the potential influence their various cultural forms possess (McManus 1994; Murdock 1990). An increasing reliance on news agencies and the development of new technologies look set to continue these trends (Katz 1992; Paterson 1997). Yet, the processes involved in the selection and structuring of news remain hidden from the audience, which tends to accept conventions based on a self-evident professional wisdom rather than as definite social and political ways of understanding the world.

How have writers on Islam understood this process as a way of explaining its media image? Most make reference to the non-Muslim journalist working within specific conditions. This ranges from deliberate 'disinformation' or provocation by governments, media institutions and/or media personnel (Ahmed 1992; Morris 1989) to cognitive values, national identification and professional laziness all playing their part in asserting and maintaining the post-communist hegemony (Esposito 1992; Said 1981).

This type of individualism, however, is grounded in theories that argue that interpretations of Islam are based on vested interests and a will for power that are reflected out to the culture at large (Karim 2000; Said 1981). Images of Islam in the news therefore correspond with what prominent sectors take them to be, the purpose being to circulate antipathy, positioning people by news items that are, according to Dahlgren and Chakrapani (1982: 62), evidence of 'an implied commitment to a particular form of global order'. This results in readers who are unable to consider the real causes of confrontation but who are provoked to imagine a 'clash of cultures'.

In developing a conceptual framework, I have established a hypothesis that images of Islam will form a 'particular symbolic universe, a relatively stable and recognisable world of (TV) news' (Dahlgren and Chakrapani 1982: 45). This 'constitutes a communal core of interpretations' (Said 1981: 43), a consensus definition of what is important in relation to Islam, outside of which other issues are deemed irrelevant to our understandings of 'Islam'. These news frameworks or 'facile labels' are seen as radically limiting knowledge of Islam and are therefore obstacles to understanding (Esposito 1992: 163). Each event is seen as characteristic of Islam rather than as an event in its own right. And, as we have seen in this chapter, there are many reasons why it may not be in each paper's interest to question the way we see Islam.

In an examination of theories of racist ideology, Cohen (1988) warns of the reductionism in the reification of either institutional racism or the individual. To subsume one under the other, he argues, is to ignore the multiple dimensions of its articulation. By providing a multi-level analysis in theories of ethnocentric discourse in relation to Islam, I have shown how representations cannot be examined apart from economic, political, social and cultural factors. Said's theory of Orientalism has been particularly influential in framing this debate. Explanations for the absence of diversity in media images of Islam are apparent in theories on the interplay of politics and society, on the historical conflictual relationship between Islam and the West, on current political processes including globalization and fragmentation, on the politics of differentiation and ethnicity, with religion adding an extra dimension to hostility, and on institutional news practices operating within a market environment. Within these frameworks, we can begin to understand current manifestations of Islam in a British context, rather than relying on historical stereotypes for evidence.

2. Framing Islam: a quantitative analysis

I n this chapter I make transparent *the framework of reporting* of British Islam. In *Race as News*, Hartmann et al. (1974: 145) refer to a 'news framework' as 'the set of inferences about what it is related to, that define an area of subject-matter, and provide the terms in which it is discussed'. Using this notion, I will show how portrayals of British Muslims are limited in the daily coverage of the British mainstream quality press.[1] Questions of concern include, what does coverage of British Islam look like and in what ways is it newsworthy? How often does British Islam make the news? Where does the action take place? And who is allowed to speak for or to represent Islam?

Introduction

Clearly, the number of articles a newspaper publishes on a particular subject gives an indication of its editorial policy, the attention and thus importance attached to this subject, and the degree to which a paper has informed its readers. To identify the sort of material and patterns of coverage in different papers over a period of time, two broadsheets, the *Guardian* and *The Times*, and their sister Sunday papers, the *Observer* and the *Sunday Times* were chosen for their differing political/ ideological stances, the *Guardian* being left of centre and *The Times* conservative. Critics of media coverage of Islam often draw on tabloid articles for their evidence. Would coverage in the 'quality' press be fairer and more diverse given that the broadsheets are supposedly characterized by an 'objectivist' epistemology of news?[2] Attention to these newspapers provides wider and more detailed coverage of stories related to Muslims and at least some of the range of ideas circulating on Islam and being disseminated by Establishment and elite groups.

The Times is one of the longest established newspapers in Britain and is known internationally. The media mogul Rupert Murdoch's News International, whose newspapers constitute 35 per cent of national daily sales, owns it. Though perhaps it is less influential than it was 30 years ago, circulation has increased from 285,000 in 1965 to 718,213 in 2000 and the *Sunday Times* is now selling approximately 1,411,942 copies compared with its 1,275,000 in 1965.[3]

The trustees of the Scott Trust, which was set up to ensure its continuance, control the *Guardian*. A non-profit making organization, the revenues made from its *Manchester Evening News* provide financial support to the *Guardian*. A paper that supports liberal causes such as the rights of minorities, it is, however, somewhat less radical now than in the past.[4] Accounting for only 3 per cent of UK national daily sales, the *Guardian* sold an average of 401,567 dailies in 2000 compared with its 276,000 in 1965, slightly lower than its circulation numbers in the 1980s and early 1990s. The *Observer*'s readership has almost halved in this time.[5] And both papers draw their readership from the higher socioeconomic groups.

The focus on British Muslims, of course, raises the problem of placing boundaries around definitions of 'British'. Is it possible to draw a line between 'foreign' and 'home' news? Categories of identity have significant fluidity because multiple attachments are increasingly the norm. A recent letter to the *Muslim News* (A. F. Khan, 'Not A British Muslim', 28 May 1999) argued that the category of 'British Muslim' could be applied only to people born as British Muslims. Since this would not include British converts or immigrants, and the objective here is to examine the discursive construction of Muslims in the British context, this would leave us with a much narrower framework of representation than desired. I chose to incorporate stories about British Muslims (and their activities internationally), and about 'Muslims in Britain' (non-British Muslims in the UK), which offer an opportunity to examine nuances in discourse based on differing signifiers.[6]

The data presented here reveal not only a narrow framework of reporting but also a close correspondence in the types of issues covered between papers, indicating the assumptions (cultural consensus) being made about what constitutes news in relation to Islam. What is illustrated is not only the limited range of topics associated with Islam but also the predominant themes that run through the coverage, a closer analysis of which will be examined in the next chapter. The subjects of interest can be regarded as cultural units in that they provide valid cultural indicators of symbolic content. Thus, a comprehensive picture is provided of current manifestations of British Islam as represented in two UK broadsheets at a particular historical moment.

Global to local

To contextualize the British situation, a comparison with coverage of Islam in its international entirety provides additional valuable insights. In the late 1990s, international events dominating the news media's attention included conflicts in Algeria, Afghanistan, Bosnia, Chechnya, Kashmir and Kosovo; the initial trials for war crimes of mainly Serbs in Bosnia; political coverage of elections in Bangladesh, India, Indonesia (resulting in sectarian violence), Iran (which also saw the withdrawal of European ambassadors after accusations of international terrorism by Germany and the monitoring of relations following the election of moderate Mohammed Khatami), and Pakistan, which also celebrated its fiftieth year of independence in 1997; the visits of various dignitaries, for example the Queen's visit to Pakistan and Princess Diana's visits to Pakistan and Bosnia; the disastrous fires in Mecca at the time of the pilgrimage and an equally destructive earthquake in Turkey; the ongoing Israel–Palestine peace talks; the death of King Hussein of Jordan; terrorist bombs in Pakistan, Israel, France, Nairobi and South Africa; the build-up to further conflict with Iraq in the Gulf; and American air strikes in Afghanistan and the Sudan following attacks on US embassies in Africa. This appears to validate the claims of the authors cited in Chapter 1 that coverage of Islam (and the 'Third World' in general) revolves around conflict, terrorism, social and political turmoil, and disaster.

The extensive coverage of international events in relation to Islam is significant in sustaining public awareness. This data illustrate that the main significance and focus on Islam is global. Given that over the three-year period analysed (1994–96), there were 6507 articles on Islam and only 837 of these were about British Muslims, just 12 per cent, images of Muslims abroad will therefore be at the forefront of people's minds. This is further compounded by a consistent reference to world events in the articles on British Islam, implying that Muslims are to be thought of as one and the same.[7]

Due to the specific focus on British Islam in this study, it has not been possible to identify correlations between the reporting of global and British affairs. However, it is evident that international events and their reporting can provide an indication of patterns of coverage of British Islam that occur as a consequence. Global events concentrating on war and aggression allow hostility towards Islam to become more acceptable and often raise questions regarding 'the enemy within'. Where there are direct links between international events and British interests, such as the American air strikes on Sudan and Afghanistan following the Nairobi bombings (1998), there is a marked increase in coverage in the British press of terrorist activity in the UK, suggesting that global issues are used to question the actions of and potentially reinforce judgements against British Muslims. It is interesting that these data illustrate how British Islam is becoming a more salient issue, despite a corresponding reduction in space given to global events (see Figure 2.1). This trend was evident up to 1997 and subsequent research illustrates a growth in news on British Islam from 244 articles in 1994 to 410 in 1999, so that it now accounts for 20 per cent of total coverage. However, the global continues to outweigh the local and interest in the global after 1997 has resumed. Further investigation of these patterns and relationships is hence required.

Figure 2.1 **Frequencies of coverage in the *Guardian and The Times*: global and British Islam comparatively**[8]

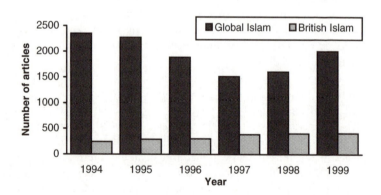

These trends are reflected in both *The Times* and the *Guardian*, although the *Guardian* covers issues relating to Islam more extensively than *The Times* (on average accounting for 57 per cent of articles) (see Figure 2.2).[9] However, *The Times* almost doubled the number of its articles on British Islam over the time period, lessening the difference in the quantity of coverage between the papers by 1999 (Figure 2.3).[10] While the *Guardian*'s coverage of British Islam therefore accounts for, on average, 56 per cent of the two papers' news items on this subject, similar to its percentage of global coverage, this drops from 65 per cent in 1994 to 53 per cent in 1999. Though a full analysis of the reasons for this difference is beyond the scope of this book, it is possible to identify areas of increased interest in the reporting of British Islam.[11]

Figure 2.2 **Comparative frequencies of the *Guardian* and *The Times*: global coverage**[12]

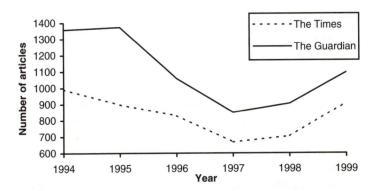

The total frequencies of British coverage excluded obituaries, reviews (television and arts), general articles about Islamic belief that were not geographically located, and articles that referred to Islam but whose substantial content was about an unrelated topic. This was due to the separate issues at work in the (press) selection of these articles. Over the three-year period, 246 articles appeared, 58 per cent of which were in the *Guardian*.[13] The numbers of these articles decreased each year, illustrating how the majority of coverage of Islam (and this is increasingly the case) consists of news rather than reviews. The two papers did, however, demonstrate a slightly different emphasis, *The Times* having a literary focus and the *Guardian* displaying a more general interest and openness to minority groups and their beliefs. This was evident in that, although both papers featured a similar quantity of all of these types of articles overall, the *Guardian* had three times as many articles that referred to Islam and a few more stories on general belief, while *The Times* included more book reviews.[14]

Figure 2.3 **Comparative frequencies of the *Guardian* and *The Times*: British coverage**

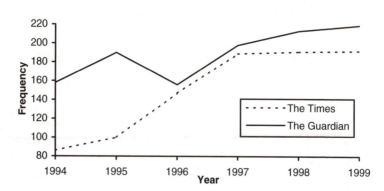

To put this coverage in perspective, I compared the amount of news on Islam to that of the other world religions (Figure 2.4).[15] Coverage of Islam accounted for 22 per cent of all reporting on the major world faiths. Islam was covered to a greater degree than the average number of 4990 articles per religion, at 6507 over the three-year period, similar to that of Christianity and Judaism, with slightly fewer articles. However, a good deal more space was allocated to these three religions than to the others, which perhaps reflects the fact that Judaism and Islam, as religions, are closer to Christianity in terms of doctrine and geography, with Judaism being thought of as having more parity within the cultural consensus. Buddhism, Hinduism and Sikhism might hold less appeal, in terms of news value, because of their distance from Christianity and Western culture, their non-threatening status and their lack of involvement in what the West sees as significant world events.[16]

The difference between papers was of little significance except in that *The Times*' coverage of Christianity included 806 more articles over the three years. This could reflect a more traditional emphasis in the paper, also evident in its domestic reporting. As was previously evident, the *Guardian*'s copy included more accounts of Islam, with 1071 more articles than *The Times* over the three-year period.

Figure 2.4 **Patterns of coverage of the major world religions**

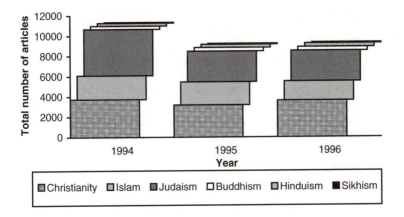

Domestic news

Table 2.1   Coverage of British Islam, 1994–96

Newspaper	No of articles	Percentage of total articles
Guardian	406	48.5
The Times	232	27.7
Sunday Times	101	12.1
Observer	98	11.7
Total	837	100

As we can see, the volume of news on British Islam reaching various audiences is highly differentiated. *Guardian* readers are presented with almost twice the amount of material as readers of *The Times* (Table 2.1). While I am unable to take account of the tone of the articles, I would suggest that the latter reflect the more traditional, Establishment news values of *The Times*, which is less likely to take an interest in items with less cultural proximity (Islam) unless they have extreme news value. The more extensive coverage assigned to minority groups and other alternative issues and perspectives in the *Guardian* is consistent with the results of other research in which the paper has been seen to express more tolerant and accommodating interpretations (Hartmann et al. 1974; Lacey and Longman 1997; van Dijk 1991). However, the differences in the proportion of space allocated to minority groups in the daily papers is not reflected in the Sunday ones, whose coverage has more parity with each other. This pattern of coverage, in terms of the percentage share of articles for each newspaper, is fairly consistent across the variables examined. For example, the number of items included on certain topics, such as education, tends to reflect the proportionate share of the total articles on Islam in each paper (in other words, there are more in the *Guardian*). This is a logical premise. Attention, therefore, is paid in particular to coverage that does not reflect this pattern.

Periodicity of coverage

Figure 2.5 clearly illustrates the changing patterns in the reporting of Islam. These patterns of coverage reflect both the event-centred nature of news[17] and news gathering processes in general, reflecting quiet and busy times. For instance, given the high number of news items that occur on policy relating to British Islam, including education and laws on religious discrimination, it is logical that there is less coverage of British Islam when Parliament is not in session. The main irregularity in this pattern of reporting is the increase in articles appearing in December each year, which may be due to an increase in dialogue and thought given to religion in general at this time, especially given the tendency uncovered by this analysis to refer to Islam in relation to Christianity. However, while patterns in the timing of coverage are shared between the dailies and their sister Sunday papers, they do not show a parity with each other (see Figure 2.5), illustrating that coverage is not just dependent on 'events' but on the differing news values of individual papers. For example, both papers have a similar number of articles occurring in December. However, these account for 24 per cent of all articles on British Islam in *The Times/Sunday Times* while only 12 per cent of the *Guardian/Observer* articles occur in this month, an example of *The Times'* tendency to invoke Islam in relation to Christianity rather than as a subject in its own terms. Some of the peaks and troughs, however, do correspond, providing evidence of an 'issue attention cycle' of news, similar to Downs (1972), but incorporating a wider range of factors in news production, which gives events their currency.[18]

Figure 2.5 **Monthly patterns of coverage in each paper, 1994–96**

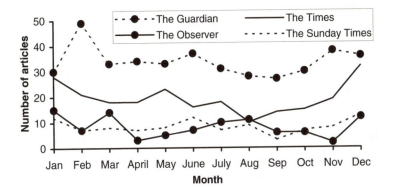

Topical analysis

To understand the content of press coverage on British Islam, particular emphasis must be given to the prominent topics of news items, by which I mean the overall subject category of an article (Hartmann et al. 1974). In addition to identifying the main topics of coverage, I also analysed the subtopics of articles (a secondary but prominent subject) and two significant references made to other related subjects. This is important if one is to discover not just what articles are about but what else is referred to in the treatment of particular topics, allowing for an identification of the type of material presented to the public on Islam and, therefore, the likely concerns and agenda of the prevailing majority groups. As well as providing a framework of reporting, therefore, this also allows us to identify what kind of subject areas occur more as topics or as subtopics. For example, crime may not be the main thrust of articles but may be an underlying theme that is often referred to in accounts about British Muslims.

Topics are selected on the basis of their news value and carried for a given time depending on their considered importance. Lacey and Longman (1997) have argued that the pressures of limited space and inter-newspaper competition determine this. In their own research on British press coverage of environmental issues, they showed how the cyclical nature of the news, structured by the market, means that some issues become marginalized or excluded from debate while others are always approached in the same ways. They refer to the work of Hilgartner and Bosk (1988), which demonstrates how different social problems have to compete for space and attention. Increased coverage, then, implies that an issue has some salience or importance to the interests of powerful groups in a particular social context. Islam's ability to be newsworthy relies on established notions of who Muslims are and what they represent to (interpretations of) British culture and perhaps even how 'useful' these representations of Muslims are to 'us' in creating a focus for anger and blame.

In what context does Islam appear in the British broadsheet press?

Islam is represented in British broadsheets in relation to a relatively restricted range of issues within which there are clear clusterings around certain topics that emerge as dominant (Table 2.2).[19] Through an examination of the most frequently occurring topics and any unusual elements of coverage, I will show how these topics are similarly framed by repetitive ideologies.

Table 2.2   Frequencies of all topics and references in total[21]

Topic	Frequency as topic	Frequency subtopic	Freq Ref 1	Freq Ref 2	Total	%
Belief	33	49	58	49	189	22.5
Education	128	26	12	18	184	21.9
Fundamentalism	57	39	36	30	162	19.3
World affairs	–	–	101	55	156	18.6
Relations to Christianity	28	50	41	18	137	16.3
Adjustment to culture	9	28	45	52	134	16.0
Racism	21	41	40	31	133	15.8
Muslim community	8	6	52	50	116	13.8
Relationships	60	30	13	8	111	13.2
Relations to other religions	16	30	29	29	104	12.4

Gender	17	*33*	27	20	97	11.5
Government	–	–	45	*49*	94	11.2
Criminal activity	43	*50*	–	–	93	11.1
Rushdie	21	21	*22*	17	81	9.6
Politics	*54*	13	5	8	80	9.5
Conversion	16	21	20	*22*	79	9.4
Freedom of speech	*28*	24	10	9	71	8.4
Immigration	*25*	17	8	17	67	8.0
Media	*41*	26	–	–	67	8.0
Religion	8	*57*	–	–	65	7.7
Cultural atrocities	–	–	32	30	62	7.4
Prince Charles	*41*	2	5	4	52	6.2
Anti-racism	10	8	15	*18*	51	6.0
Unrest	*15*	13	11	10	49	5.8
Offence caused to religious groups	–	–	25	23	48	5.7
Business	*13*	12	12	8	45	5.3
Islamophobia	*11*	*11*	9	9	40	4.7
Ethnic minorities	9	*12*	8	9	38	4.5
Health	*17*	*17*	–	–	34	4.0
Segregation	–	*28*	–	–	28	3.3
East/West relations	–	–	*16*	12	28	3.3
Muslim Parliament	7	3	*14*	3	27	3.2
Cultural/legal differences	4	*23*	–	–	27	3.2
Mosques	9	*10*	4	3	26	3.1
Anti-Jewish sentiments	–	–	16	10	26	3.1
Sport	*19*	6	–	–	25	2.9
Peaceful protest	*13*	10	–	–	23	2.7
Facts about Islam	10	*13*	–	–	23	2.7
Food	*12*	9	2	–	23	2.7
Islamic committees	–	–	10	*13*	23	2.7
Nation of Islam	–	–	*18*	5	23	2.7
Relations with host community	8	*13*	–	–	21	2.5
Rise of Islam	–	2	*9*	5	16	1.9
Mocking stories	4	*12*	–	–	16	1.9
Deprivation	–	–	*10*	6	16	1.9
Anti-Western	–	*6*	4	5	15	1.7
Conflict between Muslims	2	*10*	–	–	12	1.4
Crisis of faith	1	*6*	–	–	7	0.8
Bradford riots	–	–	<u>4</u>	3	7	0.8
'Normal' news stories	–	4	–	–	4	0.4
Population	–	1	1	1	3	0.3

It is *the framework of representation*, how topics occur in combination with others, 'subtopics' and 'references', which is considered significant, for even if Muslim groups can sometimes set the agenda for coverage, it is in the way events are framed that gives newspapers the ability to define Islam for their audience. The few themes underlying most of the topics examined here are imbued with negativity and represent Islam as a threat both to internal security and traditional values, as deviant and prone to segregation. For this reason, topics and their significance are examined first, followed by an analysis of the themes they represent.[20] Annual fluctuation and newspaper differentiation will also be examined.

Education

Education in particular has become the focus of widely shared anxieties both among Muslims and non-Muslims. Seen as vitally important in the transmission of values from generation to generation, it has become the site of struggle between competing interest groups seeking to have an influence on the curriculum. Pushed onto the agenda by all sides in the 1980s, Muslim groups through their growing dissatisfaction with the system and increasing politicization, liberal groups through multiculturalism and anti-racist policies, and conservative groups as a reaction to and in an attempt to defend tradition against this challenge. Van Dijk's (1991) analysis of ethnic minority representation in the UK press during 1989 found a shift in coverage, with education becoming a major subject in relation to Muslims. Previously a marginal subject in relation to minority groups, as their disadvantage within the system was ignored, education exploded onto the agenda following the Honeyford affair in 1985. Van Dijk (1991) found that these articles were almost exclusively discussed in terms of Islamic practices.

In total, education is a topic of concern in almost a quarter of articles on British Islam. Almost a quarter of these are about the nature and role of religious education in schools. These occurred mainly in 1994 following reforms by the then Conservative government to ensure teaching was broadly Christian in character, likewise daily worship. This resulted in a vociferous debate in the press, contained within a comparative framework, both with Christianity and other religions. Other curriculum concerns during this year were sex education, dance and music as part of the national curriculum, which led to some Muslim parents withdrawing their children from lessons. A further 13.5 per cent of the articles about education were about funding Muslim schools in

Britain. These occurred mainly in 1996, although 1994 also saw some discussion over whether opting out and becoming grant-maintained was an option for Muslim schools. The move from discussion relating to provision within the mainstream system to separate provision marked an important shift in the strength and identity of Muslim communities in the UK, alongside a recognition that the system already in place, based on multicultural policies, was not working. Muslim groups have campaigned consistently for state support for Muslim schools on the basis that Anglican, Catholic and Jewish religious schools receive funding. The debate is symptomatic of the idea that giving Islam equal status to Christianity is a contentious issue and while government rhetoric supports the idea of multiculturalism, this issue is represented as a problem for British society. Christianity is discussed within 38 per cent of articles on education and Islam, showing how the debates will often come back to the values of the majority culture. Christianity is referred to in 16 per cent of all articles on British Islam, further illustrating this point.

Belief is also prevalent in relation to these articles. It is evident that such discussion tends to refer back to Muslim belief, which is seen to be the point from which the dispute is driven. The problematization of this issue results in the problematization of the Other's beliefs, depending on the ideological position of the paper. Another prevalent subtopic is the ability of Muslims to adjust to the majority culture, implying that these problems may also be caused by Muslims' difficulties in adapting to the values of British society. Both subtopics suggest that the blame lies with Muslims' beliefs, culture and ability to fit in. One example of a story that had a high profile at the end of 1995 and beginning of 1996 was the 'outburst' of a Muslim teacher who disrupted his school's assembly, shouting at Muslim children for singing Christmas carols. Coverage concentrated on the upset caused to the 'innocent victims' of this 'senseless' attack.

Coverage of education has a fairly tight structure and framework of reference. For example, education and its relation to religion, Christianity and segregation always appears as a main topic with the others as subtopics (except in one case). Christianity is more likely to be put to the forefront, while belief and relations to other religions are secondary. This reflects the position of Christianity in religious education in schools and how it will be affected by teaching about a wider diversity of faiths. When education is the topic of an article about British Muslims then the form becomes predictable, consistent and restricted within the framework presented here.

There is space for some more open debate within the papers; racism, equal opportunities and offence caused to other religions are also discussed in articles on education in addition to the problems for female Muslims in mixed schools. However, it is not evident whether the beliefs of Muslims are seen to be causing the problems (and offence) or whether it is the beliefs and policies of others (governments and other religious groups) that are affecting Muslims. All these subtopics, except offence caused to other religions, which is spread across papers, appear only in the *Guardian*, which is illustrative of its general approach. However, discussion of education in these terms is minimal; *The Times* and both Sunday papers' education articles are strongly confined within the main areas of religious education, separate schooling and the role of Islam in relation to Christianity.

The consistency with which world affairs (which have the highest frequency as a reference, in 18.6 per cent of articles), the government, political activism and the Muslim community, are referred to in conjunction with all other subjects demonstrates their considered importance when discussing Islam in Britain. Hovering in the background, they constantly feed our 'understandings' of Muslims. The presence of world affairs as a reference in articles on education is most marked during discussion of the activities of Islamic fundamentalists in universities and the funding of Muslim schools in the UK by other countries, for example Saudi support for an Islamia school in London. This has the effect of conveying Islamic movements elsewhere as making threats upon, impinging and infiltrating British institutions. The British government also has a presence in these articles, implying the necessity for state intervention when dealing with British Islam, which needs to be managed (allowing prejudicial practices to continue).

Relationships

The relationships of British Muslims are featured on the following terms, namely that a British person converts to marry a Muslim, particularly if this person is in the public eye, or it is suggested that there is some kind of deviant, culturally abominable or criminal action related to the relationship. Criminality is more significant in the coverage of personal relationships than any other subject, perpetuating the idea that

Muslim law and practice is deviant in its difference from British values and customs, for example, in the practice of arranged marriage. Thus, the purpose of articles on relationships is to emphasize cultural difference. The association with conversion then secures the cultural threat.

The type of stories covered include the conversion of Jemima Goldsmith to Islam in order to marry Imran Khan in 1995; the conversion of schoolgirl Sarah Cook after a holiday in Turkey in 1996; and recurrent stories of British women who marry Muslim men and then have to 'escape' from their brutality (coverage of abduction cases can be a consequence of this). Media celebrities have a high news value and the marriage of Imran Khan, a popular sportsman, and Jemima Goldsmith, an archetypal Western beauty and daughter of a billionaire businessman of Jewish descent, who then converts to Islam, has many elements of interest to the press. British people who convert to Islam are often viewed with a mixture of curious fascination and incomprehension. The required adjustment to a new way of life and redefinition of identity is a curiosity to the British press. These stories are framed in a way that implies the inevitable breakdown of the relationship. However, the word British usually means 'white'. Black British (African-Caribbean) conversions are not newsworthy despite accounting for more than half the converts to Islam in Britain (Nielsen 1991b). Although the subject of conversion only appears explicitly in 20.7 per cent of the 111 articles on relationships, once a couple becomes newsworthy for this reason their activities tend to remain in the public eye for some time. Conversion is then often not explicitly referred to but is the initial reason for the news story. As a subject in itself, it is referred to in a total of 79 articles. Halliday (1995 and 1996) has previously argued that the concentration on conversion by the press is alarmist in trying to provoke fears about an expansionist force. However, I have found no explicit association with the rise of Islam and conversion (although it may be inferred). The focus on numbers and population growth is low over this period of time and in any case the press nullifies any possible threat of this kind through derision and scepticism towards the converted.

These relationships are seen as problematic in particular ways as we can see in the frequent references to the requirements of converts to adjust to a different culture, occurring in 21.6 per cent of the articles, and to the cultural differences or even atrocities that occur in these relationships, a reference to how women are treated in Islam occurring in

14.4 per cent of the articles. Islamic belief is again a feature of these articles, indicating that it is this that is behind these actions.

There is evidence of the press having 'ideological scripts' about this topic so that even when stories concentrate on different issues they are related to the same recurring associations. For example, coverage of Imran Khan's political career in Pakistan nearly always refers to his relationship with Jemima and her conversion.

The variation of articles on relationships over time again depends on events occurring that fit into this framework. In 1995 articles relating to conversion are more frequent because of Jemima Goldsmith's conversion. In 1996 articles relating to criminal activity increase because of the illegal religious marriage of Sarah Cook and Musa Komeagac in Turkey.

Few other subtopics appear in articles on relationships, though more diversity exists than between those on education. While the emphasis is as described here in all papers, there is slightly more attention to conversion and all articles on gender appear in the *Guardian*, perhaps because of its feminist/human rights stance. A few more articles appear on criminality in *The Times*, which is also more likely to highlight cultural difference, work within a comparative framework (with Christianity and other religions) and conflict between Muslims.

Islamic fundamentalism

This topic has relevance and, as a result, a presence due to its high media profile in terms of foreign news. These stories usually follow an international event that provokes press speculation on the Islamic fundamentalist presence in the UK (it is associated with world affairs in half of all articles). This could, to some extent, be seen as recognition of the worldwide community, the *umma*, and a reflection of the problem of reconciling the multiple identities and loyalties that transcend national boundaries. Consequently, because of concern about the activities of legal dissidents who take refuge in Britain and are the focus of these articles (mainly Arabs and, for example, members of Hizb ut Tahrir or Hamas), this subject is frequently linked to immigration (consistent throughout the time period). The government is also a key player here as it attempts to deal with the 'problem'.

In 1995, when the activities of Islamic groups in Britain's universities became a focus of interest, the subject of fundamentalism was often discussed in connection with education. In later years, as global events increased the coherence of the dissident framework (coverage of political refugees residing in the UK), this story moved off the agenda. Dissident activities are often linked to deviance (through crime), the Muslim community in general and its role in aiding fundamentalists (in a quarter of articles). This has a further homogenizing effect as the associations imply that all Muslims can be thought of in these terms. The connections made between fundamentalism, the Muslim Parliament and Islamic committees similarly link extremists to non-extremist groups. Belief and cultural differences again act as explanatory factors. These stories represent Islam as a global threat to security, fundamentalists in the UK being the political and physical threat within. In addition, fundamentalists are seen to be intolerant through antagonism to other groups, usually religious, in 21 per cent of articles.

As well as being a central focus of an article, Islamic fundamentalism often occurs as a subtopic in discussions about immigration (19 per cent). This is illustrative of the narrow framework within which these subjects are reported (in relation to Islam), in that if one is raised, it is highly likely that the other will be referred to. Immigration is frequently related to the difficulties Muslims have in adjusting to British culture. The shift from seeing minorities as immigrants to labelling foreign dissidents as immigrants is an indicator of changes in the perception of minorities, recognizing that they can no longer be defined in these terms. This accounts for the lower number of articles on immigration than in previous research where it tended to predominate (Hartmann et al. 1974; Troyna 1981; van Dijk 1991). The preoccupation in these articles appears not to be, as in previous decades, with the mass migration of peoples and prevention measures, but with concern about the assimilation of those residing within, hence recognizing their permanent settlement. However, the presence of Islamic 'fundamentalists' has allowed the issue of immigration to re-emerge acceptably, given the possible, but in most cases imagined, security threat.

Immigration, when it appears as a main topic, occurs within a similarly limited framework to that of fundamentalism. *The Times* places slightly more emphasis on this along with other subjects bearing negative connotations such as crime, cultural differences and the Muslim Parliament (which is perceived as an extreme organization). This is consistent with previous research that shows *The Times* to be generally more interested in population figures (Hartmann et al. 1974).

However, as previously identified, attention to the rise of Islam and population composition are limited in this coverage and are more likely to be an issue of concern in the *Guardian*. It is clear that these anxieties in relation to Islam are being expressed in different ways. The *Guardian*, while having an equally restrictive framework, illuminates issues of health and racism along with immigration. Given the likelihood that immigration and fundamentalism will appear together, these articles are mainly discussed in similar terms.

The same pattern is apparent in articles on peaceful protests (which generally involve rallies planned by Islamic groups in the UK, for example the Kalifan in 1994 and Hizb ut Tahrir in 1995). In seven out of 13 articles where the main topic is a protest, the subtopic is fundamentalism. The limited number of subjects discussed in articles on fundamentalism is evidence of the news framework that has been established for this topic. Other topics arising have negative connotations. In the *Guardian*, for example, fundamentalism is also associated with the rise of Islam, conflict between Muslims, and unrest. *The Times*, again, has a slightly narrower framework, but the topic of fundamentalism also occurs in relation to unrest and gender. The only occurrence of gender issues in *The Times* appeared in an article on fundamentalism. This was an indication of the paper's negative presentation of the treatment of women in Islam. Other references made in these articles were equally negative — cultural atrocities, anti-Western sentiments, the growth of Islam, tension with the authorities, population composition, East–West relations. This results in a negative association with Islamic fundamentalism and the consequences of this infiltrating from abroad into the UK, the invasion of British culture by extremist tendencies.

However, within the structure of these articles, fundamentalism is more interchangeable (in terms of the degree of focus on it) than, for example, education. Fundamentalism often occurs as a subtopic or is referred to in other articles (occurring in total in 162 articles, see Table 2.2). This is an illustration of the close association of fundamentalism and extremism with Islam across a range of issues.

Political activity

This subject denotes a shift in the representation of ethnic minorities through recognition of their increasing presence in the public sphere. The long struggle for Muslims and other groups to be represented politically led to coverage of their campaigns for selection for candidacy within a competitive framework. However, what could have been a positive move turned into an association with criminality (in a quarter of the articles). This suggested that when Muslims are involved in politics, illegal activity takes place. It also illustrated a tendency to undermine what few Muslim politicians exist in Britain. The central focus of these articles was corruption in politics, with accusations of bribery and vote rigging during a by-election involving the first Muslim MP in Govan, Scotland in 1995 and consequent activities in 1996. The low occurrence in 1994 suggested that Muslim political activities have little news value unless they show them in a negative light and gaining some power (a possible reason for the negative framing). In such articles, Muslims were often shown in conflict with other groups and individuals, with internal disagreements in various constituencies over which candidates were chosen to represent the community. The links with the Muslim community in 28 per cent of the articles implicated their involvement. The British quality press closely followed the entry of a Muslim MP into the political arena and it continued to be newsworthy up to 1999 (see Chapter 3). In many articles on Muslims and their political activities, no other topic was mentioned, indicating a closure of the subject around these issues. Politics, however, was also linked to racism in 24 per cent of the articles, though it was unclear who was engaged in racism, Muslims or non-Muslims. Some of these stories arose over a controversy surrounding Muslim applications to join the Labour Party, leading to accusations of racism within the party.

Significantly, though politics has so far been associated with wider ranges of subjects than other themes, these tend to concentrate on ethnic and race issues — racism, gender, conversion, marriage and stories about Muslim candidates helping the community over these issues. This verifies arguments that contend that minorities are not shown to be speaking on, or represented in relation to, everyday concerns such as economics. The few references to the government in these articles illustrated the localized and 'unofficial' associations around Muslim political activities rather than the national or legitimate politics of the country.

An association with world affairs allowed questions to be raised about Muslims' motives for political action, their loyalty to Britain and the possibility of foreign political practices being transferred to Britain. Political activism was mainly represented as fundamentalism, an indication of the sort of extremist politics in which Muslims are shown to be involved. Coverage of this topic represented Muslims as deviant and extremist, in conflict with other groups for political power and concerned only with minority interests.

Politics occurred most frequently as a main topic, an indication of its central place for media interest. Politics always has a high news value, with the involvement of scandal and a novel element such as the first Muslim MP increasing its salience.

This framework applied quite rigidly to all papers except the *Guardian*, which again had a slightly wider framework that included articles on racism, gender and anti-racism. All other subtopics appearing in *The Times* had negative connotations, including anti-Western sentiments and conflict between Muslims.

Criminal activity

Crime, like politics, has a high news value, particularly in relation to minority groups (Hartmann et al. 1974; Troyna 1981; van Dijk 1991). Events in which Muslims are involved in criminal behaviour rather than regular activities, therefore, have a higher probability of making the news. Everyday topics such as relationships, the media and employment become more newsworthy if crime is involved. Deviancy among British Muslims is represented by criminality and suggests that they are a threat. Muslims were associated with criminal behaviour in 93 articles. The connections made between crime, relationships and cultural atrocities give the impression that the Islamic law that governs relationships leads to illegal activity and what may be judged atrocities by Western standards. The newsworthiness of this combination of topics was evident in the attention given to the illegal religious marriage of a 12-year-old British girl to a Turkish Muslim in 1996. Again, Islamic belief becomes the driving force for action and the ability of Muslims to adjust culturally is seen as a problem coming from within the community expressed through deviant behaviour. To quote Gilroy (1988: 54), the criminal subculture of a group is seen to 'violate the laws and customs which express the civilization of the national community and in doing so provide powerful symbols which express black difference as a whole. To be a criminal is to fulfil cultural destiny.' The representation of Islamic fundamentalism and Mohammed Sarwar, Britain's first Muslim MP, similarly expressed this criminal culture.

These findings demonstrate that although Muslims as a minority group were similarly associated with crime, the type of crime reported differed from that of 'black' groups. Occurring largely as a subtopic, the criminal activity of Muslims was represented in relation to their deviant relationships and political activities (fraud and bribery). There were few images of the stereotypical violent street crimes traditionally attributed to black people. This was partly due to particular stereotypes applied to Asians (which constituted the main body of representations of British Muslims), equally on a worldwide scale corruption in politics (for example in Pakistan) and stereotypes associated with Muslims arising from Orientalism (such as sexual deviancy).

A comparison of Muslim criminality with white hostility (racism and Islamophobia) gave an idea of the marginal coverage of attacks on Muslims compared with articles that highlight Muslim deviance (3.5 articles to one) (and this did not include all the articles in which crime was a subtopic).

Riots did not figure highly in relation to Muslims over this period. Despite the Bradford riots in 1995, when an increase in coverage was noted, these events were mainly discussed within a racial paradigm. Articles that did appear were set within a framework of criminal deviance (47 per cent) or cultural difference (40 per cent). However, there appeared to have been some shift away from traditional ways of representing riots (as in Cohen 1988; and Solomos 1988) to more exploration of the reasons for their occurrence in terms of racism and cultural alienation, though it is impossible to elaborate on this here without a more detailed qualitative analysis. These articles also had a lower visibility than those that expressed the deviancy of Muslims.

Criminal activity was reported in relation to various subtopics, which illustrated a general tendency to associate Muslims with crime. Both *The Times* and the *Guardian* displayed a similar framework of reporting. *The Times*' association of this topic with gender again represented how gender issues and Islam were treated in *The Times* (also in the *Guardian* here). This was consistent with the findings of previous studies that showed that liberal newspapers did not necessarily report less on crime (van Dijk 1991). It should, however, be noted that a small number of these articles were about Muslim actions against crime, for example their campaigns to clear prostitution from the streets of Birmingham in 1994.

Prince Charles

Prince Charles's pronouncements on many subjects are newsworthy, but his speeches on Islam have been of particular interest given his future role as head of the Church of England and press fascination with the peculiarities of Islam. The findings illustrated what issues the press placed at the forefront in an agenda set partly by the speeches of Prince Charles — relations between religions, belief, and the importance of understanding East–West relations. However, the response to these was overwhelmingly negative. David Dimbleby's documentary on Prince Charles in 1994, which embraced a variety of topics, was followed by press coverage of his remarks on his desire to be 'defender of all faiths' in Britain. Particular attention was paid to his speech in December 1995 describing the attractive features of Islam, and in 1996 his support for funding Muslim projects from the millennium fund.

Comment on Prince Charles's opinions occurred most frequently in *The Times*. The newspaper's references to cultural atrocities were a reflection of the cynicism with which some commentators treated his ideas because of what they believed to be the real nature of Islam (expressed in terms of human rights abuses across the world). Since 1997, this topic has slipped off the agenda as Prince Charles has tried to improve his media image following the death of Diana, the Princess of Wales. The negativization of Prince Charles through his speeches on Islam and his recent silence on the subject are indications of its controversial nature.

The Times has consistently presented its coverage of Prince Charles and Islam within this narrow framework, though, because of its greater interest in royalty, it did provide more space for wider discussion of the subject. Excluding this factor, news items in *The Times* and *Guardian* are similar in content, focusing on particular speeches and issues, visits and their interpretations. Although Prince Charles was usually the main focus, his previous close association with Islam was enough for him to be referred to when these issues appeared as main topics (injecting the articles with elitism and, at the time, increasing their negativity and thus adding to their newsworthiness).

Belief and religious rituals

Articles on Islam frequently alluded to Muslim beliefs or religious practices (a total of 189 articles), making this topic the most commonly referenced of all issues about Islam. This subject was more likely to be referred to in relation to other main topics but occurred as the main thrust of the articles as well. It had a wide framework, being dispersed throughout a variety of subjects in both papers and equally across all years. Where the main discussion of an article was about British Muslims and their beliefs or rituals, it was likely to be compared with both Christianity and other religious groups, and often prompted a discussion on the ability of Muslims to adapt to the dominant culture of their host country. This comparative aspect was more prominent in *The Times*' newspapers, particularly in relation to Christianity.

News on this subject contained articles on pilgrimage, beliefs, practices around gender and the preparation of food, including ritual slaughter, and government regulations relating to these. References to world affairs suggested that uncultivated cultural practices were being transferred to British society through migration. As a subtopic, it most often and disturbingly appeared in articles on criminality. These articles were included if certain cultural practices could be shown to be barbaric and the people practising them were polarized in a negative value system. This illustrated the tendency of the press to use a religious belief in Islam as a 'universal cover' (Halliday 1995), as a key to understanding Muslim behaviour in both social and political arenas. This is not usually the case with the majority of 'Christians' in this country except in extreme cases. Equally, Christianity is not used to explain the actions of non-practising 'Christians' as it is with non-practising Muslims.

Islam's relation to Christianity

Islam's relationship with Christianity was discussed within a similar framework to that of belief, for the positions of both these topics in articles (as topics, subtopics or references) were fairly interchangeable. The topic was raised in a total of 137 articles, again mainly as a subtopic (50 times, mainly with education). This illustrated a tendency to frame debates about Islam comparatively. It was fairly evident that, from an ethnocentric perspective, discussions about religions other than the established one of the country tended to be compared with it. This theme was widely dispersed in both papers and remained consistent across the three years.

Comparisons between Islam and Christianity also provided a context in which to compare other religions and beliefs. Such topics often occurred together when a prominent person in the Church of England (in these articles chiefly the Archbishop of Canterbury) discussed religion and Christianity in relation to other religions and called for increased tolerance both at home and abroad to improve East–West relations. Articles on world affairs also alluded to Islamic fundamentalism as an intolerant face of religious belief. Some of these reported on the reactions of British Muslims to speeches by the Archbishop of Canterbury during his visits to the Sudan in 1994 and 1995. Other public figures were also newsworthy, particularly Prince Charles, as we have seen. The call for increased tolerance demonstrated that, in some instances, the topic could be interpreted as having positive connotations. However, reference to the growth of Islam showed how it was often seen as a threat to Christianity, especially in its extreme form. This expansive force could then be constructed as a threat to Christian values, and the call for tolerance a veiled call for assimilation. Further qualitative analysis would be necessary to clarify this point.

Freedom of speech/the Rushdie affair

Although, due to its more general nature, freedom of speech occurred more frequently as a main topic than articles specifically on Salman Rushdie, I will deal with them together because of the frequency with which they appeared conjointly in the press. The Rushdie affair continued to be topical and to be associated with the British Muslim community. Eight years after the event, there were still 81 articles referring substantially to Rushdie over the three-year period under review. What was most interesting about these was the frequency with which the debate about freedom of speech would be referred to in association with Rushdie. This occurred even in stories unconnected with British Islam. It was apparent that, to some extent, the Rushdie affair came to symbolize the debate about freedom of speech in the press. Of a total of 21 articles in which Rushdie was the main topic, freedom of speech was discussed as a subtopic in 20. Where freedom of speech was the main topic of debate (28 articles), Rushdie was the subtopic in 15. This narrow framework was further revealed by the few other topics associated with these subjects. Freedom of speech in relation to British Islam was linked to only six other topics, including conflict between Muslims, the Muslim community, criminal activity and Islamic fundamentalism. These related to the involvement of Muslims in censorship, in which they were judged to be extreme, even by the right-wing press (which is hypocritical given its usual moral stance on censorship, but in this instance, due to the specific content, it shifted the attention to the extreme activities of the victimized group). Articles on Rushdie also focused on Islamic fundamentalism and criminal activity. An article appearing on his health could have been seen as inferring its deterioration because of the pressures put upon him by extremist groups. Articles also continued to debate the issue of blasphemy and whether laws protecting Christians should be extended to Muslims, an issue closely related to this topic since it first arose.

In relation to this issue then, the Muslim community in Britain was discussed only through a highly consistent negative framework in both papers, though there was a subtle difference between them on which aspect of the issue was brought to the forefront. The *Guardian* was more likely to focus on Rushdie, subsequently raising the issue of freedom of speech, while *The Times* paid more attention to censorship, through which Rushdie was then invoked. Attention to Rushdie was particularly high during 1994/5 due to the fifth anniversary of the *fatwa* (religious decree) and a spate of action prompted by progressive trends towards the European Union (prompting fears for his safety because of the increased movement of peoples). Subsequently, freedom of speech became prominent as articles attended to other extremist groups and their activities in which (their position on) Rushdie was referred to in the process (for example, al-Muhajiroun and its Rally for Revival).

That Muslims were continually associated with the issue of freedom of speech illustrated the considered threat from irrational, antiquated Muslims to British liberal values and democracy. The Rushdie affair has become an ongoing news story because of the Iranian *fatwa* and, as a result, has affected relations with Iran. Debate throughout this period focused on the annual renewal of the *fatwa* and measures taken by the British government to put pressure on Iran and support Rushdie. Some 71 per cent of the articles on Rushdie referred to this issue. Again, this suggested that Muslims outside Britain were dictating the agenda for Muslims in Britain, that Muslim (foreign) values were impinging on British society and were a constant reminder of the global menace and Iranian terrorist threat. These images sustained and maintained in the public mind ideas about extremist and fanatical Muslims determined to create an Islamic theocracy in Britain, which marginalized the moderate and pragmatic position of the majority of British Muslims.

In his own research, van Dijk (1991) found that the Rushdie affair was significant in the late 1980s (along with issues of education based on the Honeyford affair) in pushing Muslims to the forefront of ethnic minority coverage. Through this, a channel of news was opened with regard to Muslims that can often be artificial. In his content analysis of five British newspapers' coverage of ethnic minorities in 1989, education and Rushdie were the two most prominent topics. He argued that this was also part of a negative shift in approaches to the reporting of ethnic minorities to 'affairs' or 'scandals' into which these events neatly fitted. A key aspect of this approach was the over-reporting of an event that symbolized a 'sudden national panic' (van Dijk 1991: 88). This took place within a general trend towards this type of coverage as commercial pressures increasingly prevailed and the reporting of scandals became more attractive. The continuing coverage of Rushdie so long after the event was indicative of the 'panic cycle', which will become increasingly apparent in my qualitative analysis. The qualitative data (1997) and an ongoing monitoring of the papers used for this analysis (1998/9) provided evidence that anxiety about education and freedom of speech persisted nearly ten years later. This represented unresolved anxieties and the continuing struggles of all groups to establish hegemony.

Race relations

Although not a consistent topic in the representation of Muslims, I consider it of benefit to compare the frequency of articles that say something about the problems the Muslim community faced with articles that were indicative of the problems they caused. Of all the articles, 5 per cent discussed racism, anti-racism, Islamophobia or deprivation as a main issue, and 92 per cent of these appeared in the *Guardian* and/or *Observer*. However, these issues *were referred to* in articles 240 times, 73 per cent of which appeared in the *Guardian*. Critical discussions of inequality were therefore severely limited even in the quality press, particularly the right-wing papers. This bodes ominously for tabloid coverage. However, a more in-depth analysis would be necessary to determine whether Muslims themselves are implied in their own deprivation. In fact, although racism was widely dispersed among topics, references to Islamophobia occurred mainly in articles on Islamic fundamentalism. This implied that Islamophobia was a result of Islamic fundamentalism and could therefore be justified. Articles on anti-racism are frequently used by the right-wing press to attack progressive policies, so cannot be assumed to be positive.

Some 49 articles appeared to show Muslims involved in daily activities that were similar to those of the majority population, with topics including health, business, sport and 'normal' news stories; 58 per cent of these appeared in the *Guardian*.[22] In the majority of articles then, events involving Muslims were selected and constructed to fit a prevailing image of them that highlighted their problems of assimilating and relating to mainstream society. There was little allusion to Muslims participating in the day-to-day lives of the majority, to the problems they face through not having facilities that are available to the wider public, and to unemployment and deprivation, despite constituting the group most likely to be living in poverty and disadvantage (Runnymede Trust 1997).[23] This was also illustrated by the topics selected as categories for this analysis. My own familiarity with coverage prior to analysis, through pilot studies, found no need for categories on housing, unemployment and similar issues often selected for content analyses of ethnic minority coverage in the UK. Although scant coverage of these types of concerns was found (Hartmann et al. 1974; Troyna 1981; van Dijk 1991), the total absence of reporting on them in relation to Muslims illustrated the differing associations made with Islam. An event or action has to be indicative of some kind of essential 'Muslimness', an idea of Islam, to be featured as such.

Topical structures

It is clear from the evidence so far that articles on Islam have topical structures. That is, some topics have their importance as main events and others are used to frame them. Some are discussed within a narrow framework, frequently occurring in a predictable and specific form, such as debates on education, relationships, and Rushdie. Others, for example on criminal activity, belief, world affairs and Islam's relations with Christianity, are more diffuse, applying across subjects or events associated with Islam and with wider frames of reference. These can be said to have formed part of the frames of reference within which British Islam was discussed in these newspapers (regardless of topic). This accounted for the relatively low occurrence of some subjects as the main topic, such as conversion, gender, and cultural differences, which, according to the literature, were prevalent representations in that they were more likely to constitute part of an article than its substance. The qualitative data provided here reveal how such subjects (like conversion) were more likely to be key discourses relating to topics on Islam.

Crime, fundamentalism and cultural atrocities all symbolized deviant behaviour that appeared to be based on Islamic beliefs (rather than on customs). This took place within a comparative framework in which the values and beliefs of majority Britain (often Christian) were contrasted and in which their differences were pronounced, thereby creating problems for integration. Articles often referred to world affairs, reflecting Islam as a worldwide (possibly uniform) phenomenon. This association also promoted ideas of not belonging, allowing questions about loyalty to be raised and thus working to accentuate difference. The presence of discrimination in articles and references to the Muslim community may have resulted from the increasing politicization of Muslims. However, this was outweighed by concerns about the ability of the community to adjust culturally and by cultural atrocities committed. It illustrated how these different values were framed and how often Islam was presented as an alien culture in opposition to a 'Western' life.

The stress on the Muslim community and its beliefs may be an indication of blame discourse, namely that Muslims are to blame for their discrimination and deprivation through their own antiquated practices. Romer et al. (1998: 286–7) define ethnic blame discourse as 'ethnocentric bias in blaming "outgroups" for social problems'. The authors' findings on a study of crime news in Philadelphia, which compared coverage on homicide statistics, suggests that the media had engaged in a discourse of ethnic blame that was independent of realistic group conflict.[24] Their research also suggests that the media framed the behaviour of ethnic Others as intergroup conflict and accentuated the harmful effects for the in-group, which was also apparent in my findings. By focusing on the problems of the out-group, the discourse perpetuated the belief that they have interests and values that conflict with those of the in-group and can be blamed for these problems. This theory appears to be particularly applicable to the representation of Muslims in the UK with its emphasis on cultural differences, interpersonal relations, integrative concerns and deviancy. A clear example of this was reference to unrest in articles that reflected on Muslims' ability to adjust culturally.

The implication here was that Muslims' own difficulties in adjusting to life in the UK was causing unrest in Britain's towns and cities, a cause that has been much less prominent in previous content analyses of ethnic minority coverage. The subject of unrest, as has been found in previous research, was more likely to be related to criminal causes than deprivation (van Dijk 1991).

Topics that occur infrequently can be accounted for in other ways. The visibility of the Muslim Parliament, for example, has faded somewhat but has been used as a source of Muslim comment (given that extreme sources have more news value and fit neatly into the two-dimensional oppositional structure of news debate).[25] One positive finding was the absence of stories blatantly ridiculing Islam. However, this type of story was more common in a tabloid format, which can be more explicit. The conveyance of ideology tended to be subtler in the broadsheets.

The continued attention to the limited set of topics found in this analysis precluded attention to others, made explicit by the frequency of articles occurring outside this framework, only 2 per cent. Equally, no stories involving Muslims reported on 'normal' events (see note 22). This could also represent a movement away from labelling people when religion and race are irrelevant to the article.[26] For a quarter of all articles I was unable to find any references to a third or fourth topic. This illustrated the simplified presentation of issues relating to Islam in that they required discussion only within the bounds of two to three concerns. It also provided some idea of the length of articles. These results, then, are a clear indication of the restrictive frameworks that have developed in relation to the reporting of Islam. Once frameworks such as these have been established, it requires more effort to include different topics, to think about Islam in a different way.

Themes and meanings of British Islam

The framing of news on Islam has allowed for the effective clustering of topics that connote several dominant symbolized meanings. Topics that are not numerically important, however, are not insignificant. By analysing the number of articles on particular topics rather than the tone of the articles, I have been able to identify any 'central defining themes that might be taken as indicating the meaning and significance' given to Islam in the newspapers (Hartmann et al. 1974: 108). How these topics were discussed together in the newspapers created particular meanings, which can be summarized as:

- Muslim involvement in deviant activities threatens security in the UK;
- Muslims are a threat to British 'mainstream' values and thus provoke integrative concerns;
- There are inherent cultural differences between Muslims and the host community, which create tensions in interpersonal relations; and
- Muslims are increasingly making their presence felt in the public sphere.

Other topics identified as significant here are race relations and belief. Appendix A shows how the topics are most likely to be conceptualized through thematic discourse. These themes are actually inter-related in that belief and practices lead to charges of cultural difference that present integrative concerns and may constitute a threat to the security of the country.[27] This demonstrates how the press handle material on Islam and what it symbolizes. For example, the debate on freedom of speech and Rushdie symbolized concerns about the conformity of Muslims within the UK and the threat from global Muslim forces. Relations between the host and Muslim communities are significant elements in all themes.

Through some topics, it is evident that Muslims are having an increasing impact on public life in the UK (Appendix A: public sphere theme). This raises questions about whether Islam is becoming more newsworthy because, as their public voice increases, Muslims are increasingly able to set agendas. Restriction in the public space led to politicization. However, most of the topics that could be seen to be an expression of this have a predominantly negative framing. For example, the Muslim Parliament is an example of Muslims attempting to create a political space for themselves within the UK as a result of their exclusion from the wider political process. The framing of these stories and their association with fundamentalism, however, mean that they often symbolize a threat from within. Education, a concern of minorities that the press has systematically ignored in the past, is now firmly on the public agenda, substantially because of the activities of Muslims. Again, however, the framing has shown how often it is represented as an issue of integrative concern to the majority. Islam's ability to be newsworthy, then, appears to rely on established notions of who Muslims are and what they represent to 'British' culture.

Although there are a (restricted) number of topics associated with Islam, the way these topics are framed in the press shows that they are systematically associated with the same sort of meanings. When applied to British Islam, these meanings are extremely limited, effectively amounting to a concentration on the negative consequences of the presence of Islam in the UK and the reification of difference. It was argued earlier that news about Islam has become more salient because of its propensity for cultural identification (for example as 'Muslims' rather than 'Pakistanis') by both themselves and others, and as both a defensive strategy and an attempt to construct coherent identities, 'filtering out the threats in social experience' (see Sennett 1971 in Chapter 1). This, however, has allowed a comparative framework to evolve in which Muslim differences are defined as deviancy from the norm, with their cultural practices interpreted as backward and based on archaic beliefs. These beliefs and practices are made to look strange in relation to the majority culture, while the practices of the dominant groups are never discussed or challenged, but presupposed. News coverage, then, contains underlying assumptions about the natural behaviour of homogenous polarized groups, which in every instance encounter a conflict of interests. Even other ethnic groups are used as a contrast to the separatism of Muslims.

What is clear from this framework is that Islam in Britain is most likely to be reported if it clearly affects or is seen to impinge on the lives of what are considered 'normal' British people. Educational debates are extensive because the incorporation of other religions threatens the traditional Christian values of the country, having the potential to change them. The consistent association of British Islam with fundamentalism and criminal activity implies deviancy and a threat from within. These themes illustrate how Islam is understood across a variety of topics. Integrative concerns are established as more important than race relations when discussing Muslims in Britain. Although it is evident that Muslims are seen as a threat to security, this is deemed less so than in the global construction of Islam. Due to the local context, other issues take precedence. However, that it has such currency on a local scale, does illustrate the strength of the image. A discourse of conflict, deviancy, difference and backwardness runs through these themes, illustrating the closeness of the arguments on the global and the localized media image. This is also due to the mixture of discourses relating to ethnic minority groups and Islam.

Despite the slight differences between papers in topic coverage, there is little difference in the overall themes that occur. It is the ways in which articles are framed (how topics appear together) that really tells us something about images and meanings relating to British Islam in the press. These meanings will now be extended to look at other aspects of the representational framework.

The role of British Muslims: the standing of principal actors [28]

The social role, faith and gender of the main actors in the articles can tell us something of the type of people associated with or allowed to speak for British Muslims. This kind of analysis is essential to an understanding of media roles in social representation and power relationships in society. Two main findings emerged: that Muslims are denied legitimacy in the roles in which they are represented, and that women are marginalized as significant actors.

(1) Muslims are denied legitimacy in social representation

Figure 2.6 shows how Muslims and non-Muslims are represented in articles as occupying particular social roles. It is evident that community members are most common in these articles, as are Muslims. It is also apparent, from the peaks and troughs, that actors of different faiths are represented in very different roles. Additionally, people with no faith affiliation are highly likely to be represented while Christians appear mainly as royalty and religious figures and those from other faiths have a low occurrence overall.

To illustrate the patterns of representation in terms of power-based roles, the social roles were merged into Establishment and non-Establishment positions to provide an idea of the position of Muslims given coverage in the press. The following have been included as Establishment figures: heads of state, religious figures, political figures, academics, media workers, media figures, educationists, royalty, medical figures and the police, accounting for 48 per cent of coverage. Members of the public include community spokespeople, community members, business figures (as these tend to be small businessmen not big corporations), and political activists, 31 per cent of coverage. The conclusions (Table 2.3) are interesting.

Figure 2.6 **Social position of actors**

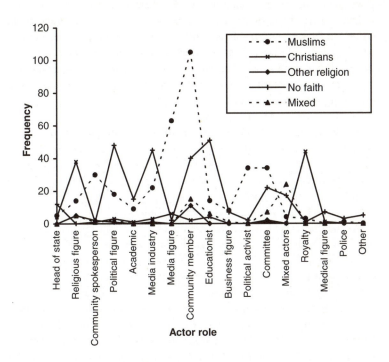

Table 2.3 **Social position of actor by religion**

	Establishment positions		Non-Establishment positions	
	Frequency	*%*	*Frequency*	*%*
Muslims	149	17.8	177	21.00
Christians	69	8.2	3	0.35
No faith given	184	22.0	50	6.00

It is clear that Muslims are far more likely to be represented in positions of little authority than are people whose faith is not identified.[29] Though this can partly be explained by the secular nature of institutions in Britain, it also means that it is likely that the secular perspective will prevail on issues concerning the Muslim community. Typically, actors who are not affiliated by faith are educationists, politicians, academics, media workers, the police and medical people. Christians who are specified are easily identifiable as such (religious figures and royalty); otherwise journalists see it as inappropriate to do so. It is, however, considered appropriate to label minority groups because the majority of articles relating to them deal with minority issues. Despite this, the percentage of Christians in Establishment positions is comparatively higher than in non-Establishment positions, indicating the legitimacy of Christians compared with Muslims in these roles. This aspect of press coverage, using Establishment figures to offer expertise, is usual. Coverage of British Islam appears to revolve around the views of the (non-Muslim) British Establishment (it can also be assumed that they are mainly white because in these articles ethnic actors tend to be positioned within a faith framework). By setting the agenda on how the Muslim community is represented, Muslims are subjected to Pnina Werbner's 'external definition' (1991).

As may be expected, *The Times* and *Sunday Times* allocate far more space to Establishment figures than do the *Guardian* and *Observer*. So, while Establishment figures are the main focus of 51 per cent of *Guardian* articles and non-Establishment figures 42 per cent, 61 per cent of *The Times* articles attend to Establishment figures and 34 per cent to non-Establishment figures. This is in part a result of the focus in *The Times* on traditional elites — royalty, heads of state and religious figures (who are mainly Christian). It features 68 Christians compared with the *Guardian*'s 41 (see Table 2.4). Media figures (celebrities) also account for a higher percentage of its articles than the *Guardian*'s. The *Guardian*'s elites on the other hand are more likely to be educationists and media workers, in addition to the greater access assigned to ordinary voices and other faith groups. This represents the authority that *The Times*, in general, gives to more traditional voices while the *Guardian* has a more secular outlook.

Further analysis, looking at the content of the article (topic) in which these different actors appear, provides a richer picture. Given their higher occurrence overall and that they are the focus of the research, Muslims obviously appear in articles covering a wider variety of subjects. So, while it is probably inevitable that more than three-quarters of all articles on relationships are about Muslims, these only appear if they feature elites or relate to a 'topical' issue such as conversion. Further, three-quarters of the articles on criminal activity involved a Muslim as the central actor, with a slightly lower fraction showing Muslims involved in fundamentalism. Compared with other actors, Muslims have a significant presence in articles on politics, a topic that is also frequently related to crime. This can be compared with the small number of articles on education that involve a Muslim as the central character, fewer than a quarter, which in this case tends to be a secular educationist or policy maker since faith is unlikely to be specified unless it is a religious school. However, it does indicate an institutional perspective over and above the views of Muslim parents.

Table 2.4   Frequency of actors occurring: faith position

	The Times/ST	Guardian/Observer	Total number	%
Muslim	144	220	364	43.5
Christian	68	41	109	13.0
Other	7	15	22	2.6
No faith	100	180	280	33.5
Mixed	14	48	62	7.4

Apart from articles on Prince Charles, Christians are most likely to be the main actors in articles that compare Islam with Christianity; otherwise, they are also dispersed across a variety of topics.

Articles that provide equal space to different faith groups are most likely to be about education, relations between Islam and other religions, belief, and issues pertaining to ethnic minorities. Where the central character is a member of a religion other than Islam or Christianity, the article is most likely to be about the relationship between this religion and Islam, belief, *criminal activity* or health. These associations fit neatly with theories about religious and ethnic minority coverage.

The few stereotypical roles allocated here to Muslims — community members, media figures, political activists, business people, community spokespersons and committees (which are associated with more controversial subjects) — illustrated not only the limited framework applied to British Muslims but also the lack of authoritative and 'normal' roles in which they were represented in the press. Even religious figures discussing Islam were more likely to be Christian. This framework showed consistency throughout the time period. Typical news values were also applied to British Islam. Community members were more newsworthy if they were seen to be causing trouble, but the elite approach was prevalent too. The frequency with which politicians occurred as the main actor in all articles was also indicative of this.

(2) Women are marginalized as significant actors

It is not unusual to find that women are marginalized voices in the news media since more authority, in general, is given to male expertise. However, it was evident that the marginalization of women's voices (Muslim and non-Muslim) in the coverage of British Islam had some significance.

Table 2.5   Gender of principal actor

	Frequency	*%*
Male	492	58.8
Female	119	14.2
Unclear	153	18.3
Equal status	73	8.7

Figure 2.7 shows the social roles of actors in articles and their gender and in all these positions, men far outnumber women. They also occupy a wider range of positions than women, whose representation is more limited. In articles on British Islam then, the central character was most likely to be a male community member. Women were also most likely to occupy this position than any other social role. Other than this, women also featured in a small way as media and political figures. This was probably because there was a female education secretary at the time, Gillian Shephard. Women were mentioned infrequently in all social positions and in every position less frequently than men. Women did not appear at all as community spokespeople, business figures or members of the police.[30]

This was an indication of the authority of men as commentators in the press, particularly in this area, but it also reflected the number of women in these positions in society. Women were not represented as figures of authority at all in relation to Islam in Britain, featuring mainly in less authoritative roles (men hold more than 80 per cent of the Establishment roles). One might expect there to be a higher percentage of women educationists, reflecting the make-up of the profession, but men are still given more opportunity to represent a field in which they are outnumbered by women because they hold higher positions within it. This was amplified by the fact that, where it was possible to identify authorship, nearly three-quarters were men. A male perspective, then, is more likely to be given on the subject of British Islam.

Figure 2.7 **Social position by gender**

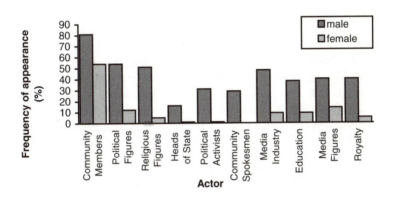

These findings are indicative of the lower status of women in newspapers in relation to the subject of British Islam. It was especially apparent in that many articles were more likely to be about individuals or groups in which gender was not specified than about women. This could be related to the lower public visibility of women in Islam and the difficulty journalists have in getting information. It is also partly related to the type of topics considered newsworthy in association with Islam.

In terms of the type of subject matter with which women are most likely to be associated, this included, with the highest frequency first, personal relationships, education, criminal activity, conversion, gender issues and politics.[31] It is of some concern that, apart from the subjects with which women were often associated, criminal activity featured frequently, giving an indication of the news values that operate with regard to ethnic groups. Even in potentially neutral subjects such as health and belief, as well as the traditional male domains, women featured less frequently, which suggests that Muslim women are being regarded as victims of male aggression, at the mercy of men's deviancy, rather than being deviant themselves.

Muslim women (and women from other religions) were relegated to the private sphere and were most likely to feature in articles on relationships. Over half the articles in which religious women were mentioned involved private matters, compared with a quarter of articles on public issues. These figures were reversed for women without a faith affiliation, who have a much greater chance of being represented in the public sphere, particularly in articles on education.[32]

An examination of the combination of the faith and gender of the central actors (Figure 2.8) in press articles on British Islam showed that male Christians were more likely to appear than female Muslims. However, male Muslims were dominant as the central characters of articles. If a woman featured, she was more likely to be a Muslim, although almost as many women had no faith attributed to them. Similarly, actors from all other religions were more likely to be men.

Figure 2.8 **Faith and gender of main actors**

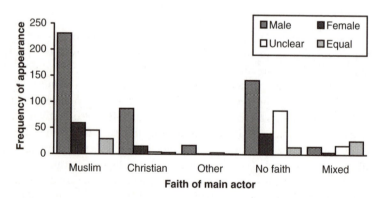

What is clear from these results is that, even when discussing customary female roles and topics, women were marginalized to the traditional, private sphere in the coverage on British Muslims. Few articles appeared in which men and women featured equally; and those that did tended to be about relationships or education. The few articles in which gender was not specified were general ones on education, fundamentalism, belief, racism and minorities. There was a slight difference between the papers. Although all categories of gender appeared more frequently in the *Guardian*, as a percentage of all its articles, more men featured in *The Times* (62 per cent compared with the *Guardian*'s 57 per cent). However, they both included a similar number of women, with the *Guardian* containing more articles in which the sexes were awarded equal status.

Is this a reflection of Muslim values and its power hierarchy, how the press represents Islam, a reflection of Western values in journalism, or a mixture of all three? This is a question for consideration but not one that can be answered here. The aim here is simply to say how Islam in Britain was represented and here women were far less visible than men except in relation to a few specific subjects.

The lack of diversity and of normal and legitimate roles occupied by Muslims within the narrow framework has contributed to accusations of non-assimilation being aimed at Muslims (when in fact it constitutes an example of exclusion). Islam will only be represented when it fits in with these narrow definitions. Non-Muslim groups and institutions dominate definitions of Muslim affairs in the news. This is consistent with previous research on the main actors presented in the news, which shows that important issues are defined for the public by powerful institutions and interests, and that 'alternative' voices are marginalized or unlikely to gain access. This is an indication that, in an attempt to maintain power relations, Islam is presented from a dominant ideological perspective, which the media then express and construct for their readers. Van Dijk (1991) argued that the high occurrence of white politicians and educationists as main actors in ethnic minority coverage is related to the attention that the quality press devotes to policy news, primarily involving white authorities. Similarly, the predominance of men is related to the high amount of crime news.

The prominence of British Islam: article type

News coverage of British Islam reflected the quantity of coverage overall, given the amount of space allocated to different types of articles within a paper (Figure 2.9). News stories occurred most

frequently, followed by features, then editorials. It is logical that few
articles should appear as news in brief, in which foreign coverage
dominates. Letters tended to be of a general nature, offering facts and
information about Islam. However, newspapers also often used letters
to balance their coverage, hence the greater number of defensive than
critical letters (they also act as a substitute for analysis). There were just
24 front-page news stories, accounting for only 1 per cent of front pages
available in the papers in the three-year period (and, inevitably, there is
often more than one story on the front page).

Figure 2.9 **Type of article in which stories appear on British Islam**

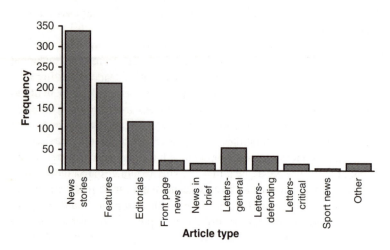

The reason for examining the type of article is to assess how different stories are located in the papers. Indicating the importance
assigned to a topic gives us more information about what news values
are placed on issues relating to Islam. As we may have expected, front-
page news stories often focused on elite people. Some 37 per cent of the
articles focused on either Prince Charles (mainly in *The Times*, for
example David Dimbleby's television interview with him appeared on
the front page); the relationships of members of the elite (Jemima and
Imran Khan), which both papers covered along with her conversion and
the wedding; or the conversion of Darius Guppy (gaoled for the Lloyds

insurance fraud). This was confirmed by an examination of the central actors appearing in these articles. A quarter of front-page news stories focused on celebrities and 17 per cent on royalty. A similar number of political figures featured, as well as one article on a head of state. However, relationships also hit the front page when some negative aspect could be applied. In 1996, both papers covered the anticipated return of 'child bride' Sarah Cook to England. Community members were more likely to feature in controversial topics such as fundamentalism and criminal activity, which also accounted for 17 per cent of the front-page articles. Front-page news stories about fundamentalism in *The Times* included a government plan to deal with terrorists taking refuge in London following Iranian bomb raids on Israeli targets, and plans for an Islamic rally by the extremist group al-Muhajiroun. For crime, it covered the Bradford riots and a murder inquiry in London involving Muslim perpetrators and victims. The *Guardian* did not cover any of these. It reported the use by the extremist group, Hamas, of London as a base for terrorism; political fraud in Birmingham involving Muslim groups and the Labour Party; and Guppy's release from gaol (including references back to his conversion). It is therefore evident that negative associations with Islam reach the front page. The threshold of these events and the news values of the papers contributed to their location, for example *The Times* focus on Prince Charles and its law and order framework. However, both papers undermined and derided Muslims by focusing on abnormal pursuits; ridiculed tensions between practice and belief (lottery winner shunned by his community); feared the Muslim terrorist threat; attended to and detailed unusual practices (food, underage marriage and the Rally for Revival) and treated their activities with scepticism and ridicule (the Rally for Revival and conversion). What is more, they placed these aspects of Muslim life at the forefront.

The positioning of events in other articles reflected general news practices, namely the difference between 'soft' and 'hard' storylines. News stories are more likely to feature hard topics like crime, fundamentalism and politics, with 74 per cent of articles on crime being news stories. Features were more likely to focus on the media, belief, conversion, and gender issues.

Comment on Islam had a slightly different emphasis. Although education was most likely to be editorialized, 'harder' coverage on the whole was ignored. Opinion is more likely to be formed on softer issues, people and their activities: relationships, cultural differences, crises of faith are more likely to raise judgements. When events occurred in relation to British Islam, it was these sorts of events that provoked the expression of particular viewpoints (and more so in *The Times* than the *Guardian*). It is noteworthy that there was little comment on Islamic fundamentalism (only three articles). Were these articles so explicit that journalists felt little need to comment?

Perhaps some attention should be paid here to letters. Letters are normally written in response to an article that has been published in the paper. Most of these letters focused on the supposed inherent differences of Muslims, differences that were negatively evaluated. A quarter of these letters criticized Prince Charles and his attitude to Islam, others criticized the way in which women were treated in Islam, compared Islam negatively with Christianity, and attacked the Muslim Parliament, in particular the pronouncements of its leader, Kalim Siddiqui. All these issues appeared in both papers but to a greater extent in the *Guardian* (except articles on Prince Charles).

Letters defending Islam had a different focus. They tended either to be corrective, offering information on Islam's position on women, the *Satanic Verses*, human rights and intolerance, to contest accusations of separatism and difference, to dispute any cultural threat, or to focus on discrimination towards Muslims. They also offered reasons for why Muslims were seeking legislative redress. Again, such letters appeared more often in the *Guardian*. Their presence showed a willingness to present an alternative perspective but raised questions about the articles that prompted them. The idea that the impact of these letters balanced the overall effect of negative coverage, however, is questionable.

Letters were more likely to be of a general nature, expressing neither a like nor dislike for Islam but offering facts and information; or they were critical of policies, laws, aspects of the British system, Christianity or some other element without articulating attitudes towards Islam. Letters of this kind covered a variety of topics. Some offered to correct a newspaper's translation of the Koran, to define the meaning of the word Semite, to criticize a paper's interpretation of Christianity, or to offer examples of interfaith cooperation and tolerance.

Many of the letters of all types focused on issues around the media, freedom of speech, censorship, gender and discrimination, or they compared Islam with Christianity, all topics that are clearly areas of debate. This illustrated the news convention of dealing with controversial issues by printing letters with opposing viewpoints.

Academics were the most prominent letter writers when it came to subjects of a general or defensive nature. This reflects the tendency of newspapers to feature letters written by academics, giving them greater authority. These mainly appeared in the *Guardian*, 80 per cent (perhaps indicative of the liberal, leftist outlook of many academics). Community members also defended or wrote in general about Islam, as well as community spokespeople, committees, religious and political figures and educationists. As might be expected, more non-Muslims wrote letters that were critical of Islam while more Muslims defended it. Letters of a general nature were more likely to be written by non-Muslims.

The geography of British Islam

Regions that are significant in reports on British Muslims reflect both the localities in which newsworthy events take place and newsgathering processes. London occurs most frequently, in 29 per cent of articles (and has a significant hard news 'law and order' focus), followed by other big cities with a significant Muslim presence, such as Birmingham and Bradford. Birmingham schools were a particular focus for educational debate during this time, along with unrest in Bradford in 1995. To some extent, this reflected the distribution of Muslims throughout the UK. Anwar (1993) estimated that 60 per cent of Muslims lived in London and the southeast (mainly outer London), closely followed by the West Midlands and West Yorkshire. However, this was not merely a straightforward reflection of the ethnic mix of the country; he also found south Lancashire to be highly populated yet marginalized in press coverage. Other cities with large Muslim communities also slip through the news net (Tuchman 1978). Bolton, Bristol, Coventry, Leeds, Leicester, Liverpool, Manchester and Sheffield all have substantial ethnic minority communities, yet none of these cities had even ten stories about their Muslim communities featured (and some none at all). This is an indication of how certain geographical 'spaces' become associated with particular groups. It also illustrates the tendencies of journalists to revisit known sources and familiar faces for information.

Of the articles that centred on a variety of locations (13.5 per cent), many reflected the link between home and abroad, and focused on relationships (35 per cent), politics (27 per cent) and criminal activity (17 per cent). Significantly, the home country of British Muslims was the setting for 8 per cent of the articles. This again reflected an idea of the 'foreignness' of Muslims whose loyalties are located elsewhere. The ties between countries are seen as threatening, as part of Islam's global nature (which allows it to be homogenized). However, more articles were not spatially located at all (16 per cent).

Other sources showed a wide variety of Muslim activities taking place throughout the country (see BMMS,[33] which reports monthly on activities covered in both the national and local press), yet this diversity was not represented in the national press. For a journalist to make the effort to report on an unusual location, highly newsworthy events must be taking place. For example, Essex is Sarah Cook's home county (6 per cent) and Scotland (3 per cent) was mentioned because of the Govan by-election and Muslim efforts to elect a candidate.

Regional specification added to the narrow framework of reporting on Islam, especially in relation to particular topics, for example, the focus on Islamic fundamentalists (immigrants) living in London.

The main findings in this part of the research then are as follows:

- Coverage of British Islam is increasing. However, it only accounts for a small proportion of coverage on Islam, most of which is concerned with international events.
- British Islam consistently takes on a few limited forms in the press, albeit with a wider diversity of representation than its global image due to political and social necessity. However, coverage of British Islam is strongly tied to countries and people abroad, delineating networks and implicating British Muslims with events overseas, allowing them to be seen as part of a worldwide phenomenon.
- This narrow framework of representation is further bound together by a restricted number of meanings. These reflect the anxieties of differing elite groups who represent Islam as a threat to majority British political, social and cultural interests. The major topics associated with Islam fluctuated in their emphasis over the three-year period due to particular events, but remained the most dominant topics in each year. This consistency continued in 1997 and 1998. Actors featured in articles tend to be identified as Muslims only if the story explicitly expresses themes specifically associated with Muslims.[34] If not, the story will be represented within a racial paradigm.
- However, coverage is not homogenous and spaces for oppositional

perspectives are present. These are mainly found in the *Guardian*, which pays more attention to minority views. However, both papers have remarkably similar news values and categorization in relation to British Islam.

- The current manifestation of British Islam in the press has been pushed onto the agenda partly by Muslim groups (reflecting the struggle for representation in public life). However, at the point of production, they lose control of the meaning, which tends to be framed within a dominant ideological framework based on an agenda of maintaining and protecting sacred values and institutions, be they traditional, conservative (*The Times*) or liberal (*Guardian*).

- Events selected for coverage of British Islam fit within a framework of dominant news values, that is they feature elite personnel or institutions, they are predominantly negative in content and the extent of this negativity is significant, they are consistent with previous frameworks of understanding, they are unambiguous in their meanings and have continuity with previous events, and they can be personalized (Galtung and Ruge 1965). However, articles are more likely to appear if they match the news values attached to minorities in general, namely negativization and problematization. Representations of British Islam are composed of a mingling of perceptions and attitudes related to ethnic minorities in Britain with current and more established notions of Islam on a wider scale (Orientalism).

- British Islam is presented within an ethnocentric ideological (secular) framework. A non-Muslim official position is given legitimacy in defining British Islam to the public. Women's voices are further marginalized in this process.

Conclusion

Thus, Muslims are not seen as an integral part of British society. The absence of 'normal' stories in which Muslims appear, and the narrow diversity of roles that results from the selection of stories seen as specifically dealing with 'Muslim affairs', results in a consistently narrow framework of representation. This firmly established itself in the 1990s, but stemmed from events in the late 1980s (the Rushdie and Honeyford affairs) that defined 'what it meant to be Muslim' and that attempted to construct a closure around these definitions. These factors,

combined with images of the global fanatic, with xenophobic tendencies and with anxieties about minorities in general, which were
exacerbated by Muslim attempts to preserve their culture and traditions
being interpreted as Muslim separatism, have resulted in the images of
Islam made explicit here.

Islam is understood across a limited number of topics and framed
within a narrow definition of Islam, thus constituting a particular
'symbolic universe' (Dahlgren and Chakrapani 1982: 45). Press
coverage is linked to specific events and to the general framework, but
the consistency of coverage over the three-year period and beyond
suggests that a consensus of news values has been established and
events will be selected only when they fit into this framework.
Although the mainstream press displays a high degree of homogeneity
in themes associated with Islam, total homogeneity should not be
assumed. The dominant themes are represented and delivered in an
assortment of ways depending on the news values, style and target
audiences of the various newspapers. In addition, both slippages and
contradictions in content occur both between papers and within articles.

While focusing on these topics, the aim has been to establish the sort
of 'material made available to the public as a whole' (Hartmann et al.
1974: 117). They argued that newspapers, being widely read, have
some influence on topics of public discussion, which become 'part of
the shared perspectives that people use to make sense of their world'.
On this basis, it is the overall picture that matters. Newspapers, through
the selection and inclusion of topics, frame social reality, constructing
social meaning for their readers, and promote particular 'ways of
seeing' Islam in Britain. They provide a description of the world
produced within a specific interpretative framework, located within a
limited social, historical context. This framework should not be taken to
be deliberate distortion but generated from complex processes in news
production and rooted in cultural assumptions.

The purpose of the next chapter is to explore these conclusions
further, to examine whether the framework shown here subsumes
nuances in the discourses, to look at the subtle differences in the representation of different papers and to establish how far patterns of
representation of Islam can be collapsed into these few meanings.

3. British Islam: a discursive construction

The aim of this chapter is to identify and place the dominant social meanings of British Islam to be found in sections of the British press at a particular historical moment, 1994–1997, within the wider context of the findings so far. The extent of coherence between papers is examined along with the subtle differences, the contending discourses that represent a struggle for symbolic and actual power. Contextual knowledge is vital in understanding the interests underlying the ideologies found in competing formulations of an event.

Introduction

An approach based on discourse analysis was employed for its incorporation and development of both ideological and structuralist approaches. In analysing the texts, it was necessary to use an ideological approach to gain an idea of the 'preferred meanings' present. Although the meaning of a text cannot fully be understood without the varying interpretations of the audience, research findings have revealed that texts do have an ideological stance reflecting the particular 'myths, meanings and values of society' (Hindmarsh 1996).

Discourse analysis stems from the work of the French theorist Foucault, who conceptualized discourse as the production of knowledge through language that has a will to power. According to Foucault (1980: 201), power is exercised over those who are 'known' through discourse. Those who produce discourse, therefore, have the power to enforce its validity so that it effectively becomes a 'regime of truth' (Hall 1992a: 295).

The shift from ideological to discourse-based explanations of ethnic tension (Goldberg 1993; van Dijk 1983; Wetherell and Potter 1992) is based on a definition of ideology that makes a distinction between true statements about the world (science) and false statements (ideology). Foucault argued that statements are rarely simply true or false because facts can be construed in different ways (through language). Rather, discourse acknowledges the ideological dimension in all statements. Competing discourses therefore represent a contestation over power in which the outcome of the struggle, according to Hall (1992a), decides the 'truth' (based on real effects). Ideology cannot, however, be dismissed. If defined, as by Sapsford and Abbott (1996: 332), as 'a coherent set of propositions about what people and/or social institutions are like and how they ought to be — generally presented to one group of people that certain behaviours are in their own interests and concealing the fact they are more so in the interests of another, more powerful group', it can be usefully incorporated into Foucault's notion of discourse as an expression of ideology, 'a framework within which ideas are formulated' (Sapsford and Jupp 1996: 332).

The media then contribute to 'discourse environments' (van Dijk 1991), having the authority based on institutional power (and structured by unequal sets of social relations) to reproduce 'moral norms', theoretical 'explanations' and 'techniques of (social) control' (the three aspects of social regulation) (Foucault 1982 cited by Jupp 1996: 308). This means that through the discursive practices of newspapers, the norms, values and interests of dominant groups, which legitimate a certain conceptualization of an event, its social meaning and a preferred solution, are reproduced, confirmed and diffused (van Dijk 1988b: 110). Its power then, lies in its contribution to the maintenance of social relations and discriminatory practices.

Discourse analysis has the advantage of taking into account and revealing social processes in its incorporation of all aspects of communication: a text's author and therefore intention, its authority, and its audience (Worrall 1990: 8). It therefore allows the researcher, through a critical analysis of the text, to reveal the prevailing knowledge among sets of people held about another set of people at a particular historical and political conjuncture, and provide an alternative reading. Given that official (state) discourse is only one among a 'multiplicity of interacting discourses' (Jupp 1996: 311) involved in the production of knowledge, an examination of the variance between papers in the placement and construction of subjects into the public domain allows for the identification of the social priorities of differing groups.

I employ a classical qualitative method of 'content analysis', which is refined by a particular method of discourse analysis that draws on aspects of critical linguistics based on the functional linguistics of Halliday (discussed in Fowler 1991) and 'structures of news discourse' (van Dijk 1983; 1988b; 1991). The theoretical basis for these procedures maintains that aspects of linguistic features, both syntactic and semantic, contain ideological significance (Bell 1991; Fairclough 1995). By examining the deployment of lexical choices, sentence structures, structural transformations and photographic imagery in texts, I shall make explicit the implicit assumptions contained in them, the cultural indicators of the current political epoch (in the UK). Underpinning this is the theoretical conception that all texts are discursively constructed, reproducing available discourses in society. Meaning is never fixed, for it shifts at different moments in the communication process. However, discourse analysis aims to show how practices of representation attempt to secure meaning by favouring certain constructions over others.

Inevitably, the complexity of media discourse and the sheer number of articles retrieved in a study such as this require massive data reduction and simplification in the presentation of the results. In concentrating on the important findings then, I do not intend here to explicate fully the exact methods of analysis; some linguistic procedures will, however, be drawn on to demonstrate the extraction of meaning.

As well as the broadsheets, I have looked here at two tabloids, the *Daily Mail* and the *Sun*, in order to include a wider selection of the type of information made available to the public on Islam, especially given the readership of these tabloids, which were chosen as representing the most popular and influential papers among the tabloids (Lacey and Longman 1997). Both papers express conservative ideologies. The Daily Mail and General Trust, part of the Northcliffe Newspapers Groups, owns the *Daily Mail* and is the second largest regional paper owner. It currently sells 2,391,229 papers daily, and a similar number on a Sunday, constituting approximately 12 per cent of the newspaper market overall. The *Sun* is part of News International, as is *The Times*. At 3,589,204, it has the highest daily sales in the UK.[1]

The focus for this study is 1997, the year following the previous analysis, allowing a comparison with these years and contributing additional depth to the news framework we see developing. The most topical stories of the aforesaid years were chosen for their consistent media interest — specifically education, Rushdie, fundamentalism, relationships and politics. The dominant topics (with subtopics) ascertained from the 1994–96 quantitative analysis were as follows:

- education and religion;
- Rushdie and freedom of speech;
- education and segregation;
- Islamic fundamentalism and immigration;
- relationships and criminal activity; and
- politics and criminal activity.

Quantitative context

Before focusing on these topics specifically, I feel it is important to provide the quantitative context for 1997 overall, to assess the continuing relevancy of the framework that has already been established. The predominant topics and themes identified became more pronounced in 1997, providing a consonance with earlier events. This year saw a convergence in the coverage of *The Times* and *Guardian* and a correspondence in the appearance of dominant topics with previous years. However, Table 3.1 demonstrates the shift in the volume of coverage allocated to them, based on the 'significant' events of the year (resulting in different positions of dominance from earlier years). It is evident then that the same sorts of stories about British Islam are newsworthy, but appear as 'new' events.

Politics became particularly significant during the build-up to the general election and selection of the first Muslim MP. His subsequent arrest for vote rigging explained the high number of articles on criminality. The romance between Princess Diana and Dodi Fayed and their ensuing deaths and funerals ensured that coverage on relationships remained high. In addition, speculation began to circulate on the breakdown of Imran Khan's marriage. Education remained an ongoing concern with debates about funding Muslim schools, an issue that appeared to hold more salience for *The Times* than the *Guardian*. The focus on fundamentalist activities continued after an attack on tourists at an ancient site in Luxor, Egypt, by the al-Gama'a al-Islamiya extremist group, resulting in discussions about the presence of Islamic militants in Britain. Royalty was also prevalent during this year, with reports on Prince Charles's visit to Bangladesh (rather than of his speeches) and the Queen's visits to Pakistan and India. Norman Tebbit's remarks about multiculturalism at the Conservative Party conference caused a furore. The Rushdie debate continued with the renewal of the *fatwa* and

Table 3.1 Topics occurring in 1997

Topic	The Times Frequency	%	Guardian Frequency	%	Total frequency
Politics	52	27.5	34	17.0	86
Criminality	27	14.2	40	20.0	67
Relationships	17	8.9	24	12.0	41
Education	20	10.5	11	5.5	31
Fundamentalism	9	4.7	19	9.5	28
Royalty	15	7.9	7	3.5	22
Censorship/Rushdie	14	7.4	14	7.0	28
Multiculturalism	6	3.1	12	6.0	18
Christianity	12	6.3	5	2.5	17
Conversion	10	5.2	2	1.0	12
Discrimination	4	2.1	5	2.5	9
Total	186	98.4	173	87.3	359
Total articles on British Islam in 1997	189	100.0	198	100.0	387

in relation to discussions on freedom of speech, which coincided with the launching of a report on Islamophobia to fight religious discrimination (interpreted as blasphemy). Conversions during the year included those of Chris Eubank and Prince Naseem's new wife. Articles on Christianity in *The Times* compared the decline of Christianity in Britain with the rise of Islam, and both papers carried the story of a bishop reading the Koran for Lent. A comparative framework thus ensued. Finally, articles on discrimination were included in the analysis (racism and Islamophobia) to illustrate the continuing lack of attention given to these issues. The topics mentioned here (excluding discrimination) accounted for 90.4 per cent of all coverage on British Islam in that year, evidence of the framework appearing to narrow.

The differing degrees of emphasis reinforced some of the variations in the papers' news values. Tebbit's right-wing views on multiculturalism were more controversial for the *Guardian*. *The Times* focused on traditional stereotypes such as conversion and maintained its royal and comparative slant. However, there were some shifts in emphasis, the diminished focus on politics and increased attention to criminality in the *Guardian* and vice-versa in *The Times*.

The *Mail* in 1997

For the qualitative analysis, I decided to include two tabloids, both aimed at the middle and lower-income market, to examine the consistency in news values with the quality newspapers. On the basis of the findings from the broadsheets a more restrictive and marginal framework of representation could be inferred, whereby given their different criteria for newsworthiness the tabloids focus more on entertainment than politics and foreign affairs. Their scope, then, is often more limited, presenting a jingoistic picture of the foreigner. This initial quantitative analysis showed that the *Mail* found the same topics and stories newsworthy, but that a lack of depth and fleeting coverage marginalized them further. Much less space and attention was allocated in the middle market tabloid press, but the agenda appeared to be the same.[2] While global coverage accounted for less than one-third of that of the broadsheets in this year and British less than half, British coverage accounted for a higher percentage of the tabloids' reporting on Islam (34.6 per cent) compared with the broadsheets. This remained consistent in subsequent years (see Chapter 5). This is partly to do with tighter restrictions on space in a tabloid, but also with a lack of interest in foreign news and minority affairs, which are thought to have little to do with the lives and interests of the target readership. It is of note here that approximately half to three-quarters of the *Mail* articles in each year (both global and local) used the derogatory term *Moslem*. While this served further to exoticize and distance the Other, any patterns in this lexicalization would require further investigation.

Three-quarters of the *Mail*'s coverage addressed topics that were prominent in the broadsheets (Table 3.2). Again, royalty was of interest to this right-wing Establishment paper. Apart from Lord Tebbit's views, multiculturalism was unlikely to be given much space. However, it is important to ask what this means and whether it fits into the meta-theme of integrative concerns identified in Chapter 2, raising questions about the place of minorities in British society. The question of education was notably absent from the *Mail* in 1997, which reveals a reliance on official sources to make the topic newsworthy. Although of growing significance to the community in that year with negotiations with the government on state-funded Muslim schools in progress, in the absence of any firm action or policy decisions being made in this area, the paper did not take up the subject. It was, however, discussed when the government released plans to fund two Muslims schools early in 1998.

Table 3.2   Topics covered in 1997 by the *Mail*

Topic	Frequency	%
Politics	28	24.3
Relationships	28	24.3
Prince Charles	10	8.6
Fundamentalism	9	7.8
Christianity	6	5.2
Blasphemy	3	2.6
Multiculturalism	3	2.6
Total	87	75.6
Total articles in 1997 on British Islam	115	100 (34.6)
Total articles in 1997 on Islam	332	100.0

Figure 3.1   **Comparative frequencies in the *Mail*: global and British coverage**

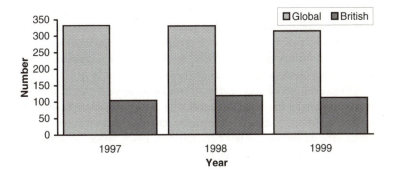

The *Sun*'s coverage will be examined through the stories selected for analysis to see if these emphasize similar meta-themes to the other papers but express them according to the paper's style and audience.

Due to its different emphasis on story selection, however, I will look further into the *Sun*'s coverage in a separate section later in this chapter.

Taking, specifically, the *stories* selected for the qualitative analysis, Table 3.3 shows the number of articles on these stories carried in each paper. A total of 128 articles from 1997 were analysed plus 31 extra articles from 1996 (on education) making 159 in total.[3]

Table 3.3   Number of articles covered on each story by paper

Newspaper			Topics			
	A	B	C	D	E	Total
The Times/Sunday Times	23	9	8 (+18)*= 26	2	3	63
Guardian/Observer	18	19	6 (+13) = 19	11	2	69
Mail/Mail on Sunday	8	5	1	3	3	20
Sun	5	0	2	0	0	7
Total	54	33	17 (+31) = 48	16	8	159

A = Crime and politics (Sarwar); B = Fundamentalism; C = Education; D = Rushdie (blasphemy); E = Relationships

*Bracketed figure = articles examined from 1996.

There were some variations between the papers. They all followed the 'Sarwar saga',[4] a political scandal involving the first British Muslim MP and the New Labour government, resonating highly in the news values of crime and politics. The *Guardian* paid particular attention to the religious discrimination laws, which was understandable given its liberal position on freedom of speech. However, its attention to fundamentalism was more unexpected.

It becomes increasingly evident throughout this chapter that the legal legitimization of the Muslim community is an issue over which a number of competing groups struggle to attain hegemony. Of all these articles, however, only 8 per cent could be described as outwardly *supportive* of Muslims. Just over half of these are letters, 21 per cent are news items and only 7 per cent are editorials. It is evident, then, that the newspapers themselves made negative evaluations of events involving Muslims while using letters (of which people may take less notice when competing with the authority of the paper) for balance. Almost three-quarters of these were in the *Guardian*, slightly less than a quarter in

The Times and the remainder split equally between the tabloids; almost half were about educational issues. One-quarter of the *Guardian*'s coverage of the blasphemy debate and of fundamentalism presented an alternative viewpoint, or was at least balanced. All other coverage, apart from that of Sarwar, could be described as portraying Muslims in either a critical or negative light. While most articles on Sarwar could be said to be critical of Sarwar himself, it was not possible to say that they were outwardly critical of Muslims. Only two articles, however, could be said to have been wholly supportive of Sarwar.

Qualitative analysis of relationships

Stories about relationships in 1997 followed a pattern that was very similar to those of previous years. Mainly involving the relationships of non-Muslims with Muslims, often members of the elite and their ensuing conversion, they included speculation about the relationships of the Princess of Wales, the Khan's marriage, which was increasingly seen to be under strain, and John Birt's son (who had converted following a relationship with a Muslim). Due to the celebrity focus of these stories, this is one topic relating to Islam that is highly likely to be featured in the tabloids. Items involving non-elite people include stories of 'Shirley Valentines' who have married Muslims abroad and consequently had to flee from their brutality. The single feature in which both partners were Muslim focused on their feelings about an impending arranged marriage (*Mail*).

The story of Sarah Cook developed in 1997 from previous years, this being the only story on relationships that could be described as continuing into that year and hence was the most interesting for analysis. This focused on the relationship of a 13-year-old girl from Essex and a Turkish waiter, Musa Komeagac, who met on holiday, got married and had a baby. She was made a ward of court and sent back to Britain while he was charged with having unlawful sex and arranging an unofficial religious ceremony by the Turkish courts.

Coverage of the story in that year included, first, her decision to remain in Britain (August), second, his punishment in the Turkish courts (October) and, finally, his second marriage to a Turkish Muslim (December). While the *Observer* broke the story, the *Mail* and *The Times* then covered all aspects of it. The *Sun* did not cover the story in 1997, which was surprising given its typically tabloid constituents —

namely associating sex and crime with the Other. The *Sun*, which bought the initial story from Sarah Cook's parents following the marriage, would appear to have had a number of reasons for running it. Yet, the broadsheets *did* cover it, an illustration of their increasing tabloidization.

The coverage of relationships is characterized by an Orientalist discourse relating to sexual deviance, primitivism, gender, generation, illegality, immorality and perfidy (fraudulent faith), which formulate a meta-discourse of cultural incompatibility.

Sexual deviance/generation

Sarah's age was significant in the newsworthiness of this item. Thus, all papers categorized her lexically as a 'schoolgirl' and 'child bride'. These labels featured in five of the eight headlines, so could be considered significant in defining the event for the audience, providing conceptual solidity and memorability, which are important in cognitive processing (van Dijk 1991). This is obviously a general ploy the tabloids use when referring to any articles that include young women and sex, a mixture of 'titillation' inherent in the tabloids and 'moral outrage', but it was the religious (and foreign) aspect producing the combination of exotic cultural practices and crime that gave this story a particular news value.

In the first *Mail* article, Sarah was referred to as a schoolgirl four times and her age was cited five times. By classifying her as such, the articles appeal to a consensus on child abuse, which allows her to be subjected to state action. His nationality and age (18) lent themselves to the construction of a discourse on deviant and excessive sexuality harking back to historical images of the cruelty and suppression of the Arab harem. He was therefore subjected to a form of fetishism in which he was reduced to an essential (corrupt) sexuality endemic of 'the primal fantasy ... [of black sexuality, which] projects the fear of a threat not only to white womanhood, but to civilization itself, as the anxiety of miscegenation, eugenic pollution and racial denigration' (Mercer 1994: 85). These anxieties were then dissipated by his 'failed sexuality' in her ultimate rejection of him (Said 1978: 315).

The final article in the *Mail* confirmed his sexual deviance when he married 'the daughter of a prostitute' 'secretly' and without his parents' consent. References to his 'latest' and almost as 'controversial' marriage confirmed his 'natural' status as a consistent offender.

Cultural clash

This macro-proposition was expressed both explicitly and implicitly.[5] The caption 'culture clash' appeared in the *Mail* beneath photographs twice, making explicit the inferred meaning to be read from the article. The incompatibility of the two cultures was also signalled by the short duration and inevitable demise of the relationship, 'she proved the sceptics right'. The marriage was declared as 'over' in all three initial headlines. The texts worked to reinforce and fix these conditions by the use of definite terminology, she 'vowed', she would 'never go back'. This was contrasted with his state of 'bewilderment', further adding to his apparent weakness (see failed sexuality). The cultural clash was constructed through a number of binary oppositions in the texts:

Freedom versus constraint: constructed through a discourse on the treatment of women, this was achieved through reference to her 'imprisonment' compared with her comfortable 'suburban home in Essex' and to giving prominence to Sarah saying 'it wasn't the life for me'. That she felt 'like an old woman rather than a teenager' was highlighted by a presentational strategy of bold typography.

Muslim clothing was deemed symbolic of these restrictions and referred to in all articles: '"I feel freer ... I'm much happier now" she insisted.' The *Guardian* described how 'she has reverted to Western clothes.' The relations between propositions here establish this as a positive move and result in a negative inference by 'but [she] is still a practising Muslim.' As the most visible signifier of difference, Sarah was veiled in six of the seven pictures of her. The veil signifies patriarchal Islam rather than, as many Muslim women feel, a factor in their freedom (Holt 1996).[6]

However, while the heavy black *hijab* dominates the representation of Muslim women internationally (thereby reducing them to its significations: objectified and eroticized within male-centred fantasies, a gendering discourse associated with historical views of Arabs and the harem), British Muslim women, as here, tend to be dressed in their regular clothing with the addition of a headscarf. This signifies their status as incomplete Muslims; their state of conversion represents transience as opposed to the absolute, permanent and threatening nature of the full *hijab*. This functions to delineate a line between the 'exotic' and the British subject, allowing the papers to overcome the problematic issue of conversion and allowing for reader empathy. Sarah certainly looked uncomfortable in her headscarf and her release from it confirmed its fleeting status.

The focus on Sarah's age, in particular, and being categorized as a 'child bride', constructed an idea of a little girl playing with dressing-up clothes. Thus, Sarah's sexuality was suppressed and displaced to him to ensure the continuance of this racialized discourse (Mercer 1994). This characterization of a woman in terms of her relation to a man is typical of the 'female paradigm' within which women generally, and particularly Muslim women, are represented (Fowler 1991).

However, a further difference in coverage of the British convert is the agency given to the British participant. This can be determined by an examination of the syntactic process in the transivity of clauses (see Appendix B). An examination of the initial headlines shows Sarah as the syntactic agent in leaving him, 'Child bride says marriage is over' (*The Times*, 12 August).[7] Or, he is subject to the actions of the authorities, and now defined as being in her possession, 'Child bride's Turkish husband fined £5' (*Guardian*, 10 October). However, when the associated actions become negative, he becomes the central agent, 'Turk weds again' (*The Times*, 24 December). She was, therefore, the passive victim of his negative actions (in previous coverage) until she is proactive in ending the relationship. This occurrence in the sequence of events and Sarah's attitude to it are ideologically closer to the papers' views on the relationship, meeting their initial expectations. This is illustrated by bringing Sarah's quotes to the forefront, while marginalizing his by placing them at the end of the article or undermining them with cynicism.

The *Guardian* and *The Times*, however, give Sarah less responsibility for her actions, emphasizing the enforced culture by implying that she was at the will of the Komeagacs, converting 'at the family's request'. The syntactical structure of these clauses emphasizes her subject position, 'Komeagac, who married Sarah in Turkey', 'she was returned to GB'. By rendering her helpless in this way, the papers reinforce her status as a child, making the abuse more explicit.

Significant in these headlines is his categorization as a 'Turkish waiter'. All papers used at least one of these two terms to define him in nearly every single instance. This had two effects: first, as a waiter he was defined by his menial, low status occupation and second, he was seen to have abused a position of trust. This 'over completeness', adding extraneous detail, was also illustrated by the papers' continued attention to how they met, a holiday romance, which functions to devalue the nature and feelings experienced in the relationship (van Dijk 1991: 185). His Turkishness allowed his actions to be attributed to his 'natural' disposition. However, these are displaced to his 'Muslimness' (Halliday 1996) by the Turkish authorities' negative evaluations of his behaviour. This label does, however, appeal to xenophobic tendencies, further marginalizing his perspective.

Rationality versus irrationality: this is evident both in the implication that Sarah has regained her sanity after a bout of momentary madness and by denigrating the Turkish legal system. That normality (by press standards) has been restored is symbolically illustrated in terms of clothing; 'Gone is the Moslem clothing. ... Back in Essex, she is once again.' The inadequacies of the legal system are made manifest by focusing on the length of the trial, indicating it has 'dragged on' and by expressing dissatisfaction with the punishment Musa received. Both the *Mail* and *Guardian* consider his punishment 'a trifling amount even by the standards of a provincial village. The court had decided that there was no unlawful sex despite intercourse with under 15s being illegal in Turkey'.

Morality versus immorality: all the articles expressed a morality based on an ethnocentric perspective of the event, which made assumptions and reproduced an institutional discourse about what was right and wrong. Thus, the papers established a consensus around specific norms relating to sexual relationships. This was expressed by emphasizing the *illegality* of the marriage, it was 'never officially recognized in either country' and 'merely religious' (as opposed to civil law), stressing a lack of importance. The papers reinforced the unofficial nature of the marriage by putting inverted commas around the words 'husband', 'bride' and 'marriage'. *The Times* defined the sexual relationship as 'rape' in its final headline. By referring to the fine imposed on both the imam and Musa's father, the *Mail* reinforced the illegal context.

A discourse of *primitivism* based on what are deemed to be backward cultural practices runs through these macro-semantics and allows for the reification of 'British' values, which are presented as common sense. This is achieved through specific lexical choices that address the audience inclusively as 'we', 'It was a marriage which *defied belief* and

shocked the nation' (emphasis added). By referring to widespread outrage, the ideology becomes naturalized. When this consensus is broken,
as in the conduct of Sarah's parents who supported the marriage and her
father's conversion to Islam, it is constructed as aberrant, achieved by
the papers by setting up a division between the sensible majority and
the irresponsible few.

Part of the rhetorical strategy the papers used to ensure a dominant
reading was in the characterization of Musa. We saw that he was the
agent of negative actions and thus penalized by the authorities. As well
as being oppressive and abusive, he was depicted as unsupportive of his
son, sending 'just £180 to support 10-month Mohammad'. This selfish-
ness, particularly with regard to money, is a discursive construction that
reappears in the analysis of further topics. Any indications of behaviour
that may counter this construction, such as Musa's declarations that he
would return to England to be with his family, were quickly undermined by setting them against her more definite and prominent pro-
nouncement that it was over (*Mail*, 10 October). Quotation marks are
used to distance his remarks from the views of the paper. His subsequent second marriage provided global coherence to the story, as
evidence of the shallowness of his comments.[8]

The explanatory factor for these events being Musa's Muslimness
was constructed through the local coherence of propositions in the articles.
By detailing Islamic clothes, ritual and belief, the articles provided a
cultural register that insinuated religious motives. One example of this
was to quote Musa saying, 'Before Allah and my people I am proved
clean' (*Mail*, 10 October), a statement which, when juxtaposed against
the trial and punishment and the newspapers' derogatory evaluations,
negativizes Muslim belief. That these values were deemed to be Islamic
(rather than attributed to traditional patriarchal cultural practices) was
also constructed through the religious ceremony, which is illegal in
Turkey. His people's condemnation of his actions allowed the papers to
deny that there were any racist motives in their portrayal.

However, the religious absolutism expressed here in adherence to
strict cultural practices was undermined by a further significant discourse, namely that of perfidiousness. Muslim dogmatism in following
a strict religious code was confuted by their criminal, immoral behaviour. As fraudulent Muslims, their adherence to Islam was presumed
to be for manipulative reasons. An explicit example of this (in *The
Times*) was when Sarah asked of Musa, 'What sort of Muslim are you?'

She, a British convert, was seen to be morally superior to him. This also worked to neutralize the ideology by attributing it to the focal actor as an evaluative statement in the form of a question.

There was little variation in coverage between papers on this topic. All highlighted the same details, agency and quotes. Global coherence was provided between articles by duplicating and highlighting the same 'facts' about the unlawfulness of the event and the groom's negative actions. This functioned to secure that the public's reading was around a single ideological position.

The conformity in this instance, even in the *Guardian*, also reflected the existence of norms about the exploitation of underage girls by older men. However, concern for the victim cannot be seen as the primary motive in this coverage given the number of juvenile relationships, teenage pregnancies and oppressed wives that go unreported in Britain and the tabloids' hypocritical use of sex to sell papers. Fears about the rise of teenage sexuality in Britain were displaced in this case to problematize Musa's Muslimness as a reason for his behaviour.

Differences, then, occurred in rhetoric and style, with the *Mail* allocating extra space, details and visual support to its articles, its message being more explicit through the use of dramatic lexicalization. However, the journalistic modality was explicit in all papers despite these articles consisting solely of news items, an example of the strong ideological concordance.

The only other reference to this topic was in the *Mail on Sunday*, 18 May, in a Travel Mail item on Turkey. The story of Sarah Cook became associated with Turkey along with its discourse. The story was used to introduce the feature but, with the criteria being to sell holidays, the stereotypes formulated in the initial story were introduced but then replaced by others, 'Child bride? The young Turks here prefer football.' Western females were again the dominant agents, seeking pleasure, not marriage. Although the waiters were presented as predatory, this was firmly placed in the context of traditional Muslim family values with parents maintaining control. This shows an approval of Muslim values when they accorded with British majority values. Their passivity (and inferiority) was reinforced by the idea that their men made poor matches for English women. Though set in a leisure framework, the discourse reiterated the stereotypes of the Muslim threat in order to dispel them for economic reasons. The discourse therefore contained fewer moral overtones and was more light-hearted.

Although I have attempted here to examine the discourse prevalent in these stories discretely, they are obvious overlaps. For example, the discourse employed in relation to deviant cultural practices, such as gender and generation, allowed for a meta-discourse of immorality to be inferred. The synergy between the discourses within this coverage gives them greater strength and increases their 'reality', making it harder for competing discourses to gain assent.

Coverage of conversion represents both a fear of Islam as an expansionary force, despite the main reason for its growth in Europe being migration (Halliday 1996), and an attempt to fix boundaries between what are considered to be mutually exclusive categories: Muslim and Briton. Converts are not treated as 'real' Muslims and coverage is constructed to indicate their return to British values forthwith. Coverage of relationships works to highlight exotic cultural practices (which from an ethnocentric perspective are deemed negative), thus enhancing the superiority of the nation.

Subsequent coverage of this topic relied on ongoing incidental articles that focused on cultural differences and repressive practices towards women. The dominant ideology was apparent in intermittent coverage of the Khan marriage when visits by Jemima to London alone were interpreted as evidence of 'tension' in their marriage caused by cultural differences (apparent in 1998/9). In 1999 coverage was dominated by articles on the 'problem' of 'forced' marriages brought about by the honour killing of a young British Muslim woman by her family, which led to an inquiry into arranged marriages.

Education

Education as an agent of socialization is a principle element in the transmission of culture and values between generations. According to Gilroy (1988), it has thus become a battleground for protecting the national culture on which minority groups are conceived to be making an assault. To Muslims, education is an issue of empowerment, cultural autonomy, identity and acceptance (BMMS, 5 October 1997).[9] The Westernization of Muslim youth, as the youngest of all population groups in the UK, raises further concerns about secular education (Modood et al. 1994). Thus, since the mid-1980s Muslim groups have become increasingly visible in this arena, lobbying for changes in the system. At the time of analysis (1996/7), the policies in question concerned the teaching of religious education. Muslims saw the Conservative government's decision to marginalize the multicultural agenda of the past, by recentring Christianity, as an indication of their peripheral status in the education system. This led to direct action, in this case a boycott of religious education lessons (January 96); 81 per cent of coverage on education in 1996 focused on RE. However, the failure of these actions in articulating Muslim positions and achieving their goals, Nielsen (1991a) suggests, led to a recognition that these can only be achieved outside the system. This resulted in a shift in attention by lobby groups from internal reform to the funding of Muslim schools. The shift was visible in the coverage, with the percentage of articles on funding increasing from 10 per cent in 1996 to 78 per cent in 1997, while coverage of RE dropped to 21 per cent (*The Times* and *Guardian* only).

Press coverage of education can therefore be seen as having been pushed onto the agenda by minorities themselves, for the press react to the measures they take and to government attempts to resolve them. However, the ability of Muslim groups to influence further than this has been limited, for the core of the British press interpreted the situation as an attack on traditional white majority values and reporting has been defensive. The fluctuation in coverage on education illustrates this limited influence. An increase in coverage in 1998 was a result of government action; coverage has since decreased despite the limited funding that has been made available. There is evidence here to suggest that Muslims' own actions have more chance of becoming news when they are (interpreted as) controversial or negative, such as the boycott of lessons, about which discussion on the event and surrounding issues extended for three months over 15 articles in *The Times* and four months over ten articles in the *Guardian*. These actions can then be framed as illegitimate as opposed to the official discourse of the government and press.

This struggle has created a 'battleground' on which competing discourses are played out. A 'consensus' in this instance (as opposed to the previous topic) cannot be taken for granted. Individual papers attempt to fix preferred solutions based on their own ideological positions. All papers therefore have to work hard to establish a consensus when it is clearly not apparent. The strategies and arguments each paper adopts to achieve this are elucidated below.

Rather than merely being regarded as a struggle over the place of

Muslims in the education system, I would argue that this topic provides a microcosm of the British societal context. Questions about our national identity and a place for Muslims in it proliferated when 'multiculturalism', the British model of incorporating its minorities, went into crisis. The funding of Muslim schools, then, was symbolic of the legitimization of Muslims in political and public spaces.

The key first-order discourses to be found in coverage of education include nation, history, morality, economy, integration and absolutism. This construction gives expression to the second-order discourses of anti (anti)-racism, irrationality, illegality and homogeneity.

The Times

Coverage of this topic revealed specific beliefs about the paper's model of education and society and the appropriate accommodation of minorities within it. Prevalent in *The Times* discourse is an integrationist, anti-multiculturalist, moralizing approach. Britain is assumed to be a Christian country, which schools must reflect. The action of Muslims is considered divisive and the standards of their schooling poor. *The Times* therefore uses the boycott to disparage the current multicultural state of RE and advocate a return to Christian values. Thus, the situation is referred to as 'an unhappy commentary' on multi-faith teaching, 'a challenge to the future of our multicultural society' (David Charter, 23 February 1996).[10] Lexical items such as 'muddle', 'mish-mash', 'indoctrination', 'instruction', and 'values/morals' illustrate the extent of the confusion and debate surrounding RE.

Part of the strategy *The Times* adopts is to suggest that a lack of spirituality in the country has led to a decline in morality. Quoting Dr Nick Tate, the government's main curriculum adviser, it warns that Great Britain is 'far advanced towards becoming a religiously illiterate society' and criticizes the 'secular liberalism of the West which declines to defend absolute values' (23 February 1996). The global coherence between articles leaves one feeling that the presence of Muslims has contributed to the demise of Christian values and thus moral disintegration.

According to *The Times*, 'this country is not Muslim' (Susan Elkin, 3 March 1996). It consistently reinforces the Education Act, which states that RE 'must reflect the fact that religious traditions in Great Britain are in the main Christian while taking account of the teaching and practices of other principal religions' (23 February 1996). This is also used to augment the illegitimacy of Muslim action. When the Educational Institute of Scotland called for a change in the law that requires assemblies to be comprised of a broadly Christian character, the commentary appealed to Scotland's identity as a Christian country, arguing that the plans 'deny our history' (8 June 1997). It appropriated all the arguments supporting secular or multifaith assemblies and refuted them on the basis of the commonsense of the majority culture. It alluded to a particular nostalgic view of Britain located in past times. It was therefore dismissive of other religious traditions, referring in the article to 'Islam or Hinduism or whatever', lumping them all into one category of little importance.

To support its argument, *The Times* presents Muslims as irrational and uncompromising. This can be seen in the individual discrediting of a Muslim teacher who interrupted carol singing in assembly. The report highlighted quotes by children and parents who were upset by the 'outburst'; 'ever since he'd been here, he'd been preaching Islam to us when he should have been teaching maths' (19 December 1996). This was followed by a letter from a Muslim, congratulating the teacher, which argued 'we are unapologetically very obstinate in following Islam (Karim Chowdhury, 30 December 1996). Another letter referred to 'the thoughtless actions of a religious zealot' (Om P. Midha, 30 December 1996). The relations between these articles frame the meaning — disapproval. The ethnocentric discourse of *The Times*, then, formulates expressions of cultural identity as irrational absolutism. Muslim concerns are further trivialized by being reduced to the level of a playground squabble. This denies structural discrimination and places the blame on the community. Thus, there is an over-lexicalization of semantic concepts relating to confrontation, which creates a division between 'them' and 'us' and works to foreclose any discussion of alternative interpretations and reform — like 'controversy', 'waging' a 'battle', 'frustration', 'squabbles', 'dispute', 'row', and 'arguments'.

The ideology of consensus appeals here to the government as well as to the readership. *The Times* wanted government intervention and referred to Muslims as 'being allowed segregated Religious Education'. The headline 'Shephard refuses to order inspection of Muslim lessons' included the implicit proposition that they needed to be inspected and it was harder to refute it in this format than as a straightforward statement. It suggested that the government had 'caved in' to Muslim demands

(Wark, 25 February 1996) and referred to these 'squabbles' as 'hindering the development of British schools' (23 February 1996). This demonstrated a key strategy in this ethnocentric discourse, appealing to economy on the basis of limited resources.

In terms of funding Muslim schools, *The Times* supported the status quo, arguing that such a move would encourage separatism. This was illustrated in a letter from an OFSTED inspector who argued that teaching girls separately led them to be 'inculcated into a traditional way of life' that prevented them from integrating into British society. This made negative assumptions about what 'a traditional life' consisted of and was in opposition to British tradition to which *The Times* frequently appeals to establish its consensus. The umbrella headline that encompassed the three letters, 'Tradition bars way to funding', also implied that belief (and practice) is the reason for action by Muslims and appropriate non-action by government. A discourse of ethnic blame prevailed: 'If the Muslim community could show that they do not handicap their daughters in that way, my view would change' (3 June 1997). This is typical of a right-wing strategy in proclaiming egalitarian motives to protect the balance of power (their tolerance juxtaposed against Muslim intolerance).

Another strategy *The Times* used was to draw attention to poor standards in Muslim schools. It consistently referred to previous rejections for state funding, which begged the question why? (25 May 1997). Although it mentioned only twice that these schools might foster fundamentalism, there was some emphasis on Muslims being demanding and threatening. Om Midha Gosforth referred to 'the veiled threat' of the Muslim community to Labour if it failed to meet their demands (3 June 1997). The terminology used here obviously has a double meaning, invoking the dominant symbol of Islam, the veil and all it represents. The threat was also perceived numerically as 'Muslims set to outnumber Anglicans', which was framed in the context of *Christian* Britain (Michael Fake, 3 June 1997). The conditions in Muslim schools are 'a threat to pupils' health and safety' (7 June 1997). By focusing on unhygienic conditions in Muslim schools and recommending government action, these articles implicitly implied primitivism, that Muslims did not care about their own children and that they required outside intervention. They suggest that Muslim tradition (belief) is unequal to British standards and should not be legitimated by being awarded official status.

The *Sun*

The *Sun* occupied a similar ideological position to *The Times*, but able to assume a stronger consensus it had less need to create an impression of balance or to work as hard to persuade its readers. Though its coverage was limited to two editorials about RE, with only one explicitly referring to Muslims, its message was remarkably clear. In a rhetorical and authoritative style it constructed an argument to establish Britain as a Christian country. The current state of RE, then, had betrayed British children. Its editorial voice was both appealing and directive, '*Christians should never be shy about proclaiming their faith*', reassuring people about the right way to think. Its construction of 'us' as the white Christian majority was achieved in several ways. Rather than using the symbol of a Muslim girl with her headscarf (most commonly used for this topic), the *Sun* deployed a picture of a young white girl praying. The picture symbolized sweetness and innocence in the nation's hands, she represented 'our own' children who form the core culture of Britain and this interacted with the headline, 'The betrayal of Christianity in our schools'. It therefore established a form of reverse racism in which 'our' British traditions and social institutions were under attack.

The *Sun* attacked white groups it saw as agents of left-wing propaganda — RE is 'a politically correct multi-faith mish-mash' and it appealed to the government not to play into the hands of 'trendy teachers'. The current situation was declared 'illegal' because the law was interpreted as 'instruction into Christian values'. Its claims to be a guardian of Christian values is clearly a defence mechanism, and hypocritical given the paper's secular outlook, subjecting stories about religion to ridicule.

Part of the agenda of this article was an anti-Conservative campaign, written following the election of the New Labour government, which the *Sun* supported. By discrediting the previous government's policy on RE, it served as a warning to the present government that if it were to retain the support of the people (and paper) it should act in majority interests. The article opened with, 'School children are to be given lessons in morality, Prime Minister Tony Blair has pledged', but closed with the imperative: 'He must act quickly before it is too late'.

The article illustrated how editorials interpret events according to their specific ideologies using consensus-building strategies, in this case appealing to values of morality, history (Christian) and nation, which, aided by presentational elements and strong modal expression, culminated in a call for action. Thus, it was an expression of a social process, reproducing an ethnic consensus in order to restore the status quo (Trew 1979). In this case, then, it should be seen as a manifestation of socially shared dominant ideologies rather than personal opinion (van Dijk 1991). The strength of its strategy and brevity ensured closure around this perspective. In this format, Muslims were just one of a number of groups of people who did not deserve any special treatment but should be excluded from full participation in society in the interests of the majority.

The *Guardian*

As Said (1978: 118) argued previously of the *Guardian*, it has greater 'sympathetic identification' with minorities than other papers. However, he suggested that its more negative attitude towards Muslims was based on a human rights philosophy that saw Islam as a social evil. Equally, in its coverage of education, it was unable to reconcile its stance on secular education with what it interpreted as Muslim demands for religious separatism. Its overall strategy was to appeal to a rational Enlightenment view of history that aimed to elevate non-denominational education over any form of religious instruction. Thus, the *Guardian* was equally unhappy with the current state of RE, which it described 'as clear as mud' (27 March 1996). This, for the *Guardian*, created 'an unease about religious instruction' whereby 'fundamentalist Christians could also jump on the bandwagon' (25 February 1996). The *Guardian*, therefore, supported a pluralist approach, providing an example of how the current system should work, 'successfully balancing the needs of the syllabus and the local community' (9 April 1996), and consistently reinforcing the idea that 'education should not turn itself into propaganda' (11 February 1996). The boycott of lessons, then, as in *The Times*, was considered illegal, and the school had 'gone against government guidelines' in 'abandoning National Curriculum rules' (5 February 1996).

In its support for balanced secularism, the *Guardian* constructed Muslim demands as uncompromising and irrational. These were referred to as 'the Islamic proscription' even in an article that was otherwise fairly positive (21 January 1997). The case of the Muslim teacher who objected to Muslim pupils singing carols was treated exactly as it was in *The Times* (19 December 1996). Equally, the boycott was reported within a similar linguistic register of conflict and confusion. There were elements in its discourse that assumed that the norm was Christian when it referred to the teaching of 'non-Christian faiths' (5 January 1997).

However, in relation to both RE and Muslim schools, the *Guardian* featured the Muslim perspective more, referring to parents' 'fears', 'grievances' and 'discontent'. When this did occur though, the situation was conceived of as a problem. These conflicting discourses within the *Guardian* were illustrated in two features on funding on 21 January 1997. Bruck (1989) suggested that features as 'soft news' could more readily include accounts from unofficial and less credible sources. The longer length and 'human' angle also allows alternative perspectives and some of the complexities of the debate to be aired. This is evident even if the 'whole structure' of the article was 'designed to discredit it as a political argument' (Schlesinger et al. 1983: 91). This format was apparent in both features. A Muslim, Fazil Malik, who wrote one of these and stressed the community's alienation and cynicism about the 'proposed support', which was 'too little too late' (repeated twice in the article). However, while quoting different factions of the community, he distanced himself from these, saying that 'there are many in the community who find it contradictory to teach Islam and adopt the "secular" national curriculum simultaneously ... although they think nothing wrong in accepting government funding.' The connective here raised questions about double standards and economic gain prevalent in the discourse of fraudulence, which, expressed by a Muslim, could not be labelled racist. This was juxtaposed alongside a fairly positive article on the Islamia School in Brent, whose work was praised, but once again undermined by, 'but there is room for significant improvement' (Kingston, 21 January 1997). This was the only article in which Muslims were treated inclusively as 'British'. These two features were united by the headline, 'Living in Harmony'. Such nominalization of headlines on education, in which agency is made ambiguous, was typical and added to the confusion and constant ideological slippage in this paper; the headline's presupposition contradicted the content of the articles in which the situation for Muslims, the majority population and the government were seen to be problematic, alluding to the difficulty of accommodating Muslims, with their specific religious identities, in a country the *Guardian* desired to be plural but secular (11 February 1996).[11]

Other examples of counter discourse in the *Guardian* included highlighting the 'valuable contribution' of the community, and criticizing the government in that it 'should be recognized and funded by the government' (27 February 1996 and 28 December 1996). These also tended to be undermined by subsequent and overall coverage alluding to the 'serious weaknesses' in the teaching at Muslim schools.

For the *Guardian*, then, institutions in society are secular and religion should be a purely private matter. This philosophy excludes Muslims from the public sphere and represents them as irrational and uncompromising: 'It is perfectly possible to identify with two cultures: a common civic, British culture. But that common culture is crucial because without it there is no reason for minorities to compromise their sometimes mutually incompatible demands' (11 February 1996). However, due to its sympathy for minorities, the struggle in the social domain was reproduced in the discourse.

Counter discourse

Elements of counter discourses were prevalent in all papers except the *Sun* but, as we have seen, were more evident in the *Guardian*. *The Times* included one commentary that ran against its own discourse and was more typical of *Guardian* coverage. It advocated the multi-faith, non-sectarian model of RE as the best, appealing to a consensus that drew on a discourse of moral necessity, rationality and a version of history based on the European Enlightenment. However, this constructs Muslims in the same way, exposing their 'ignorance and superstition ... to the light of rational discussion' (10 October 1997).

The Times also covered the Islamia School's continued lobbying for funding in one fairly balanced article: 'Muslim school may sue Labour' (3 December 1997). However, the principal agenda of this article (and in its relation to others) was to problematize Labour and its numerous broken manifesto pledges.

The main examples of explicit counter discourse could be found in letters, both in the *Guardian* and the *Mail*. These were both written by Muslims (the *Guardian*'s was actually an advert in the form of a letter from a group of influential Muslims in an attempt to counteract negative coverage) and highlighted the positive contribution of the Muslim community to British society. Both appeared at the end of 1997, mark-ing another year's passing in which the situation appeared hopeful but funding had not materialized. The *Guardian*'s letter incorporated the discourses of participants, the readership and the government to counter previous arguments against funding and to persuade otherwise, for example achievements in Muslim and other religious schools. A coun-ter strategy was employed in which the elements of discourse used by the objectors were appropriated and their meaning 'transcoded' (Hall 1997b: 270).[12] History was transformed into the opportunities of the present and the future rather than the past. The specificity of nationhood shifted to be incorporated into international significance. Britain was constructed as a plural and democratic society that was in need of 'moral regeneration' to which Muslim schools could contribute. It appealed to a consensus of shared values, equality, respect and integra-tion through a discourse of inclusivity and unity, which the legitimiz-ation of their status would create (and thus their participation in society). This had the specific function of putting those who opposed funding as equally rejecting as those whose values were expressed in the letter.

Although some positive coverage existed then, this tended to be drowned by the negative. This is particularly important if we consider the differentiation in the volume of news reaching audiences, given the readership of the right-wing press and particularly the tabloids. What this illustrated was that where the topic appeared to be solely about British Muslims, there was more evidence of a struggle in the discourse (there was only one reference to any foreign element, that of the incapability of foreign imams working in mosque schools).[13]

That the alienation of Muslims, in their lack of ability to participate fully in British society, may have been increasing extremism was omitted from the discussion. Nor did the debate about the separate teaching of religion encompass all the issues for Muslim parents who were also often concerned about the teaching of 'secular' subjects such as science from which children could not be withdrawn. Specific initiatives by the Muslim community to gain publicity, such as the petition handed to Downing Street by children from the Islamia School, were ignored by the press (BMMS, 5 December 1997).

Coverage up to this point appeared to have followed a pattern over several years, constantly predicting that Muslim schools were on the verge of receiving funding, yet this never occurred. Was this a way of keeping Muslim interests in the public eye, a way of placating Muslims? Or was it a scare tactic used to ensure continued opposition to change? Whatever the answer, for ten years this method of shelving problems deemed to be unimportant severely disadvantaged Muslim groups (Lacey and Longman 1997). It has demonstrated a lack of willingness by British society to accept the need to accommodate Muslim requirements within multiculturalism and to accept Muslims as fellow citizens.

However, this situation changed in early 1998 when two Muslim schools were awarded state funding. This was reported in all papers, most extensively in the *Guardian* and least in the *Sun*. Coverage of this event was more balanced. With its discourse of equality, inclusivity, rights, identity and integration, the *Guardian* showed particular support. A commentary by Roy Hattersley grounded the problems in the fears of the majority, a discourse rare in even *Guardian* coverage. Criticism was concentrated mainly on the negative consequences of separatism.

This 'balance' was more evident in *The Times* and *Mail* in this year; both papers, for example, covered the first day of the Islamia School's official grant-maintained status, stressing its inclusivity and commitment (21 April). However, coverage in these papers was more muted, cautious, tantamount to conditional acceptance. While reassuring readers that the government would ensure that these schools met required standards and enforced equal opportunities, they introduced negative aspects, raising fears about the promotion of extremism and separatism, the cost to the taxpayer and the degree of equality, standards and stringent punishments in the schools (see *The Times* 26 April, *Guardian* 29 April and *Mail* 26 April). *The Times* again introduced a Christian response. The broadsheets continued to utilize the Muslim girl as a visible signifier of Islam, while the tabloids preferred official figures.[14]

Response to this policy within the community was mixed and ranged from jubilation to a cynical view that it was only a token gesture to appease Muslim groups. The situation was presented as a 'battle' in all papers except the *Guardian*, with two homogenous opposing sides, so that the variety of responses within the Muslim community were not expressed. However, coverage on this occasion was more positive than previously and might have represented a shift in position that is yet to be borne out. Ibrahim Hewitt, development officer of the Association of Muslim Schools, in a letter to the author, suggested that this new positive line was partly due to 'better' relationships with journalists having developed over the years (6 March 1998). Increased Muslim activity in 1998 saw campaigning concentrated around this issue. Groups united to establish themselves as a credible lobby, acceptable to the government for negotiation. Through a process of attrition, the shelving of this issue could no longer be justified in what was deemed to be a democratic, multicultural country.[15]

What was largely omitted from coverage, however, was discussion on the contribution these schools might make to the majority, rather than just their own community. As Muslim-led rather than Muslim-only schools, others could benefit from their specific cultural and moral approach in the same way as many non-Christians benefited from church schools. The Muslim Council of Britain pointed to a number of characteristics that religious schools could offer, theirs included, these being strong educational leadership, high expectations, parental involvement, discipline, respect for authority, traditional values and team work. The popularity of these values among the middle classes was verified and affirmed by the positive appraisal of the then Conservative leader, William Hague, in a speech made to the Muslim Council on 20 March 2001.[16] Equally, those on the left perceived the academic success and 'community ethos' of church-run schools as offering benefits to those in socially deprived areas.[17] Also, in 1997 and subsequent years evidence had been put forward that suggested that boys were falling behind girls educationally, resulting in discussions about the benefits of single-sex schooling. Following the A-level results in 2001, the *Guardian* published an article detailing the research of Graham Able, the head teacher of the independent boys' school Dulwich College, which showed that boys did 6 per cent better in single sex schools (21 August 2001). Yet these policies were only denigrated in relation to Muslim schools for encouraging sexual and racial apartheid.

From these sorts of omissions and subsequent coverage (which in late 1998 and early 1999 concentrated on a school run by the Nation of Islam that was eventually closed due to poor standards), it must be concluded that allowing Muslims two state-funded schools and press coverage was a way of managing the community. This was evident in the *Mail*'s only commentary, which conceded to the funding of Muslim schools as 'an act of fairness' provided they were tightly monitored by the state (10 January 1998). This acknowledgement avoided not only imminent confrontation but also having to implement further and more controversial legislation such as that on religious discrimination (see below).

Although Muslims had made substantial advances in gaining influence at both local and national levels, particularly in the educational domain, this sort of press coverage illustrated their ongoing struggle (Nielsen 1992). The increased publicity such issues received perhaps reflected a recognition of the Muslim community's increasing self-confidence and political organization. As a reaction to this, the community was sometimes able to get its views represented in the press, but at other times it received bad publicity in an attempt to negate or mobilize public opinion against it, resulting in a struggle in discourse. Apart from marginal expression of the Muslim perspective, the overall message was clear and reflected educational policy in this area. Muslims were minorities, their concerns marginal, and their place in the education system was as an exception (Nielsen 1991a).

Rushdie, blasphemy and religious discrimination

In a similar vein to the coverage of education, the issues this story raised and the way they were represented here by different papers were symbolic of minority relations in the UK, specifically the accommodation of Muslims into the supposed British way of life. In particular, they were symptomatic of uncertainties in relation to secularism and cultural pluralism in postmodern society.

The Rushdie affair (1989) could be described as the catalyst that brought to the surface tensions representing a crisis in contemporary cultural evolution (Green 1990). It has been argued that the affair exposed the strong assimilationist thrust in liberal society with which Muslims, with their specific religious identifications, were deemed incompatible (Modood 1990).[18] Secularism could no longer, therefore, be hailed as the philosophy able to hold society together (Giddens 1991). Subsequent debate in the press on the operation of a multicultural society proved to be extremely narrow, with the right emphasizing an inherent cultural clash and the left freedom of speech.[19] Much of the discourse worked to recentre the dominant hegemony of various elite groups.

The continuing interest in Rushdie was symptomatic of the sociocultural significance the Rushdie affair had for the groups involved. Representing an ideological threat on all sides, coverage represented a struggle to retain hegemony. In 1997 articles on Rushdie included the annual renewal of the *fatwa* (religious decree) in all papers except the

Sun, his increasingly public persona (*Mail*), his third marriage (*Mail*), Sri Lanka's ban on the BBC film of his book *Midnight's Children* and a dialogue in the *Guardian* between Rushdie and writer John Le Carré on censorship, which included a total of 13 letters.[20] The revival of the debate on the blasphemy laws in that year, which harked back to the Rushdie affair, was based on proposals by the government to introduce a religious discrimination law following lobbying by Muslim groups. Symptomatic of the increasing religiosity of Muslims, made visible and intensified by the Rushdie affair, this issue also represented the centrality of the law to Muslims in achieving political legitimization, being an expression of moral norms and outlooks (Runnymede Trust 1997), redressing socioeconomic disadvantage and allowing full participation in public culture (Herbert 1993). In not accepting the confinement of religion to the private sphere, Muslims sought to strengthen their own cultural survival.

Muslim groups argued that, due to changing perceptions in British society influenced by contemporary political processes, the religious dimension of discrimination was in ascendancy. However, under current legislation such as the Race Relations Act (1976), the Public Order Act (1986) and the blasphemy law, Muslims were not protected. The effect of the Race Relations Act has been to make race the crucial category in gauging the treatment of and provision for minorities in the UK. Because Muslims do not constitute a race and Islam is a religion of many nationalities and races, they are not protected under this law, although it extends its cover to Jews and Sikhs because they are considered to be ethnic groups. Although it may be possible for Muslims to claim indirect discrimination if the complainant is a member of a racial group in which 'Islam' is the dominant faith, this does not protect Muslims of a European background. This is unacceptable to many Muslims, in principle, due to their identification with their religion and desire to protect it. Religious groups cannot protect their religion from defamation under blasphemy laws because these only protect the Anglican tradition within Christianity.

Reform for Muslims based on laws on religious discrimination, however, represents 'a very different social and political project' from blasphemy, 'the institutionalisation of social rights', and should therefore be discussed in very different terms (Unsworth 1995). Yet, the mainstream press in Britain has transformed this issue, which is Muslim driven, to a discussion of Muslim demands for inclusion in the blasphemy laws, allowing the details and discourse contained in the Rushdie debate to re-emerge. One consequence of the grounding within this framework is that religious discrimination is perceived as solely a Muslim issue.

As Muslims strive for equal rights, by continual association with the Rushdie affair with its controversial nature and having become representative of conflict, dominant groups reproduce preferred discourses and present new developments as old and irresolvable conflicts (cultural clash). By emphasizing conflict, Muslims are represented as having separate and differing values and therefore as posing a threat to the dominant values. This breeds antipathy and social anxiety, thus preventing any changes to the preferred social system and hierarchy.

By reducing the debate on religious discrimination to blasphemy, the issue became one of freedom of speech and censorship. Having little to do with the original event, and being a value the press had a particular interest in protecting, the papers were able to construct a discourse that orchestrated public opinion to reject the primary initiative. In rejecting the 'blasphemy' law, the papers resorted to discourses of modernity, rationality, nation, history, identity, freedom, primitivism, absolutism, particularism, homogeneity and economy in their argumentation strategy.

Despite their differing motives, the papers appeared to adopt a similar secular liberal approach to establish their argument. In its first news report, the *Mail* argued that, 'we have to protect the ability in a democratic society to voice dissent.' The *Guardian*'s view was that the abolition of the law was 'the only course compatible with freedom of belief in a modern society'. Any alternative course of action was considered a 'historical anomaly' (14 August), a position reiterated ten times in this article alone. *The Times* ideology was made explicit through commentary, 'Ever since Milton's fiercely anti-censorship arguments in the *Areopagitica*, the right to publish what you want has been hard fought. This is scarcely the time to turn back' (Bar, 2 August). Thus, all papers constructed the nation as built on a particular view of history based on democracy and secular Enlightenment values in which 'having an established religion is itself an anomaly' (Gray, *Guardian*, 12 August).[21] Unusually, both *The Times* and the *Mail* also took this line. However, given that their discourse revealed an exclusionist nationalist ideology, this would appear to be tactical.

By relating their own views to a discourse of democracy, history and modernity, the press constructed Muslim demands in opposition, as restrictive, archaic and primitive. The composition of the discourse constructed secularism as the only path to modernity. Free speech was presented as an absolute that existed unproblematically alongside the discourse of Muslim absolutism. Yet the inherent universalism the press applied to its values increased their worth and added to views of Islamic particularism and irrationality. In addition, by appealing to such a strong consensual value in the operation of democracy, they were less likely to be opposed.

Both *The Times* and *Guardian* constructed the superiority of the nation in a comparative framework in which the relationship between religion and state in other countries was denigrated, 'we have avoided the ugly return into political life of the repressed religious which is common in regimes that make the separation of church and state an article of faith' (Gray, 12 August). The secular state had thus managed to control its religions by allowing them to practise. However, this was marginalized to the private sphere by the rejection of legal intervention in this instance, 'to tackle religious tensions we need courtesy and firm compromise, not more legislation', 'the law should not rush in' (Bar, 2 August). This statement is typical of right-wing argumentative rejection of affirmative action. It suggests that discrimination is a matter of integrity and morality, which is hypocritical given the paper's usual position on law and order (van Dijk 1991). *The Times* attacked powerful white groups as an argumentative move further avoiding the racist label. It criticized both the government and CRE for initiating the plans and discredited their integrity by insinuating political motives in supporting minorities, 'If you're wondering why the subject has reemerged now, it is worth remembering that the Home Secretary is the MP for Blackburn, where the Muslim vote is very important.'

Particularly important in the strategy of the press for building a consensus around the rejection of the law is attending to its unworkability, frequently providing the example of Northern Ireland. The selection of negative aspects of the debate was apparent in this scare tactic, which suggested that the law would have 'all sort of sects claiming protection' (*The Times*; *Mail* 30 July; *Guardian* 12 June). The *Mail*, in particular, used disclaimers such as 'however' after any positive balancing statements in order to negate them. Given the problems associated with the definition and implementation of all laws, this can be seen as unwillingness to discuss the full scope of the law.

Both the *Mail* and *Guardian* implicitly denied the need for any new law, the *Mail* referring to '*what it calls* Islamophobia' and that 'many Moslems *say* they suffer prejudice' (30 July). The *Guardian*, in an article entitled 'Muslim Tykes Happy Here' quoted a Muslim stating 'we are beyond that stage now'. ... 'It was a big problem in the 1960s and 1970s but it is not a priority now' (24 October).

By constructing the issue in such a way, the focus (and responsibility) was shifted from discrimination within British systems to the Muslim community and its personal beliefs, 'one price of living in this (pluralist society) is that everyone has to put up with statements that offend them, without resorting to violence or the law' (2 August).[22] The construction in *The Times* here of Britain as pluralist was exposed as purely strategic in the face of its ethnocentric discourse, questioning whether the law should be changed to suit the minority when the majority was indifferent. By associating Muslim (legitimate) action to violence here, despite its absence, Muslims were associated foremost with illegitimate negative activity. Muslims' beliefs then became the focus of blame. They were constructed as a package of rules that restricted 'our' freedom, 'rules that would have put Rushdie in the dock' (*Mail*, 30 July). This constituted a reversal strategy that attributed censorship to the victimized group while the papers presented a united front advocating freedom to discriminate. Muslims were therefore to blame for this 'so-called Islamophobia' (Walter, the *Guardian*, 24 October). Muslims were again constructed as a homogenous collectivity and as such constituted a threat to liberal individualism.

The *Guardian*

The volume of information and the speed with which this issue was introduced in the *Guardian* compared with other papers, illustrated its commitment to the great liberalist tradition, which advocates the freedom to publish and sees Muslim demands encroaching upon it. This discourse was reproduced in three news items, six letters and two commentaries. It unequivocally rejected the interference of state in religion but wished to situate this within a tolerant, pluralist stance, 'the truly inclusive move would involve the gradual withdrawal of the state from all matters of faith. These should be left as individual and community activities while the state concentrates on educating citizens to cherish and display the tolerance which allows pluralism to flourish' (Lane, 6

January). The *Guardian*'s religious intolerance is made explicit in a lengthy and highly rhetorical piece from an atheist's perspective (Carol Sarler, 3 August).[23] This employed a reversal strategy in which the non-religious were the persecuted.

Tension was clearly exhibited in the *Guardian* between its *secular* pluralism and its difficulty with religion. Its anti-discriminatory stance gave space to alternative interpretations on a discourse of equality and rights. In contrast with the other papers, this topic was initially constructed on this basis as 'human rights legislation', its focus apparent in the headline, 'Ban on religious discrimination' (12 June). Muslims were therefore seen to be 'pressing for change' rather than 'demanding' it, the lexical choice of the right-wing press. The linguistic register of this article, which lapsed into a racial framework, allowed the *Guardian*'s tensions to be resolved.[24] However, the race-relations framework constructed Muslims as passive victims, 'disadvantaged' and needing 'assistance', therefore subject to governmental action. Evidence of these tensions occurred again following the preclusion of reform by Jack Straw. Entitled 'Religious Debate' and covering two articles, one concentrating on religious discrimination, 'Straw shelves law on Islamophobia', and the Muslim response, 'Muslim Tykes Happy Here' (23 October). The *Guardian* attended to the Islamophobia document and its contents, and the positive contribution of Muslims to society, 'It is good to know the Muslim contribution is welcome. Bradford is our city and we want to help it,' says Mohammed Akram.[25] Whereas this, however, seemed to imply that Muslims had been let down, the other article appeared to contradict it by asserting Muslim confidence and identity and questioning the need for a law. What could have been a positive example of coverage was undermined by its composition and by associating the reassertion of identity with a more vociferous, and violent, youth, 'we don't get trouble, 'cos they know we'll duff them up if they try.' What appeared then in composition to satisfy the title 'Religious Debate' was just an illusion. However, the article did provide the only allusion to the heterogeneity of Muslims in the form of a pie chart that showed how Muslims were divided among nationalities.

The *Guardian*'s willingness to give space to the Muslim perspective was illustrated by a letter from Ibrahim Hewitt, the development officer for the Association of Muslim Schools (14 August). It presented an alternative viewpoint, for example on freedom of speech. Hewitt drew attention to the problematic nature of the free speech argument the press espoused, pointing to anomalies such as the current libel protection laws. He tried to draw the line between freedom of expression and offence, advocating the need for protection from 'scurrilous abuse, like that at the height of the Rushdie Affair'.

A counter to the view of religion presented in the *Guardian* also came in the form of a letter from a Christian teacher entitled 'Live and let live'. It was critical of Carol Sarler's 'blanket demonisation' of the religious (3 August). However, it opposed the blasphemy laws and, while criticizing her for her extremity by saying her article placed him in the same category 'alongside Islamic terrorists and American right-wing evangelicals', reinforced stereotypes of Muslims in the same sentence.

While the *Guardian*, then, was not explicitly negative towards Muslims, the unequivocal judgement of religion trivialized them in their strong religious identification. It was in their constructed opposition to *Guardian* values that Muslims were formulated negatively. References to them as 'hard-line' and 'fundamentalists' occurred when discussing issues of concern to Muslims (see Nick Cohen's article on 'Dead laws' in the *Observer*, 2 November). The *Guardian*'s letters revealed the shared social scripts by which Muslims have come to be known — women and their clothing (12 June), the Rushdie affair, Muslim schools (12 August) and fundamentalism (24 October). It was in this way that Muslims were ideologically fixed.

The *Guardian*'s position *vis-à-vis* religion is an example of how religions, alongside non-Western cultures, are often constructed as 'relics of primitivism' in opposition to the intellectually advanced secular world. It follows the assumption, as Michael Dummett observed among intellectuals, that the 'religious believer may properly be affronted, indeed deserve to be affronted' (cited in Modood 1993a). According to Modood (1993b), this itself is a form of cultural racism as religion is currently of greater personal value and community importance to non-white than to white people in Britain.

Mail and *The Times*

Both the *Mail* and *The Times* downgraded any discussion of religious discrimination, to the level of side comment in the *Mail* and was completely absent from *The Times*. The blasphemy laws were reconstructed as top-level information (appearing in both initial headlines). This deliberate misinterpretation of events revealed the ideological stance of these papers. Once the issue had been defined in this way, it continued to be constructed as such. *The Times* featured just one other negative commentary representing closure around the negation of reform (2 August).

The Times and *Mail* had similar ideologies. Their construction of Muslims was explicitly negative, their choice of sources extreme, Christianity was established as the central faith and Muslims were regarded as outsiders. However, the *Mail*'s discursive strategies in achieving its goal were more extensive. Assigning a whole page and two articles to the initial development, its clear modal expression did not need editorializing.[26] Its leader 'Moslems can look forward to the same protection as Christians' situated Christianity centrally and constituted a 'tease' given the *Mail*'s position that according Muslims parity with Christians was unacceptable (Cottle 1991).

The *Mail* places this new event within a well-known situational model that presupposed relevant episodic knowledge to interpret it (van Dijk 1983 and 1988b). The familiarity led to a generalization (the same as the Rushdie affair) and worked to prefer familiar solutions. The headline 'Defender of all faiths' referred to Prince Charles's previous statement that he would prefer to be defender of all faiths as king. Readers of the paper would remember how this was negatively framed previously, but they were also provided with selective reminders, it 'would chime with the beliefs of the Prince of Wales who would prefer to be defender of faith than Defender of the Faith, Christianity'. However, here, this refers to Jack Straw. This immediately placed Straw in a similar position of ridicule.

Although most of the broadsheet headlines involved non-transactive clauses, passive constructs and nominalizations emphasizing processes, the contrast was distilled in the *Mail*'s articles in which the agency was clear.[27] The emphasis on the participant's responsibility in the sub-headline, 'Straw plans to rewrite law on blasphemy', had political motives, associating New Labour with negative, accommodating 'loony left', policy. A quote from one Muslim leader saying that it was good news, 'the kind of gesture we hoped from the Labour government', worked to discredit further both the government and the law. This article then, which focused on the blasphemy laws, was framed by negative responses and criticism. We have seen some of the strategies utilized already. In the *Mail*'s tradition, the cost of the law was included (nowhere else did this occur). The article closed with quotes from anti-censorship groups that 'back Mr Rushdie'. This was juxtaposed with Muslims 'demanding' change, which invoked a more sinister effect than seen elsewhere.

Inset with this article was a report specifically relating to Rushdie. It consisted of a large head and shoulders shot, which now has currency as a visual symbol of conflict and incompatibility. The article went on to express the Rushdie affair on a selective basis, giving ideological coherence to previous interpretations. It provided the history of the death sentence and said 'Moslem countries banned the book and British Moslems demonstrated against it', homogenizing and therefore associating all British Muslims with the death sentence.[28] The *Mail* did, however, present the right-wing view of Rushdie, unlike the other papers, that he had 'attempted to enrage Moslems by writing a purposely blasphemous book', indicative of its sympathy with religious and censorship positions.

This decontextualizing of the events in the Rushdie affair was a common practice in all papers and presented Muslims as irrational, acting for no apparent reason. By keeping the parameters of debate on the blasphemy laws and marginalizing Muslim commentary, alternative, viable options to protect Muslims from discrimination were excluded from discussion, such as successful implementation abroad. Other omissions included a full debate on the problematic nature of the free speech argument, for example the non-incorporation of Muslims' current inability to practise their religion freely, which contravenes European and UN laws.[29] These 'omissions' meant that the press was not practising its own ideology of allowing free speech. The immorality of this (and the failure to protect minority groups) was not considered amid the wider moral discourse.

These strategies worked to fix public opinion around rejecting the law, 'the answer is to repeal all blasphemy laws' (*Mail*, 30 July). When the current hegemony was strengthened through non-action, *The Times* remained silent, while the *Mail*'s short article, 'Straw says no to "religious hate" law' (23 October), supported the home secretary's decision and foreclosed any discussion on this outcome.[30] This appeared to contradict the paper's previous secular appeals for abolition and suggested that the rhetoric employed by the papers was actually engaged in maintaining Christianity's privileged position (it was rejected by the government for its unworkability, a strong element of press discourse). The *Guardian*'s subsequent coverage showed some sympathy for Muslims in their 'disappointment' over its position on the blasphemy law (23 October). However, the composition of the article revealed its ideological stance on additional legislation or the extension of existing laws (constituting an unreasonable interference with freedom of expression). Its overarching title 'Pronouncing a *fatwa* on extremes' indicated some satisfaction that the government had not pandered to fanaticism. Both these articles occurred following the launch of the Runnymede Trust's report on Islamophobia. The announcement that legislation on religious discrimination would not be implemented 'in this Parliament' was just one of numerous issues discussed. Yet the law's precedence in the order of relevance represented an ideologically based transformation, again shifting the discussion away from discrimination against Muslims to Muslim censorship.

The power struggle in society over the negotiation of national collectivity, which this issue symbolized, was barely represented in the press. Those competing positions represented consisted almost entirely of the two hegemonic sociopolitical forces in society, secular liberalism and liberal Christianity. These, despite their differences, converged to exclude Muslims from public life (by not awarding them legitimate and thus equal status). Although this Muslim-driven issue now had a place in the public arena, it has not been presented as Muslims would wish and has failed, as yet, to have any effect on the law.

These contending discourses represented arguments about the *relationship* between Church and state (Modood 1997; Modood and Werbner 1997). Currently, as the Established religion, Christianity is a symbol of national identity that attributes second-class status to other religions. While this situation remains, there are structural difficulties in treating all equally. Despite their protestations, the right-wing press seemed to support this exclusion from Britishness, while the *Guardian* appeared to want to exclude public religiosity *per se*. By squeezing religion out of public culture, exponents of liberal secularism practise an exclusionism in which minority religions would be the most disadvantaged given, by comparison, the relative power and influence of Christianity in British public life. Thus, the debate on Muslims in the *Guardian* revealed the illiberalism in its own liberal rhetoric. Secular liberalism, which claims to be non-privileging and therefore a solution to all, was shown to privilege non-belief. In seeking to preserve its own identity (secular), liberalism cannot therefore satisfy the principle of equality (Parekh 1997). Yet this is at odds with its philosophy on rights provided by the same Enlightenment movement, which suppressed religious belief (Linden 1995). It is this tension in liberal theory that places Muslims of all minority groups outside the *Guardian*'s pluralist vision of society.

For these reasons neither secular liberalism nor Christian tradition-alism could accommodate Islam with its assertive religiosity within its conception of Britishness. This would require a re-evaluation of the nation. Through press coverage of British Muslims, the current crisis in national identity and attempts to recentre dominant political forces were exposed.

As an issue still firmly on the Muslim agenda for reform, reference was again made to the subject of religious discrimination (albeit fleet-ingly). This occurred as a result of discussions between Jack Straw and Muslim groups to amend the Crime and Disorder Bill in an attempt to incorporate religion into aggravated crime. However, this was discussed only in the *Mail*, which sought to mobilize support against the change (23 June 1998). The introduction of a private member's bill by Labour MP John Austin seeking to criminalize religious discrimination was not reported on 3 March 1998. Subsequent coverage appeared only in the *Guardian*, which ran six articles in 1999. While continuing to take a negative position on proposed religious discrimination legislation, a positive response was shown, for example, to proposals for a question on religion in the next census to combat discrimination. Articles on freedom of speech in that year concentrated on the censorship activities of Muslims (three in the *Guardian*; two in *The Times* and one in the *Mail*).

Rushdie once again became a story of significance, however, when negotiations between the British and Iranian governments led to Iran's withdrawal of support for the *fatwa* (September 1998). This was covered in some depth by all papers, particularly the *Guardian* (22 articles in total), which was the first to break the story. The *Guardian/Observer* categorically supported Rushdie (and in this case the government), for it saw itself as part of the Rushdie campaign. Initial coverage constructed Rushdie as a faultless victim of others' intolerance. He was the 'oppressed' and was attributed with numerous positive predicates such as 'courageous', 'brave', 'survivor' and 'generous'. Constructed as a freedom of speech issue and upholding democratic rights, the paper's rhetoric was more extreme than that of the others. It established two homogenous polarized groups. Rushdie stood for all that was good in liberal society: freedom, creativity, intellect and rationalism. Muslims were therefore constructed (and referred to) as inferior, immoral, rigid, restrictive, intolerant, misogynist, fanatical, manipulative, brutal and threatening.[31] Initially celebratory about Rushdie's (and as such their) 'triumph', articles became sceptical about 'the deal' in which the Iranian government disassociated itself from the *fatwa* in exchange for better diplomatic relations with the UK and USA, introducing the concept of a 'freelance fanatic'.[32] The use of extreme sources and Islamic 'experts' to confirm that the *fatwa* was 'irrevocable' and that it was 'the duty of all Muslims of the world to carry it out' transferred this label to all. After reporting several indicators (the instability of politics in Iran) their scepticism was confirmed when 'Radicals set new Rushdie bounty' (12 November 1998). Stories confirming Muslim unity around the world on this issue continued to filter through sporadically, as with Indian Muslims' opposition to Rushdie's application for a visa (February 1999).

The Times (with nine articles covering this story) and the *Mail* (with seven), although supportive of Rushdie, distanced themselves as being outside his 'circle of friends and apologists' (*Mail*, 27 September 1998). Although again supporting the issue for which the affair stands, they made less of it, preferring to highlight the political expediency on both sides (and were therefore less supportive of the British government). Their scepticism towards 'the deal' was immediate, particularly in the *Mail* in which its first article stated, 'Rushdie still faces death threat' (24 September 1998) and each article in subsequent coverage worked to cement this argument. These papers alluded to possible alternative perspectives, which barely entered the extensive but repetitive and closed discourse of the *Guardian*. This included questioning Rushdie's character, the cost of protecting him, suggesting that blasphemy was offensive, that liberals were hypocritical in their support for him, and attacking the government's climb down (for compromising with Iran). Generally, however, although less attention was given to the issue and the response was more muted, the same discourse and strategies were resurrected. All papers used extreme Muslim sources, featured his conversion to Islam as a 'mistake', a result of being at a 'low-ebb' (*The Times*, 26 September 1998: 7). As well as picturing Muslims burning books, visually, Rushdie was situated against a wider backdrop as opposed to the dark background against which he was usually set (the prison from which he had emerged). By seeing it as an issue caused by the 'clash of civilisations' (*Guardian*, 26 September 1998: 9), the *Mail* was able to suggest that the release of Rushdie was a high price to pay if, in backing Iran, we were to be subject to the 'terrorism of the Taliban' (27 September 1998). Islam was thus restored as the propagator of international terrorism.

After this event, coverage of Rushdie was severely limited (though retaining some presence with six articles in 1999). However, the Rushdie affair was continually deployed in numerous circumstances, as an effective way of invoking its meanings, which have resonance internationally. Equally, by introducing scepticism, the story remained unresolved and open for further attention.

Islamic fundamentalism in the UK

The term 'fundamentalism' has its origins in American Protestantism, in movements that opposed modernizing tendencies and insisted on a literal interpretation of the Bible.[33] The association of the term with the maintenance of orthodox religious beliefs and its opposition to the forces of liberalism and secularism immediately formulated a fundamentalist–modernist dichotomy, which Western journalists have used to discredit resurgent Islamic movements. However, due to its Christian presuppositions, many theorists have argued that the term is misplaced (Esposito 1992). According to the Runnymede Trust (1997), the first application of the term to Islam was in 1957 in the *Middle East Journal*. However, it only became a routine part of journalese following an influential article by Anthony Burgess in the *Observer* (27 September 1981), which stated that 'the phenomenon of the new, or rather very old, Islam, the dangerous fundamentalism revived by the ayatollahs and their admirers as a device, indistinguishable from a weapon, for running a modern state' (Runnymede Trust 1997: 7). Since then the term has been inextricably linked to terrorism and extremism, so that these terms have become virtually interchangeable when applied to Islamic fundamentalists.[34] The connotations have become so well known that the term is frequently used as a metaphor in articles that are entirely unconnected with Islam to summon up ideas of mad extremism.

Fundamentalism has been inappropriately applied in the press to a variety of political groups and governments with differing goals and beliefs that go by the name of Islam, with the result that they have been homogenized under the same label, which has allowed them to be

constructed discursively in almost identical ways. Islamic fundamentalism in Britain has been applied virtually exclusively to foreign
dissidents living in Britain while being involved in activities to support
political struggle elsewhere.[35] Coverage in 1997 was triggered mainly
by international incidents, for example the ambush at the temple of
Hatshepsut in Luxor by the extremist group, al-Gama'a al-Islamiya,
which resulted in the deaths of 60 tourists and gave the press an
opportunity to put pressure on the government to act on what was
constructed as a terrorist threat within. This is a common pattern that
recurs frequently in press coverage of fundamentalism in Britain. There
was little difference in the development of the stories in papers except
in terms of space allocated and the *Guardian* allocated the most (see
Table 3.1). The *Sun* had just one article relating to these events but did
not refer to Muslims or Islam in it.

The ideological coherence between papers and with the state is based
on the extremity of events in which terrorism is considered morally
abhorrent on a non-partisan basis. Terrorism, as interpreted by the
British power structures, can be defined as 'an illegitimate form of
violence which is a dangerous threat to liberal democracies' (Miller
1994: 4). Widely written about, this subject is considered to have a
rhetorical ideological function in which only enemies are labelled and
friendly government's terrorist actions are ignored. Those with the
power to define a terrorist act as an act of violence that is disapproved
of have thus appropriated the term. Most journalists see themselves in
alliance with the state in fighting terrorism (and crime) and therefore
texts work in unison to prevent any recognition or sympathy for the
agents of terrorism (Miller 1994).

This topic was rarely editorialized. The rational interpretation of
events as illegitimate, based on a consensual definition of violence,
renders texts ideologically sealed. The foreign and violent element
allows a reductive, simplistic portrayal of the issues in black and white;
terrorism is wrong and needs to be dealt with. Thus, coverage fits more
neatly into the foreign coverage news frame proposed by Dahlgren and
Chakrapani (1982) with its motifs of disorder, flawed development and
primitivism in contrast with the order and stability of 'the West'.

This issue is therefore constructed through the discourse of national
interests. As an issue that arises from both international politics and
internal policy (towards immigration and national security), it allows
the nation to be constructed as superior and is used to justify British

activity on an international scale that is aimed at securing Western hegemony. Out of the strategies used to discredit Islamic fundamentalists has emerged an Orientalist homogenizing discourse of irrationality, primitivism, deviance, disloyalty and violent extremism.

Because of the parity in coverage between the papers discussed, it seemed preferable to examine the significant macro-semantic conceptualizations occurring rather than taking each paper individually.[36] This macro-semantic assertion is that the infiltration of Muslim fundamentalists is a threat to British interests that requires government action. Through this assertion Muslims are constructed as fanatical yet ideologically weak, as homogenous yet sectarian. Their actions are decontextualized, categorized and naturalized. The strength of the framework that has been established on this issue meant that, in general, each article that occurred included all these characteristics. These are now examined in turn along with the strategies supporting this argumentation.

The fundamentalist threat

The fundamentalist threat was illustrated most explicitly in the coverage of a letter bomb sent to the Saudi newspaper *al-Hayat*, where actual physical violence occurred. In all these articles, the injuries to the staff were exaggerated and highlighted, as in *The Times*, 'Two wounded as letter bombers aim for London target' (14 January), the *Guardian* (14 January) and the *Sun* (14 January). The *Sun* and *The Times* resorted to dramatic hyperbole, using distinct lexical items associated with physical suffering. *The Times* incorporated a photograph of a woman wiping her eyes while talking to the police, expressing vulnerability.[37] An article adjacent to this was called simply 'The Toll' and detailed the history of Britain being subjected to violence because of Middle Eastern politics. As will become more evident, Britain was portrayed as an innocent victim attempting to mediate between irrational nations and suffering as a consequence.

The *Guardian* located the threat in central London (with a map) indicating the potential disruption. Both *The Times* and the *Guardian* credited 'Islamic extremists' with the attack although this had not yet been established. The *Sun*'s article, which was scarce in detail, did not identify the agents of the bombing.

These physical attacks are scarce, the threat being implicit in the global coherence of foreign coverage of violent terrorism and the alien taking refuge in our midst. The Islamist movements were seen as spreading and infiltrating countries. References to other countries with the same 'problem' reinforced this idea. After the letter bombing, *The Times* leader purported, 'Islamic extremists blamed after terror campaign spreads from America to Britain' (14 January). This international network was made particularly explicit in coverage following the Luxor incident. It was in the context of death that the Islamists were explicitly labelled as terrorists. The articles, following the Egyptian president's accusations that Britain was harbouring terrorists, were virtually identical, with the same sources, actors and details, although the lexical items employed in the *Mail* were more explicit (24 November).[38] The first subject position of Egypt in the *Mail*'s headline, 'Egypt blames Britain over Luxor killings', and the discursive attention to the 'killers' illustrated its tendency categorically to attribute blame. This angle was also taken after Israel made similar accusations against Britain over a charity 'that funds killers', following suicide bombings in Israel that resulted in the deaths of 13 people (*Mail*, 12 August and 4 December). Its modal expression was emphatic, 'terror suspects living freely in Britain' (12 August). The construction of the alien within allowed for the perpetuation of the myth that (non-Western) foreign immigrants polluted British society with disorder, without which the tradition of stability and non-violence would be maintained (Dahlgren and Chakrapani 1982). The attack on tourists had an extreme news value in which the British victims were seen to be innocent bystanders of foreign conflicts and represented the common person. Again 'we' are caught up in 'their' troubles.

The form of these articles, with foreign governments accusing Britain of harbouring terrorists, posed an ideological dilemma for the papers in terms of national interests. Attacks on the country's integrity were to be defended, but the presence of terrorists within its borders posed a threat to national security. The papers clearly did not want to agree with the countries, but shared their basic argument that Britain should not be protecting terrorists. As a result, the papers were cautious about accepting charges against the UK, while at the same time they condemned the activities and presence of the extremists. This hypocrisy was illustrated by the use of authoritative Saudi sources to denounce the dissidents while at the same time attacking Saudi Arabia's justice system. This ideological struggle was demonstrated in the *Mail* in a two-page spread on Saudi justice following the sentencing of British nurse Lucille McLauchlan for the murder of a colleague (25 September). This included articles condemning the Saudi justice system, featuring British people who had suffered at its hands, 'British man flogged for crime he did not commit', and conforming with its approach on 'national interest'. Yet it showed sympathy for the 'eye for an eye' philosophy (tough on law and order), but again only when it served British interests. This confusion was also apparent in the same double spread when it referred to the Saudi dissident, Mohammed al-Masari, arguing that 'the nation should not give comfort to those who seek to undermine the Saudi government', but then quoted him as saying that 'It [the trial of Ms McLauchlan] has exposed the Saudi regime for what it is.'

This conflict of interests was apparent in the *Guardian* following the Egyptian president's accusations (24 and 28 November). While incredulous towards Mubarak's claims, through use of understatement and disclaimers applying 'alleged', 'claims', 'reportedly' to Mubarak's comments, the paper also cited the presence of some dissidents in the UK. The preponderance of speech acts in the headlines and texts of these reports reflected a recognition that the situation was constantly changing since the use of speech acts avoids commitment to facts and allows papers to engage in belief suspension and political mitigation.

The 'threat', however, was also considered both material and strategic. For the right-wing press economic interests were paramount. Harbouring dissidents damaged Britain's international relations. This was evident in the coverage of Dr al-Masari, the Saudi dissident. According to *The Times*, he had 'jeopardised thousands of British defence jobs' (12 November). For the *Mail*, he was also a threat to the freedom of the Saudi nurses.[39] To the *Guardian*, he was a burden, having 'been the principal irritant to Britain's relations with Saudi Arabia for three years, is broke and virtually inactive' (11 January). Another element of the discourse was prevalent here, the 'luxury immigrant myth' (van Dijk 1991: 96), that these dissidents make use of the 'soft' laws in Britain and abuse its hospitality but give nothing back. The *Mail*, for example highlighted his dependence on the British state, 'he has debts in Britain estimated at £100,000 and is currently living on social security', yet in relation to the British nurses he had 'washed his hands of their fate' (25 September). There was no mention of what kind of lifestyle the dissidents had often given up to fight their cause.

British tolerance was juxtaposed against the fundamentalists' lack of compassion and the repression of the pursuing 'regimes'.[40] The *Guardian* of 20 November suggested that, 'Arab and Muslim dissidents come to Britain because of a tradition of tolerance that was enjoyed by Karl Marx and Victor Hugo' (see also *The Times* 14 January; *Mail* 4 December). The dissidents are seen to benefit from British laws on freedom of speech. A letter in the *Mail* (4 December) expressed pride in this tradition, but stressed that 'freedom to raise funds and incite violence should not be permitted'. This appeared particularly hypocritical in the light of arguments advanced against the blasphemy laws. The intolerance inherent in anti-immigration legislation was not covered. In this way the dichotomous relationship of 'them' and 'us' was established between a free Britain, which engaged in diplomatic negotiations, and repressive reactionary regimes. This opposition was often presented dramatically in images of place.

The papers also used other discursive strategies to discredit the dissidents in order to mobilize support against their presence in the UK. In the al-Masari articles, there was greater variation in these strategies as the event was less extreme. All three papers engaged in a character assassination through popular appeals to the distinct ideologies of the targeted audience. The *Guardian* highlighted his dubious attitudes (in relation to Jews), *The Times* his ignorance and the *Mail* his exploitation of the welfare system at the expense of the taxpayer. While *The Times* and *Mail*, however, appeared to be contemptuous of the dissidents, the *Guardian* constructed them as comical figures, impotent buffoons (see section on Omar Bakri below). This variation was evident in the photographs. Both the *Mail* and *The Times* used a mug shot, with al-Masari looking awkward (signifying criminality and guilt). The *Guardian* showed him in full size, sitting on a huge sofa, a small round figure appearing cheery. This had the effect of dispelling the threat to some extent. However, although these dissidents were not labelled as terrorists, the global coherence of the articles, in terms of the discourse that was employed in their treatment, meant that it was likely that they would be lumped together in the same category. One example of this was the penultimate article in *The Times* (24 November) concerned with dissidents aiding Egyptian extremist groups. It referred back to al-Masari as an example of the problems the government had with taking action against extremists in Britain (also the *Guardian* 20 November).

The coverage of these personal cases allowed the discourse to be repeated, providing further evidence for the case against them. By discrediting them on personal grounds, it avoided any charges of racism. This differed from the coverage of extreme violence in that here the actors were dehumanized in order to be constructed as monstrous. Once constructed as the undesirable immigrant, one course of action above others was preferred as a solution, in this case deportation.[41]

Government intervention

Because of the problematic nature of the issue, when accusations were made the papers mitigated for the authorities. The government was constructed as acting on the situation but often thwarted in its attempts by soft laws and the courts. After the Luxor incident, all papers quoted Jack Straw's promise to review anti-terrorism legislation (23 November). This reliance on official sources and therefore official discourse meant that the reports were relatively closed around the official perspective. On 24 November *The Times* devoted a whole article to measures the government was taking to prevent terrorist activities, 'London is not a terror haven say Ministers' (also *Guardian*, 28 November). This mitigation was also extended to the police who 'are powerless to act' if the dissidents do not break any British laws (*Mail*, 12 August). The repeated use of this ideology mobilized support for government action while not alienating the public from the government. They compelled action but mitigated for the authorities, conceptualized as devoid of responsibility, struggling to act to protect Britain in terms of security and its democratic principles but tied by current legislation. This paved the way for new laws on the prevention of terrorism, which made it a crime to organize terrorist campaigns in the UK and against which there was no opposition.

Omar Bakri Mohammad

A striking and lengthy feature on Omar Bakri Mohammad, the extremist leader of the group, al-Muhajiroun (the Emigrants), who was also the subject of a Channel 4 documentary, *Witness*, appeared in the *Guardian Weekend* (29 March). About a Saudi dissident who raised funds for military causes abroad while 'living off the state', this article contained not only all the semantic conceptualizations already found in news articles on fundamentalism but also other dominant stereotypical images circulating in press discourse in relation to Islam, encapsulated in the leading paragraph:

Omar Bakri Mohammad is an Islamic fundamentalist. He wants to destroy the State of Israel, says that homosexuals are abominations, and that men and women should not mix freely in public. He's waging a holy war to impose these beliefs on his country. But that country is not where you might expect it to be. It's Britain.

However, the primary journalistic stylistic dimension of the commentary was ridicule. The comedic paradigm combined with the format, a feature, allowed for greater leeway in the expression of material, in this case anti-Muslim racism that would be unacceptable elsewhere. The major propositions were therefore exaggerated and subject to over-lexicalization through the utilization of the derogatory linguistic paradigms of madness, fear, conflict, violence, prohibition, extremism and separatism. It made repeated use of Islamic terminology that had been popularized by the press, their meanings transformed, evident in the title of the article, 'Oh what a lovely jihad!' and the documentary, 'Tottenham Ayatollah'. These operated as simplistic but forceful categories of ridicule, which, through their repetitive use in the press, relied on schemas of knowledge for their meanings. This allowed 'jihad' to be recognized as a physical threat/war and 'Ayatollah' as a hard-line, authoritative extremist. This, and the other nine articles in the *Guardian* relating to the central article and the documentary, veered between extreme satire, which nullified the Islamic threat, and a sinister menace epitomized in the final uncomfortable moment that saw the Jewish journalist overlooking money that was to be shipped out to Israel to fight the Jews. The caricature that counteracted the threat was therefore never ultimately realized. The explicit ideology to be found in this article was naturalized by the acceptance in other articles of its major propositions and objectivity. Being mainly reviews, they focused on the entertainment value of the documentary.

This ideology is exposed through the counter ideology of Omar Bakri in a letter to the *Daily Jang*, Britain's largest daily Urdu paper (4 April). Having a serious and intellectual tone, it offered Bakri's understanding of the purpose of the film, 'We agreed that the film would address the struggle between civilizations in particular Islam and capitalism.' Part of the letter's aim was to expose the ideology present in Ronson's film, discrediting the programme makers by focusing on their deception, apparent in the frequent references and plethora of terms relating to the assurances that there would be no 'animosity', 'fabrication', 'distortion' and 'demonization'.

Criticisms of the use of Muslim extremists to represent Islam in the press provided the counter discourse prevalent in two letters appearing in the *Guardian* (5 and 26 April). These condemned a portrayal that 'fails to place Omar Bakri in a context of diverse and divergent schools of thought and belief within the Muslim community' (R. Tuddenham, 5 April). While appearing to accept the depiction of Bakri's character at face value, they objected to the focus on extreme examples of Islam when there were few alternative images to provide balance.

These different interpretations of the same event are useful to illustrate the ideological construction that takes place through language. The difference lies in the power of different groups to access ideological structures that enabled the dominant ideologies to prevail.

Decontextualization

A typical element of conflict coverage is its decontextualization. This was evident in all the coverage here, in which events were dehistoricized and depoliticized. Very little background was given to why dissidents sought asylum here, for example that al-Masari was involved in non-violent activities in trying to democratize a corrupt regime. To be portrayed as 'a moderate, opposed to terrorism' would have permitted audience identification (Runnymede Trust 1996: 2). This allowed political actions to be removed from the political domain, to be constructed as illegitimate and the actors criminalized. Conceptualized as random, senseless acts of violence, the agents of these actions appear irrational. Resorting to violence constructs the Islamists as primitive in the context of the legitimate political negotiations of governments. Violence is seen as a reason for action and, in the absence of any political context, appears to be an essential characteristic of the group portrayed. The discourse was therefore *naturalized*. The Saudi ambassador was quoted in *The Times* after the *al-Hayat* newspaper bombing as saying that 'those who cannot face ideas resort to bombs. This is a criminal, cowardly act, which illustrates the mentality of the perpetrators' (14 January). Any Western responsibility for the conflicts taking place was omitted; the British government was seen to be justifiably responding to the provocations of others.

Homogeneity

Only in the features on Omar Bakri Mohammed, where the extreme was exaggerated for comical effect, was there any attempt to differentiate between Muslim groups: 'the majority of Muslims who live in Britain are far from being fundamentalists, there is nevertheless a great deal of mutual incomprehension between our communities' (Will Self, *Observer*, 13 April; see also A. A. Gill, *The Times*, 13 April). These types of 'admissions' (van Dijk 1991) avoid accusations of racism; even so, the Muslim community was constructed as problematic in its 'difference'.

Many of the news articles made no attempt to differentiate and actually constructed links between the general community and militants, 'As far as Islam is concerned, he [Mubarak] is now a legitimate target. If a Muslim kills Mubarak tomorrow he is performing a legitimate act because he is responding to the court's verdict' (Omar Bakri Mohammed, quoted in the *Observer*, 23 November). About half the *Guardian* articles displayed this tendency. In relation to extremists targeting Egypt, it was said that collections were 'left inside mosques and Islamic cultural centres throughout Britain' (23 November, *Observer* and *The Times*, 24 November and 13 December). Despite the comical effects in the *Guardian*'s feature on Omar Bakri, he was also referred to in more serious news stories so that the exaggerated elements of the feature took on a more sinister reality. In the aftermath of Luxor, a *Guardian* news story listed Omar Bakri as 'an important fund-raiser' (for the group responsible). He was also associated with the Muslim community and with moderate dissidents such as al-Masari (11 January). In the global coherence of articles then, Muslims were linked together.

Despite this, Muslims were also constructed as sectarian through constant references to the splitting of factions and groups. This not only implied a conflictual nature but also added to a conception of Muslims as ideologically weak and using their religion manipulatively.

Categorization

Through an analysis of categorization, ideological bias was exposed. Through a linguistic paradigm of conflict, rather than the use of political language, terrorist and fundamentalist activities were marked out as illegitimate and thus punitive action could legitimately have been taken against the protagonists.[42] Yet this discourse appeared neutral, purely because of its institutionalized state. This categorization was essential for comprehension of these stories and, once categorized in this way, allowed a channel of continuity to be opened in which subsequent stories could be labelled as being about 'fundamentalism' and treated in a uniform manner. In the frequency of their use, the terms contributed to the reproduction and therefore the reality of the categories, having a normalizing effect.

Table 3.4 shows how newspapers gave discursive attention to terrorism. Muslims were subjected to negative labelling, associated with bombing, killing, extremism and terrorism but were not recognized as political activists. The *Mail* employed a particularly restrictive level of lexicalization, limited to extreme negativization.

Table 3.4   Terms used to describe Islamists in fundamentalism articles, excluding those on Omar Bakri

	Daily Mail	Guardian	The Times	Total
Terrorism/rist	12	23	36	70
Bomber/bombs	2	16	18	36
Killer/kill/killed	11	13	7	33
Asylum/seeker	11	12	4	28
Militant	2	11	7	20
Exile	0	3	13	16
Extremism/ist	3	4	8	15
Dissident	2	7	5	14
Radical/ism	0	4	6	10
Islamist	0	4	4	8
Fundamentalist	3	2	2	7
Activist	1	2	1	4
Total number of articles in paper	5	9	6	20

What is also apparent is that the use of the lexical item 'fundamentalism' was low in all papers, as journalists increasingly refrained from using the word because of uncertainty over its meaning, publicity over its misuse and its Christian connotations. This was particularly evident in the broadsheets. However, I would argue that the connotations of the word gained such currency that it was no longer necessary for it to be used for the event to be interpreted as such. The decline in the use of the term 'fundamentalist' has not led to the use of more positive terms in general.

The excessive use of quasi-synonymous terms is a rhetorical device that emphasized, through repetition, the meaning intended, in this case agency was clearly located and the Islamist was rendered criminal or abnormal (and in the lexical choices made, dehumanized). This allowed the 'abnormality and extremism' of fundamentalism to be contrasted with the moderation and reasonableness of Western hegemony' (Said quoted in Sayyid 1997: 31). This lexicalization was not applied to the authorities, who were attributed with positive evaluative terms such as 'condemning terrorism'.

By continually associating religiosity with crime in terms of 'Islamic terrorism', the religious aspect was signified as the chief factor of influence in these actions. In this way, Iganatieff argued that 'Muslim means fundamentalist; fundamentalist means fanatic' (cited in UKACIA 1993: 4). This position can be used to justify continuing dis-crimination towards Muslims.

Counter discourse

From a liberal position, the *Guardian* was critical of restrictive asylum laws and therefore provided spaces for alternative perspectives based on its definition of genuine need. This was a non-violent, human rights moderate activist who had not expressed any statements offensive to the paper's ideologies and was under threat from a repressive regime. Exemplifying what the *Guardian* defined as a 'real asylum seeker' was an article about a Pakistani dissident, a non-violent activist who was campaigning for democracy in his home country over the phone from the UK. Although fairly light hearted and appearing partly for its novelty value, it developed a more serious tone towards the end, listing atrocities committed in Pakistan, as he 'called for an end to the feudal, corrupt and repressive nature of Pakistan's politics' (20 January).

These men were categorized differently, either in admiration as 'martyr', 'passionate' and 'skilful', or in sympathy as 'frail, 'sadly emaciated' and 'weak'. They were conceptualized as having convic-tions rather than blind absolutism, and their activities were contex-tualized in terms of political asylum. The articles were free from the consistent and dominant themes present in the others. In direct contrast with those constructed as fundamentalist, the government's tough line was criticized; they were 'being treated like criminals' (2 February).

However, these articles tended to be incidental (there were only two that year), possibly a result of the race relations framework in the UK in which many people applying for asylum would be categorized on the basis of race. The foreign element of this coverage occasionally allowed Muslims in Britain to be constructed as moderates, as in the coverage of the bombing of the moderate Arab newspaper. However, this appeared to have political expediency, and on more occasions militants were linked with the Muslim community rather than differentiated from it.

Any alternative ideology, then, was weakened by the consistency of the dominant consensus in reporting. All papers in this year ended with a discussion of the problem of asylum seekers in Britain organizing terrorist activities for action abroad.

Subsequent coverage showed an increase in attention to this topic. In 1998 this was largely due to the bombing of US embassies in Kenya and Tanzania and the subsequent American air strikes on the 'terrorist enclaves' of Afghanistan and Sudan. Chiefly aimed at the Saudi dissident, Osama bin Laden, who had been constructed as 'the world's top terrorist', the issue was personified through his demonization in a similar manner to that of Saddam Hussein. Receiving extensive coverage, which dominated the front pages of the press throughout August and into September, this international event provoked articles detailing British Muslim reactions to the bombings and the possibility of London becoming a target for 'revenge attacks'.[43] The main press source for the Muslim response was the extremist Omar Bakri Mohammad who was quoted as 'applauding the bombing of the US embassies', and 'fully behind bin Laden' (*The Times*, 24 August 1998). Following the US air raids, British Muslims were shown protesting in London and a variety of British Muslim opinion was sought that confirmed their 'fury'. In this instance, because of the event's extremity, the Muslim threat was taken seriously, with Muslims overtly categorized as 'fundamentalists'. The climate of fear promoted here functioned to justify and prepare the public for any repressive acts against Muslims, such as the anti-terrorism legislation that was rushed through Parliament in early September. The Criminal Justice (Conspiracy and Terrorism) Act gave police extended powers and made it an offence for groups residing in the UK to plot and fund terrorism abroad.[44] The strength of the discourse surrounding Osama bin Laden meant that, by linking him to virtually every incidence of Islamic terrorism since, the international threat was maintained.[45]

Both international and domestic coverage had created an illusion of a worldwide Islamic terrorist network and articles from countries across the world depicted Muslim groups protesting against the USA and Britain and raising funds for terrorism abroad. By making complex connections between British dissidents and terrorists such as bin Laden, who was then linked to Bakri, who was further linked to al-Masari, and then to the Muslim community as 'one of many among the hundreds of Muslims groups that have proliferated in Britain in the past few years' (*Guardian*, 25 August 1998), Muslims were homogenized as being united in goals and sympathies that directly opposed Western interests. Even the Govan MP Sarwar appeared, reported as intending to visit Sudan and strongly critical of US actions (24 September). The culmination of the reporting on this topic came with a story that erupted in January 1999 and that served to confirm and condemn the role of British Muslims in international terrorism. This was the capture in Yemen of five British Muslims from Birmingham for plotting to bomb the city of Aden. Constructed as ordinary Muslims with the support of the Muslim community, they were quickly linked to a fundamentalist cleric in London, Abu Hamza, who was severely demonized, linked to bin Laden and accused of plotting to overthrow the Yemeni government from London. Hamza was then linked to Abu Hassan in Yemen, on trial for shooting foreign (including British) tourists kidnapped in Yemen earlier in the year. These associations rendered any member of the Muslim community guilty of such acts. The lack of support from the Foreign Office, in contrast with the Saudi nurses, added to their guilt, which was confirmed by a confession from one member of the 'gang' on 14 February and the subsequent guilty verdict in August 1999 (although the press was disparaging of the Yemeni authorities and accused them of torture and brutality).

I would argue that these incidents have tightened the framework of reporting on Muslims further. The repercussions of such coverage — decreasing sympathy, worsening attitudes — can only contribute to the further marginalization of British Muslims.

Conclusion

The issue of 'fundamentalism' represented Muslims as an alien force undermining British interests on a number of levels. The papers used a variety of consistent strategies to mobilize support for action to be taken to remove the threat (similarly on an international scale, the image of the Muslim fundamentalist allowed repressive action to be taken against foreign countries so that Western hegemony could be maintained).

The mixing of religion and politics with violence alienated the Islamists' positions from any sympathy with mainstream political philosophies in the UK. The discursive unity meant that there was little contestation or struggle over the language on this issue. Only the struggle to contain the terrorists through the state was represented. The repetitive discourse, in which the ideology was made explicit on a regular basis, was a feature of the coverage of this topic. Each story confirmed the patterns of behaviour of the homogenized group as they acted out their essentialized characteristics. However, the foreign element allowed some distance to be constructed between the fundamentalist and the majority of Muslims in Britain. Although people may recognize that these images did not represent the norm, enough links were made to the Muslim community to imply a connection, with few representations of moderate Muslims to balance this.

Crime and politics: the case of Mohammed Sarwar

Having been topical in previous years, this story exploded in 1997 to become the most frequently occurring and highly visible story on British Muslims of the year. Having previously been accused of underhand activities in securing the candidacy for the Govan Labour seat, following his election in May, Mohammed Sarwar was accused of trying to bribe an opponent, the unofficial Labour candidate, Badar Islam, offering him £5000 to fight a losing campaign. These allegations appeared in the *News of the World* (18 May), who had involved Mr Islam in arranging an illicit meeting with Sarwar that was taped to provide evidence. Once it transpired that Sarwar had paid the money to Islam, albeit according to Sarwar as a loan to a member of the community in financial difficulty, not a bribe, other allegations arose concerning vote rigging. He was suspended from the Labour Party in June and charged in December.

The volume of coverage on this story, 54 articles over the four papers, was due to its political nature. In particular, its news value at the time was related to its definition as the first example of 'sleaze' in the

New Labour government. 'Sleaze' was coined by the press with the function of discrediting the previous Conservative government by defining different examples of political crime, which had previous currency, under one derogatory ideological term (Lacey and Longman 1997). According to van Dijk (1983), the use of such terms deeply affect people's understanding of events by concretizing their definition, providing an artificial coherence between them. This results in generalizations being made, based on methods of newspaper reading in which full details were rarely assimilated. The government therefore appeared to be ridden with an elemental corruption.

The Labour Party participated in this categorization, fighting a major part of its election campaign on eliminating 'sleaze' from government. Tony Blair was also highly critical of John Major's 'weak leadership' in dealing with 'sleaze'. By defining the Sarwar story as an example of 'sleaze', it was used by the press as an indicator of the intentions of the new government and a test of Blair's leadership. However, other incidents of 'sleaze' in the Labour Party occurring at this time received far less press attention. I would argue that this particular incident had added news value because:

- Sarwar is an Asian and Britain's first Muslim MP; therefore his behaviour came to be an indicator of the Muslim community in Britain. Sarwar's wealth and 'rags to riches' life story also gave it an extra dimension of interest; and
- the constituency had already achieved news value from previous rivalries and infighting.

As well as being a party political issue about government standards, this story was also an indicator of minority relations under Labour. This research has, so far, shown how coverage of British Muslims is representative of their exclusion from political structures and struggle for political participation. Having finally gained political representation, their position was undermined. By attempting to fix Sarwar's guilt, the papers confirmed the ideology reproduced in other stories. The meta-narrative about Muslims in Britain, encapsulated in total coverage and culminating in this story, read that Muslims brought with them (from elsewhere) abhorrent practices that corrupted British systems. This required negative repressive action. The struggle over power in the political domain was represented in the press in a way that sustained power relations.

The reproduction of the key discourses across articles resulted in a wealth of evidence that could be employed to support my arguments. However, due to the volume of coverage, the extensive analysis of this case cannot be explicated in fine detail. Because of this, and the discursive unity in coverage of this story, it seemed appropriate to concentrate on the major articulations of the discourses occurring within the macro-assertions and how they related to each other, along with the major semantic strategies employed to discredit Sarwar without being labelled racist. Discourse employed included primitivism, sectarianism, disloyalty, cultural differences, deviance, economy, nation, identity, democracy, racism and the political.

Appearing mainly in news form (81 per cent), and being an example of hard news, this was the only story covered more frequently by *The Times* (23 articles) than by the *Guardian* (18). This may be because Murdoch's News International, which is known for its cross-media interests, owns both the *News of the World* and *The Times*. Whereas both papers carried an equal number of news reports (17), *The Times* provided additional commentary and included the only two letters that were printed. There was less frequent coverage in the tabloids, which generally focus less on political issues. The tabloids covered the breaking story and its consequences, then only significant stages in its development, allowing for the expression of political and xenophobic tendencies but without being too extensive to disinterest the reader. Breaking on 18 May with the allegations in *The Times* and *Guardian* (and picked up by the tabloids on 19 May), the reported developments in the story included Sarwar issuing a writ for libel, admitting to giving money to Islam 'but in the form of a loan', Labour launching an inquiry and suspending Sarwar (June), further allegations by the *News of the World* (June), the police releasing its report (August, but only in *The Times*) and finally Sarwar appearing in court to be charged (December). The broadsheets covered all these developments, initial coverage running for seven days up to 26 May. In the *Mail* the story ran for four days initially, featuring Sarwar's suspension in June and the charges in December (eight articles). The *Sun* covered only the initial two days (omitting the libel writ issued by Sarwar) and the charges (five articles). Neither of the papers covered Sarwar's appearance in court the following day when he issued a denial. This illustrated both the lack of political depth and analysis in these papers and the discursive closure around the accusations, suspension and charges. The event was given just enough coverage to fulfil its ideological function, but then neither did the broadsheets cover all aspects of the story. An additional 11 news articles appeared in the *Scottish Sunday Times* because of its specific interest in terms of locality. However, quantity does not ensure that a full debate ensues, and the additional coverage here worked to add extra weight to the paper's particular stance. In this case, the paper used selective evidence from witnesses to build a case against Sarwar, embedding any response from his point of view in a wealth of contrary evidence and thereby making his arguments seem implausible: 'Sarwar aide: new malpractice claims' (8 June), 'Candidate sacked for standing against Sarwar' (20 July). Part of the explicit discourse of the *Scottish Sunday Times*, which was only implicated by Sarwar's activities in the national press, was that of morality. In relation to overall coverage of British Muslims, the moral high ground Muslims are often reported to take is juxtaposed against actual behaviour.

The events surrounding Sarwar were also referred to in a further 21 articles in *The Times*, mainly in relation to 'sleaze' but also at the time of voting on devolution (Sarwar's face was used in an advertising campaign against devolution). It occurred in four other articles in the *Guardian* in relation to 'sleaze'. This illustrated the cohesive effects of the label, giving solidity to the definition and our understanding of the Sarwar story in these terms.

Corruption, sleaze: guilty as charged

The activities with which Sarwar was alleged to have been engaged consisted of a series of examples of malpractice in politics. The cumulative description of illegal activities surrounding Sarwar was one of the strategies the papers used to insinuate his guilt. Thus, the dominant linguistic paradigm employed was that of corruption. Sarwar and the constituency were associated with 'malpractice', 'corruption', 'scandal', 'crisis', 'bribery', 'dirty tricks', 'misconduct', 'impropriety', 'smears', 'back-stabbing', 'vote-rigging', 'skulduggery' and 'dishonesty'. This overlexicalization signalled the abnormality of the events while maintaining the integrity of the British political system. It also worked to exacerbate the severity of the situation, evident in the syntactical (structural) complexity of the statement expounding the charges against him. He was 'facing criminal charges relating to the late registration of voters, attempting to pervert the course of justice and contraventions of the Representation of the People Act in connection with election expenses' (*The Times*, 17 December).[46] Little linguistic variety occurred across papers, thus binding Sarwar to criminal actions.

These allegations were classified lexically as 'sleaze'. Metaphor and imagery created an impression of a vast number of allegations being involved. The *Observer*, for example, described events as 'a tide of sleaze as deep and cloying as the toxic waters of the Clyde' (25 May).

Though quickly defined as Labour's first 'crisis' (*Times*, 18 and 19 May, 17 December) or 'scandal' (*Mail*, 19 May), which escalated the impact of the coverage — for example 'Sleazy Tide Ends Tony's Easy Ride' (the *Sun*, 19 May) — because of their support for New Labour at the time, all the papers except the *Mail* distanced Sarwar from the government.[47] The papers attempted to mitigate for the government by personalizing Sarwar's activities and comparing them with 'a festering sore, which distracts attention from the Premier's positive policy announcements' (*Sun*, 19 May). While all papers took this stance, the *Guardian* was cautious at first; only when it became clear that money was exchanged did it fully distance Labour from Sarwar. For the *Mail*, however, Sarwar was an example of Labour sleaze, 'Labour will be badly damaged' (19 May). This enabled the paper to discredit the government by showing how quickly it was 'facing a sleaze crisis'.

In the *Mail* (19 May) and *The Times* (22 May, 18 December), this sleaze was to some extent related to Old Labour local councils. This raised fears about the strength of Old Labour control of local politics, and in *The Times* functioned as a warning that if Labour did not deal with these constituencies, they would equally be perceived as corrupt (and so attempting to remove the left from politics). However, Sarwar was generally perceived as a New Labour man, which accounted for the distancing of him from the party.

Part of the *Mail*'s strategy to discredit Sarwar was to make associations with sexual deviance (prostitutes and an illegitimate child), which added to the conceptualization of 'sleaze' (21 May). It attributed these propositions to a third party, another tabloid, thus maintaining some credibility above the 'gutter' press while still projecting these ideas into the public domain.

The weight given to the allegations in the macro-structure of the articles allows Sarwar only a brief denial, 'Of course it's all completely untrue', marginalized to the end, and appearing often flippant in this context. The structure worked to raise questions about his innocence and amounted to a trial by the press. Semantic strategies used to intensify his guilt included:

- uncovering subversive connections (15 June, 16 June);
- making unfavourable evaluative judgements about his character — he was subjected to a plethora of negative predicates and attributives that signalled a flawed and deviant personality;
- using negative evaluative modality,[48] 'The assertion, by friends of Mr Sarwar that moneys handed over were innocent loans does nothing to reassure observers' (*Guardian*, 19 May);
- making reference to past offences in the constituency (*Guardian* and *Mail*, 19 May; *The Times*, 20 May); and
- the selective use of evidence and sources, even where these sources were from his community, thus allowing articles to be perceived as objective and non-racist (*The Times*, 18 May, *Observer*, 25 May).

Each of these assertions added damaging new evidence to the case against Sarwar, raising doubts about his motivations and reputation, aggravating reader reproach and making alternative information less believable. Personalizing the story shielded the papers from accusations of racism and crucially individualized the crime, thus exonerating Labour but more importantly shifting blame from the system, which prevents access to some groups, to the problem of an individual (and by collectivizing the crime, problematizing Muslims generally).

Visual strategies also criminalized Sarwar. Almost half the articles incorporated photographs. These both personalized and neutralized the ideology in the texts. The majority of these were passport style photos, which created the impression of a criminal mug shot, dark and shadowy. Sarwar remains unsmiling and avoids eye contact in all but two. The captions situated the meaning for the reader, offering a quick interpretation of events, 'Sarwar: £5000', 'Sarwar: embarrassing' and were ambiguous enough to insinuate guilt. Two of these images were particularly effective in grounding the textual ideology. A side-on head shot, enlarged to enhance the expressive dimension of the photo, appeared in the *Guardian* twice, when Sarwar admitted to supplying the money and when he was charged in December (Figure 3.2). Most of his head is concealed by someone's shoulder. Sarwar peers over it. The effect was demonizing. Sarwar looked devious, sly and guilty. The other appeared in the last *Guardian* article after Sarwar had appeared in

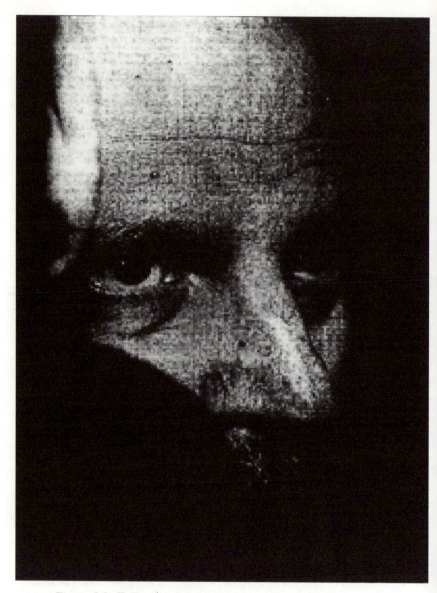

Figure 3.2 **Following Sarwar's arrest,** *Guardian*, **17 December 1997 (***photo***: Murdo Macleod/***Guardian* ©)**

Figure 3.3 **Sarwar leaving court following charges,** *Guardian*, **18 December 1997 (***photo:*** Ian Stewart/***Guardian*** ©)**

court (Figure 3.3). A large picture, it showed Sarwar leaving court disgruntled, his lawyer behind him with his hand on his shoulder. The caption read, 'Mohammed Sarwar leaves court in Glasgow yesterday, his lawyer behind him.' Given the context of the article and its positioning adjacent to another one on Labour 'sleaze' (but in that one the prime minister was seen to be backing the paymaster general, Geoffrey Robinson), this implied that Sarwar's lawyer alone was behind him. He was in political isolation. This was reinforced in all the photographs by localizing Sarwar in the street, outside any authority giving structures.

Categorization

'Millionaire MP': Sarwar's financial status was of interest to all papers. Through a lexical register of wealth he was categorized financially in a number of ways, both with negative and positive connotations. Admiration for his ambition, entrepreneurial skills and work ethic coincides with important Western values, 'Wealth from humble beginnings' (*Mail*, 19 May). However, these qualities were transformed into negative traits; the discourse of economy served to discredit him by linking his success to corruption. Any positive characteristics he was perceived to have or have had were undermined by 'political' and 'personal ambition' (formulated as a family characteristic by *The Times*, 19 May). He was therefore portrayed as an opportunist, greedy, manipulative and ruthless in his drive for power and success: 'Why was a multimillionaire who sends his four children to private schools standing in one of Britain's poorest constituencies?' (*Guardian*, 20, 25 and 26 May, 17 December).

The positive features he was considered to have possessed before the allegations were made were used as a contrast to how he should now be judged. This functioned as a warning that we should not be so gullible in the future, 'There is no doubting his achievements as a businessman. ... Immensely hard-working ... But' (*Guardian*, 18 December). *The Times* devoted its last article to this macro-assertion; 'From local hero to outcast, the tragedy of Mohammed Sarwar', which saw him discarded while the validity of the evidence against him was still untested (18 December).

That Sarwar had 'made it to the top' through corrupt and dishonourable means took on a racial element in both *The Times* (19 May) and *Guardian* (25 May) by association with political practices in

Pakistan. According to Yuval-Davis and Silverman (1998), this racialized discourse had its origins in Orientalist conceptions of the over-rich oil sheikhs of the 1970s. Shifts in their economic class positionings due to oil wealth, it was argued, led to their demonization based on envy (by the West). This was evident in the frequently used metonym 'Muslim millionaire'. Sarwar's economic and social standing was undermined by the use of low status terms such as 'cash-and carry tycoon'. Although this can be recognized as a racial stereotype in that many wealthy MPs are not categorized in such a way, this categorization is used more generally by the press in relation to political corruption as an indicator of criminal greed, provoking dislike for the central character.

'British Muslim MP': The operation of the discourse in this story relied on a cultural conception of Sarwar as a Muslim MP. Sarwar was clearly identified as a Muslim in 77.7 per cent of all articles, 42 out of 54. The mobilization of Muslim identity had specific goals, allowing the discourse relating to this topic to be associated with the formulas, evoking their meanings whenever it was used. Thus, pre-existing beliefs about Muslims could be reproduced in the evaluation of Sarwar, and popular assumptions and prejudices made what was said about him seem plausible. This categorization was based on the increasing visibility of Muslims, partly as a response to their own desire to be identified as such (we rarely see other MPs labelled in such a way). One might argue then that this identification was necessary as a cultural indicator for Muslims. However, this categorization allowed the press to associate, in their evaluation, Sarwar's inappropriate behaviour with his identity (chosen or not). The negative actions with which this label was associated here, that of corruption and sleaze, gave it its meaning and is an explanation for its persistent use. The other frequently applied metonym was 'bribe MP'. Its ambiguity allowed guilt to be derived, if little else, but top-level information, comprising either the headline or the first few paragraphs, was read. The interchangeability of these definitions of Sarwar not only inextricably linked deviant behaviour to Muslimness but also allowed the worth of Islamic values (and the sincerity of Muslims) to be questioned. This was evident in the juxta-position of Sarwar, having made his oath to parliament on the Koran, with the allegations (18 May) and then the charges (18 December).

As 'Britain's first Muslim MP', this aspect of his identity became most significant. Through this, Sarwar became a representative for all

Britain's Muslims (above his status as representative of the Govan constituency) and a highly visible indicator of their behaviour (attributed
with the 'burden of responsibility'). Generalizations were fostered
through connections with the community, 'he has raised funds for a
Glasgow mosque and was elected secretary of the Central mosque in
1986' (*The Times*, 19 May). Numerous examples are provided that
show the Asian community engaged in similar behaviour, including
Sarwar's colleagues. When Sarwar's aides sought to help him by
attempting to buy the *News of the World*'s legal files, they were quoted
as saying, 'We have got to help Mr Sarwar in any way we can. As
Muslim brothers this is our duty. If the whip is withdrawn there will be
a national outrage. We will do our utmost to make sure Muslims up and
down the country screw the Labour Party' (*The Times*, 15 June;
Guardian, 16 June). This admission or threat of Muslim action from
within, from Muslims themselves, is used to justify any suspicions the
majority may have had about Muslims in politics.

Use of the categories Asian and Muslim was interchangeable in the
reporting of this story, with no attempt to differentiate between them
(*The Times*, 19 and 20 May). The fusing of religious and ethnic identity
allowed further generalizations to be made. Sarwar was constructed as
an immigrant for this purpose; the tabloids in particular gave lexical
emphasis to his status as 'Pakistan-born Mr Sarwar' (*Mail*, 19, 20 and
21 May, 17 December; *Sun* 19 May, 17 December). Sarwar's Pakistani
origins allowed a discourse to be constructed around the myth of
corrupt Pakistani politics, which emerged as a significant explanatory
factor. The negative and homogenizing evaluation of Pakistani politics
as endemically corrupt was naturalized, making it appear to be a
consequence of the essential characteristics of Pakistanis. The
comparison of both the corruption and infighting in the Govan constituency with Sarwar's involvement in politics in Pakistan implied that
through immigration these practices had infiltrated British political
culture, thus corrupting it. This was made explicit in two articles that
appeared together in the *Guardian* that contrasted Sarwar's 'first taste
for politics in a turbulent period in Pakistan' with the statement that
'bribery claim is latest in string of Govan seat rows' (19 May). An
inherent cultural clash was implied, apparent in the headline of an
Observer article, 'The worst of both worlds met and the result was
disaster' (25 May).

Sectarianism

Part of the strategy used to reinforce the political and racial discourse was to focus on the factionalism prevalent in the Govan constituency. In the local coherence in the structure of articles and the global coherence of articles, this appeared to have two origins — political (Old Labour) and racial (Pakistani politics). In a way similar to that in which corruption was reported and asserted, this was partly achieved by accumulating evidence and information formulated within a graphical lexical register of conflict and warfare. Govan was referred to as having 'The battles of Backstab City', 'for more than 3 years ... racked with infighting' and was compared with 'open warfare' in which the actors were 'tearing lumps out of each other' (*Mail*, 19 May; also *The Times*, 20 and 22 May). Sarwar was situated as a key figure within these hostilities: 'Britain's first Muslim MP proves adept at making enemies' (*Guardian*, 22 May; also 21 and 25 May). The local coherence of this headline, which used the lexical choice of Muslim rather than Labour, attributed him with a conflictual nature connected with his Muslim identity.

This was also achieved by relating facts such as the borough's characteristics to the infighting, implying a relationship between the two. According to *The Times*, Govan had the 'highest ethnic population of any of Glasgow's seats, at about 11 per cent, 9.6 per cent of whom are Asians from Pakistan'. This appeared in an article on the 'hostilities' (20 May). Minorities were constructed as a problem for Labour and for Britain. *The Times* suggested that Labour's relationship with minorities, in particular Muslims, was 'strained' because they had 'created some unforeseen difficulties for Labour' (19 May). Labour was constructed as struggling to control its minority groups (by implication they needed controlling). They were associated with aggressive campaigning 'entryism' and irregular activities to obtain power, and there was an implication that once their goals were achieved they would act against the majority.

The political struggle then was represented as a 'row', incorporating the personal ambitions of individuals and therefore removing the political context. This continual discrediting of Sarwar's opponents did give some credibility to Sarwar. Badar Islam, for example, was subject to an Orientalist discourse associated with sexual deviance, aggression, gambling, deceit, financial ineptitude and bestial imagery (*Mail*, 19 and 20

May; *Guardian*, 19 May; *Times*, 21 May). In this way, it was implied that they might have been motivated by jealousy. But Sarwar was equally derided, indicating that neither could be trusted.

Although this fragmentation in some way acknowledged differences between Asians, it homogenized them by constructing them as all engaged in primitive conflict, conflict that was contrary to a 'realistic group conflict explanation' (Levine and Campbell 1972). However, in creating this illusion, it also works to promote tensions among rival groups, a strategy based on the concept 'divide and conquer', which encourages groups to fight among themselves rather than against the white majority. These (Asian) practices were then constructed as intrinsically primitive and undemocratic, a concern made explicit in the *Observer* in a statement like 'bribery in elections pollutes democracy itself' (20 May).

Anti anti-racism

As well as denying racism, 'it is not racist to say that many Asian members campaign more actively, some would say aggressively for their cause' (*The Times*, 19 May), the papers were quick to pre-empt any attempts to provide social and political explanations, in this case racism, for these circumstances by arguing that such a move would be an excuse for criminal activity and a way of escaping normal procedures. They constructed a watertight argument that minorities were guilty of 'crying discrimination' (*Observer*, 25 May). As it occurred, it could then be dismissed and Muslims could be accused of using racism manipulatively and shifting blame (*Guardian*, 19 May).[49] This also served as a warning to anti-racist groups and in particular to the government not to yield to this. *The Times* suggested that 'Mr Sarwar's allies have claimed that, as Britain's first Muslim MP, he is a victim of "Islamophobia". By using his faith to shield him from scrutiny they risk fanning the prejudice they fear', thus rejecting any 'special treatment' that Sarwar may have received as a result of being Britain's only Muslim MP (21 May; see also 19 and 22 May; *Mail*, 19 May, 17 December; *Guardian*, 26 May, 13 June, 17 December). Only the *Guardian* acknowledged that some of the constituency's problems might have been due to racism because Sarwar took on 'a white political Establishment' (19 May: 5).

Institutionalized racism was rejected as an explanation. By removing

the actions from the structural setting, the criminal activities of individuals and here collectivities were perceived as the problem. This was
another example of ethnic blame discourse (Romer et al. 1998), which
accentuated the harmful effects for the in-group. This type of right-wing
mitigation, engaging in positive self-representation with negative representation of the out-group, conceals power relations. The preferred
solution was not then to change the political system to make it more
accommodating to minorities but to take punitive action against them.

Appealing for tough action

The superstructure of many of these articles was manipulated to organize attention to the actions of Labour and downplay Sarwar's denials.
The papers saw it as a necessity that the government should act quickly
or otherwise become similarly associated with 'sleaze', as with the
previous government. This represented an appeal for tough leadership.
Reminders were offered of Blair's 'vow to clean up politics' (*Sun*, 19
May; *Guardian*, 20, 22 and 26 May). As an issue of government
credibility (or even the credibility of the British political system), all
papers focused on it, their modality clearly expressed through the voice
of authority, 'Crack the whip. Labour should show leadership in the
Sarwar case' (*The Times*, Commentary, 21 May; *Observer*, 18 May;
Sun, 19 May). Labour was depicted as about to act, updates were constantly supplied, with Labour sources adding to the constructed
'reality', 'Tony Blair will not be like John Major and act uncertainly ...
he will act positively, decisively and immediately' (*The Times*, 19 May;
Sun, 19 May). The pressure for action was finally heeded when Sarwar
was suspended from the party. By this time he had been constructed as
increasingly politically isolated, allowing his actions to be attributed
only to himself and thus distanced from the party. Labour's suspension
of Sarwar was interpreted as its lack of confidence and trust in him,
which was used to confirm the papers' stance.

Although this discourse was present in all papers, the main differences between them, apart from stylistic ones, were partisan. There was
some mitigation by the supportive papers in the face of government
non-action in the initial stages, whereas the *Mail* mitigated for the
previous Conservative government, alluding to the realities of govern-
ing. The *Mail* was critical, illuminating the lack of support Sarwar had
received. This political criterion did open up spaces for positive repre-

sentations of Sarwar, but in an attempt to discredit the government, Sarwar was ultimately condemned. To achieve this, the *Mail* put less distance between Labour and Sarwar, seeing the affair as 'embarrassing' for the government. While the discourse of other papers was dominated by calls for 'tough action', the *Guardian* and *Sun* were more likely to accentuate and protect Labour's good reputation. In *The Times* this approach, which was particularly vigorous and demanding, functioned as a test of Labour's ability to govern. It was therefore more likely to be critical.

Figure 3.4 **Cartoon appearing in *The Times*, 21 May 1997**
(© Peter Brookes/*The Times*)

Labour had to rid itself of troublemakers, 'purge (itself of) suspect councillors' (*The Times*, 22 May). In the guise of 'tough action' on 'sleaze' the paper addressed the government (and built a consensus) to 'suspend Sarwar' as a solution to the problem. Through the construction of these articles in which Muslims were criminal and corrupt, 'tough action' to expel them from British systems seemed the only feasible option. While the function of the discourse was left implicit, it was perhaps more evident in a cartoon in *The Times* (21 May). Free from the constraints of news reporting, it made its ideology more explicit (Figure 3.4). It showed Tony Blair transforming himself into a mullah so that he could be 'tough on sleaze' and on 'the causes of sleaze'. Apart from implicating Muslims as these 'causes', this required knowledge of pre-existing populist views about the 'mullah', its imagery mainly associated with a caricature of the Iranian Ayatollah and the associated extremism and uncompromising position. The connotations of this cartoon were that Muslims misbehaving in this country should expect to be punished as they would in an Islamic state. This ignored Sarwar's origins and homogenized Muslims worldwide, essentially constructing Muslims as 'foreigners'. It was also a reference to the enemy within, the root of the problem and the threat to British society as Muslims attempted to gain power. Blair would therefore be perceived as being in allegiance with this enemy if he did not act. Tough leadership was required to deal with minorities and their crimes, implying that if they were not controlled in the UK, they would become as wild as their counterparts elsewhere.[50]

This construction is evident through an examination of the syntactic agents in the headlines (Table 3.5).[51]

Table 3.5   Agency attribution in headlines

	Subject to action %	Sarwar actor %	Other %
The Times	60.8	13.0	26.0
Guardian	55.5	33.3	11.1
Mail	62.5	25.0	12.5
Sun	60.0	40.0	
Total	59.2	25.9	14.8

These headlines were actor focal (focusing on people rather than structures or the passive nominalizations as seen in the reporting of the religious discrimination laws, and therefore clearly attributing agency). They showed that Sarwar was mainly subject to the actions of others.

The news values and categorization of this story contrasted with the reporting of 'the systematic deselection' of ethnic minority councillors by Labour at the last election, 'fury at Labour's party whitewash' (*Observer*, 15 March 1998: 19). Although this resulted in Labour facing a 'high-profile court case' under the Race Relations Act, it was selected as a news item only once, with no follow-up on the outcome, and the right-wing papers left it uncovered. This illustrates how the press worked to promote political agendas in their attention to particular stories that could aid or force government action. Despite both candidates being Muslim, they were not identified as such. The lack of categorization here was an example of the association of Muslims with particular 'appropriate' topics.

Figure 3.5 **Following Sarwar's acquittal,** *Guardian*, **26 March 1999**
(*photo:* **Murdo Macleod/***Guardian* ©)

Counter discourse

Counter discourse occurred in relation to both Sarwar and other ethnic minority group actors, mainly in the *Guardian*. Only the *Guardian* made reference (albeit only once) to any contribution Sarwar was making to the community by helping his constituents in relation to employment at the Govan Kvaerners shipyard (20 May). The *Guardian* also detailed some possible explanations for the registration of late voters, given to the Labour investigation and excluded from other papers, such as 'apathy among Urdu speaking recruits' and 'data which suggest that the turnout was statistically unexceptional' (5 June). However, this was followed by an article on 7 June that said that 'members of the team were not convinced by the explanations they heard' and were therefore expecting to find Sarwar guilty of bringing the 'party into disrepute'.

The level of allegations undermined indicators that suggested that Sarwar had been framed (*Mail*, 19 May) and derisory personal evaluations undermined references to his positive characteristics. However, there was some indecision about whether his actions should be seen as political naiveté or stupidity rather than outright manipulation (*Guardian*, 21 May, 18 December; *The Times*, 22 May, 18 December). This did, however, continue to allude to a discourse of primitivism.

Sometimes, more positive constructions of Sarwar resulted in the negativization of Islam. The *Guardian* referred to his previous allegiance to socialism in Pakistan as an example of credibility, 'his political enthusiasm has deep roots'. However, this was described 'as an affront to Islam' (19 May). By implying that the two were in direct opposition to each other and by praising Sarwar's socialist activity, the *Guardian* made a directly negative judgement of Islam in terms of its own values. Another example of this occurred in the coverage of an incident in which Sarwar 'rescued' some Glasgow girls 'from arranged marriages in Pakistan' (referred to in all the papers, which praised his 'positive action'). This story represented Muslims as engaging in antiquated practices in the treatment of women (enforced culture) and also provided another example of feuding within their community (*Guardian*, 25 May; *The Times*, 19 and 20 May). In this way, Sarwar was constructed as a moderate acting against extreme practices, but this construction had a negativizing effect on the Muslim community.

The most substantial examples of counter discourse occurred as two letters, both from Asians in *The Times*, one entitled 'Anti-Muslim Campaign' (Haseeb, 25 May) and the other from the chairman of Overseas Pakistanis, Q. S. Annisuddin (23 May). Both were critical of the media coverage of Sarwar, likening it to 'a trial by media' based on his status as a Muslim. Haseeb also criticized the lack of support from Labour. However, in the context of other articles in *The Times*, these reinforced its arguments with regard to 'crying discrimination' and criticisms of Labour for courting the Muslim vote.

A column in the *Sun* by Norman Tebbit entitled 'Sarwar so good' took a similar stance of 'innocent until proven guilty'. This also appeared to have political (and economic) expediency, criticizing the *Guardian*'s treatment of the Neil Hamilton case before it came to trial. This is a technique papers use to boost their status in the eyes of their readers and feed their superiority by showing solidarity in their affiliation to a particular 'community of understanding' (Lacey and Longman 1997).

There were, then, slippages in presentation. Articles differed in their degree of disparagement towards Sarwar and he was sometimes presented favourably in relation to other actors. However, these threads of counter discourse tended to be fleeting and in the context of the level of negative discourse, with the global coherence of articles and their composition working to undermine any spaces of positive representation. For example, Sarwar's determination to stay and fight his case was seen as dishonourable in the face of the evidence against him. It appeared then that positive statements worked solely to give the appearance of balance and tolerance, with the problem debated and the solution rationalized.

An examination of the minority press showed how this could be alternatively constructed. In *Q-News*, Labour was constructed as difficult, repressive and associated with underhand negative behaviour, while it was suggested that Sarwar had been subjected to a witch-hunt. His perspective formed the basis of these articles and pictures of him were more attractive, showing him smiling and engaged (January 1998: 3; February 1998: 9).

Conclusion

By categorizing the story as 'sleaze', Sarwar was not only linked to wider political phenomena, but also constructed to appear as an abomination in the Labour Party, upsetting the social and political order. This construction, which in this case personalized criminal behaviour and thus removed it from political structures, was employed in coverage of other political actors involved in 'scandal', with the perceived Other in general, for example, homosexuals, and across news reporting. However, the racial angle in this coverage allowed the behaviour to be explained on this basis. It therefore appeared as ultimately different from other constructions of sleaze and had greater coherence with racialized stories, although it should be remembered that the construction of this story had political (attachment) grounds, which partly resulted in Sarwar's negativization. While he was to an extent a victim of this factor, other examples of Labour 'sleaze' such as Geoffrey Robinson and Fiona Jones (April 1998) at the time were treated with less attention and derision. This story had particular news value in its mixture of political and racial elements.

Sarwar was initially given conditional acceptance based on presumptions about what constituted acceptable behaviour. Cultural value judgements were made in relation to 'unacceptable' practices and were accorded racial and religious origins, thus implying that the minority group was confirming its natural tendencies. The strong argumentation of the press worked to build a consensus around Sarwar's culpability. Through his categorization as a Muslim representative, his identity was hijacked by a number of groups for ideological purposes. In this case his behaviour was transferred to all Muslims. Given the visibility of the case, this coverage therefore diminished the struggle of Muslims for political recognition and resulted in political shame, which further marginalized their chances of participation.

Coverage of Mohammed Sarwar continued as his trial at the High Court in Edinburgh commenced (on 27 January 1999) and it lasted for nine weeks. Initial coverage of the trial (in all news articles) formulated the story in the same way as previous coverage, although it was much reduced. There was also evidence of selective reporting because all the papers failed to report Sarwar's libel action against the *News of the World* (May 1998). The amount and seriousness of the evidence against him was emphasized as top-level information. Elaborating the charges in this way without providing any history of the constituency conceptualized the events as isolated cases of criminality.

Following this initial coverage, which highlighted the evidence of the prosecution, there was a gap in reporting of a month until 9 and 11 March when Sarwar was cleared of two charges. These articles appeared only in *The Times* and *Guardian* (with previous categorization dropped in *The Times*); the first charge was reported in the 'News in brief' sections and the second on a similarly small scale.

Coverage took a different turn following Sarwar's acquittal on all charges on 25 March 1999, which all the papers covered. However, while *The Times* and *Guardian* presented a whole page of analysis, the *Mail* and *Sun* afforded only a couple of paragraphs to relay basic details (on page 29 in the *Mail* and on page 31 in the *Sun*). Their lack of interest was an indication of their ideological position on the story, illustrated by the *Mail*'s only other article on the trial, which featured

Badar Islam's evidence in which he said that Sarwar was fully aware of the circumstances of his actions, having 'joked about the election bribe' (4 February 1999). While the tabloids continued to categorize him in the same way, except that the *Mail* dropped its categorization 'Labour MP', the broadsheets paid less discursive attention to it, so shifting their construction of Sarwar. Evidence supporting him was highlighted and new information was introduced, for example that Sarwar had wished to call a press conference to proclaim his innocence but that Labour had not allowed him to do so. This had previously been formulated as ignorance and guilt on his part. He was characterized positively as a 'pioneer MP' and 'characteristically optimistic' in the face of charges (*The Times*, 26 March 1999). Photographs showed him no longer po-faced, but out of isolation and with his head held high (Figure 3.5). At this stage, both papers concretized their conceptualization of Sarwar as having been foolish rather than criminal. The *Guardian* drew stylistic attention to this and concluded its analysis by saying that, 'Mohammed Sarwar has surrounded himself with all the wrong people. I think he knows this. He is not a bad man but he has made some silly mistakes' (26 March 1999). Sarwar's contribution to events was further attended to by *The Times* and *Sun*, which included his apology to Labour for misleading them on the circumstances of the loan.

Through this characterization of Sarwar and by focusing on rivalries in the Asian community, however, the papers still located the problem within the community. The background to the constituency was virtually ignored (as were the white players involved in it) because the explanation preferred for Sarwar's predicament and the current 'infighting' was 'jealousy' in the Asian community. Some of Sarwar's practices were seen as an 'affront to Islam', which fuelled antagonism against him and allowed the incident in which he 'rescued' two Asian girls from a forced marriage in Pakistan to be retold as an illustration of this. While this worked to separate Sarwar off as a moderate, slippages still ensued between Muslim and Asian identities. There was also some insinuation that the motive for these positive acts, judged by the papers, was political ambition. While *The Times* paid more attention to these negative strands of discourse, it also displayed a more balanced approach to Sarwar's background, by providing new information, and to the racial hatred he experienced on the 'hard road to the Commons' (26 March 1999).[52]

Despite a more positive approach to Sarwar following his acquittal, the practices (both business and familial) of the Asian community were still seen to have caused the situation, for which he too was still partly to blame, 'he has always played the politics of the outsider' (*Guardian*, 26 March 1999). The significance of the coverage both before and after Sarwar's trial was highlighted by this quote from Colin Wallace, an ex-army press officer in Northern Ireland: 'the important thing is to get saturation coverage for your story as soon after the controversial event as possible. Once the papers have printed it the damage is done. Even when the facts come out, the original image is the one that sticks.' (Miller 1994: 238).

It has since emerged that this news story was the result of a series of entrapments of public figures by the *News of the World*. It paid £45,000 for the story, yet the press, which universally condemned Sarwar, failed to disclose the payment.[53] This was not the case when England rugby captain, Lawrence Dallaglio was similarly snared, for that incident provoked media debate into the paper's journalistic practices.

On 30 March 1999, the *Guardian* carried (solely) a photograph of Sarwar juxtaposed against the background of the Houses of Parliament. This may be testament to a greater willingness now to accept him (now categorized as a Labour or Glasgow Govan MP). It is perhaps signifi-cant that subsequently there has been a lack of attention awarded to the conduct of Sarwar's daily activities; only his reselection to stand as MP for the party was briefly covered (in *The Times* and *Guardian*, 28 August 1999).

Sources

Van Dijk (1983) argues that the production of news is 'the reconstruc-tion of available discourses' as journalists seldom witness events them-selves. The selection of sources and actors chosen to speak clearly has an ideological basis but context is also important. It is evident from this research that the press relies on official, particularly governmental dis-courses partly because of the political and institutional context of stories in which matters of law are involved (Table 3.6). This 'authority orientation' (Hansen and Murdock 1985) has been widely recognized as giving credibility and authenticity to the arguments being propagated, resulting in 'official formulations' of events (Tuchman 1978). Given that these sources are often the 'primary definers' of a situation for a journalist, carrying with them as they do the 'common sense of (the) institutionalized status quo' (Fowler 1991; Hall et al. 1978), this appearance of neutrality conceals the power differentials that inhibit change.

Table 3.6   Sources and actors by topic

Sources	*Cook* *Actors*
Sarah Cook	Sarah Cook
British government	British government
Turkish court	Turkish court
Turkish press	Musa Komeagac
Education	
government reports	teachers
schools	local councils
government	councillors
	government officials
	Muslim spokesmen
	parents
	children
Blasphemy	
government	Home Secretary
Runnymede Trust	government
academics	academics
	CRE
	Runnymede Trust
	lobby groups
	censorship groups
	Muslim community
Fundamentalism	
Home Office	Home Office
government	government
police	Home Secretary
	President Mubarak
Egyptian government officials	Egyptian government officials
dissidents	dissidents
	Arab newspaper

Although official sources and actors dominated, there was some evidence of spaces for alternative voices. The *Guardian* was more likely to represent the voices of the Muslim community. However, most of the Muslim sources or actors were used to articulate the dominant ideology in the article, as with President Mubarak's quote on the possibility of dialogue with the extremists, 'What kind of dialogue? It will be a dialogue between the blind and deaf.' This occurred in all papers and was also achieved by the use of militant sources like Omar Bakri Mohammad whose outpourings appeared blatantly ideological and confirmed arguments about extremists. In other cases, Muslim actors or sources were undermined by the structure of the article in which credible white actors or sources had prominence. More positive or balanced minority voices were likely to follow the initial definition of events by white official sources or actors.

With those topics brought into the public domain by Muslims, one may expect more Muslim voices. This was so but they were limited. Said (1978) argued that one of the characteristics of modern Orientalism is that the subjects are not able to represent themselves. This was apparent when credible mediators became necessary to speak on the Muslims' behalf (Runnymede Trust, CRE, Sarwar's lawyer) (van Dijk 1991). The situation was particularly difficult when the actors were categorized as criminals or terrorists. The illegal status of terrorists allows government policy to set the terms of reporting by placing boundaries on interviewing in the 'public interest' (Officials Secrets Act, Prevention of Terrorism Act). Evidence based on research on the reporting of Northern Ireland showed that an 'atmosphere of caution' prevailed in which journalists were aware of what was appropriate and acceptable (Miller 1994: 57). However, incidents of foreign terrorism make it is even more likely that the press will work in allegiance with the state to achieve ideological coherence and protect democratic interests.

By criminalizing the Muslim actors in these articles, their voices lost credibility and sympathy was promoted for the groups who were seen to be protecting social order. The lack of Muslims in official positions reinforced an idea of their place in society.

Does this reliance on unsympathetic sources mean that the articles reproduced their perspectives? This often depends on the main actors selected to put forward their point of view. An examination of the Sarwar coverage illustrated this point (Table 3.7).

Table 3.7   Frequency of actors quoted in coverage of Sarwar case

	Times	Guardian	Mail	Sun	Total
Labour Party: official	6	5	5	1	17
Unofficial/unnamed	8	4	1		13
Other parties' MPs	6	4	1	1	12
Total politicians	20	13	7	2	42
Sarwar/spokesman	5	1	3		9
Police	2				2
Sarwar's supporters	1	4			5
Community members	1				1
News of the World	1				1
Other	2				2
Total official sources	25	13	7	2	47
Total other sources	7	5	3	0	15

Note: Sarwar was included as an unofficial source because his perspective was seen to be coming from outside the Party.

Three times as many official actors were quoted as unofficial. The majority of these were MPs who were critical of Sarwar. Unnamed Labour MPs were involved in unofficial 'leaks' for the government, which was unable to condemn Sarwar unless he was found guilty. This aided what Said (1978: 129) calls 'subjective restructure' whereby sources are used to speak for the paper while it continues to appear objective, in this case functioning as mitigation for the government, reinforcing its policy of 'tough action' while it awaited further evidence before acting. Actors and sources were therefore extremely limited and confined to a tight framework around institutional perspectives.

Correspondents covering these stories included the education, political and Scottish correspondents for articles about Sarwar, the home affairs correspondent for coverage of blasphemy, and foreign affairs correspondents for fundamentalism and the Sarah Cook story. No specialist religious correspondents were used, which could only have contributed to the lack of understanding of the important and sensitive aspects (of religious belief) involved.

Nationality/ethnicity

While there was an overall tendency to homogenize Muslims, there was some differentiation in the discourse based on constructions of nationality or ethnicity. Most British Muslims have their origins in South Asia. These origins may not be attended to where stories involve collectivities or cannot be implicated in behaviour (blasphemy and education). However, where personification and racialization were feasible, there was a tendency to link behaviour to the stereotypical characteristics of an ethnic group. While Muslims were criminalized, Muslims involved in crimes traditionally applied to black minority groups of a violent, physical nature such as mugging were not especially newsworthy. By applying these racialized discourses, Muslim identity was bound up with ethnic identity and stories were selected that showed groups acting 'true' to their 'nature'. Shifts in representation also occurred with political agendas, with sleaze and fundamentalism being more topical at this time than mugging. Figure 3.6 shows a simplified diagram of ideological groupings of Muslims in the press based on apparent national origins/ethnicity.

Figure 3.6 **National/ethnic ideological groupings according to the British press**

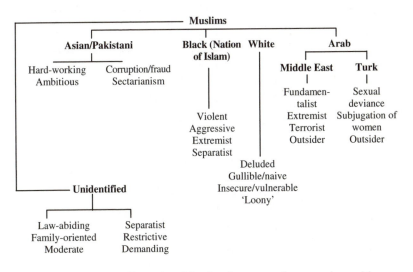

These could be differentiated further in terms of economic position, the poor or wealthy Pakistani, for example, or the differences between Iranian, Saudi, Egyptian and Middle Eastern dissidents. Arabs were constructed as having their citizenship outside the UK, with the result that British citizens with origins in the Middle East were barely visible in the press (Yuval-Davis and Silverman 1998).

Table 3.8 Most prevalent discourses in reporting British Islam

Relationships	Education	Blasphemy	Fundamentalism	Sarwar
Orientalism			**	*
Sexuality				*
Primitivism				→
Gender	*			*
Generation				
Criminality/illegality	*	*	**	**
Irrationality				→
Immorality				
Naiveté			*	**
Foreign element			**	**
Homogeneity				→
Restriction			→	
Manipulation			**	**
Threat to values				→
Insincerity				→
Nation				→
History		**		
Loyalty				→
Multiculturalism		**		
Participation		**		**
Separatism		**		
Economy				→
Absolutism				→
Anti anti-racism		**		**
Identity		**		**
			Physical threat	
				Sectarianism

Key
The discourse runs through each topic →
A large part of the discourse on this topic **
An element in the discourse of this topic *

Table 3.8 shows how this occurred in relation to the topics analysed here and identifies the discourse most prevalent in the reporting of British Islam. It clearly shows the different treatment of events according to the degree of foreign element in them. Where a topic constituted an entirely British focus, it contained a discourse of nation and identity, whereas topics with a foreign element relied more heavily on an Orientalist discourse. However, this clearly showed the evaluation of Muslims in terms of primitivism, deviance, disruption and irrationality, and as intransigent yet perfidious.

However, despite these ethnic and national divisions, the results showed an intersection of discourses relating to Muslim identity. In this chapter I have explored each topic separately and the discourses emerging within these rather than deal with the significant discourses and provide examples from each topic. This holistic approach in presenting the data has been necessary not only because it is difficult to separate complex overlapping threads of discourse but also because texts should be examined in the context of similar texts because the accumulation of meaning is important. However, the inter-textuality of meaning across topics was clearly illustrated here, providing us with a full 'representational paradigm' of British Islam (Hamilton 1997).

Coverage in the *Sun*

Apart from its stylistic differences, the *Sun* showed little interest in minority issues, with coverage being minimal (see Table 3.9). There was some parity with the news values of other papers, particularly with respect to foreign news, in which its Oriental discourse emphasized the aggressive, authoritarian nature of Islam and alluded to Arab sexuality. Its headlines tended to be actor focal, making transivity clear, for example, 'Muslim fanatics butcher 30 Algerians' (27 August). The paper gave more space to stories about relationships, Princess Diana having particular commercial value for the tabloids, and sex, for example 'Saudi Prince obsessed with Brigitte Nielsen' (24 June). Only the Saudi nurses reached the front page. The type of topics covered revealed the *Sun*'s populist rather than strategic discourse, and meant that, for example, the issue of 'fundamentalism' in the UK was rarely covered (Halliday 1996).

Coverage of British Islam was mainly included for its entertainment value and comical effect, which trivialized Muslim beliefs through ridicule. In their analysis of the *Sun*'s coverage of environmentalism, Lacey and Longman (1997), found that the paper's major tool in build-ing 'a culture of (mis)understanding is humour'. They suggested that humour and lack of interest encourages a culture of avoidance, relieving the individual of any responsibility for understanding any problems society faces. The number of puns used in the (limited) text illustrated

Table 3.9   Topics covered in the *Sun*, 1997

	International news	*Domestic coverage*
January	Saudi nurses (3 articles). Islamic punishment in Chechnya	
March		Mother 'furious' at Muslim tattoo on son (painted on at school)
April	Muslims die in pilgrimage fires	Eubank in Muslim dress. Speculation over Princess Diana's relationship with heart surgeon, Hasnet Khan.* John Major visits mosque
May	Muslim women fight to cover face on ID cards, France	Sarwar (4 articles)
June	Saudi prince obsessed with Brigitte Nielsen (actress)	'Allah' written in 'Holy Tomato' (2 articles). Education (2 articles)
August	Muslim 'fanatics butcher' 30 Algerians	Relationship between Princess Diana and Dodi Fayed suggesting conversion
Sept.	Saudi nurses (7 articles)	
Dec.		Sarwar
Total articles	15	14

* Not identified as a Muslim.

this: the boxer Chris Eubank (in Muslim dress) was set to 'Mecca an impression' and made a 'handsome Prophet'; when John Major visited a mosque, it was 'Mosque the merrier'. The composition and structure of articles directed the reader to the absurdity of Muslim belief and behaviour, demonstrated by the articles on the 'Holy Tomato'. The headline, 'Muslims queue for a glimpse of amazing "writing",' the inverted commas juxtaposed against a hazy photograph rendering the 'writing' illegible, 'which we have highlighted' and that 'hundreds of Muslims are flocking' to see. These strategies of derision of a (homogenized) group of people encouraged general disrespect for them and their values.

Serious articles functioned to reinforce this and highlighted Muslims' attempts to impose their beliefs on 'us' and provoked opposition to change. This was illustrated by a story about a boy who was given a henna hand painting of an Islamic symbol at school as part of Ramadan celebrations. The headline screamed 'fury at Muslim tattoo', and the grievance of the white parent was attended to with no attempt at balance. In these articles, a strategic pattern had developed that attempted to defend Britain as a Christian country and ensure positive presentation of the in-group. The boy's mother was quoted as saying 'I'm not racist *but* Steven is a Christian' (emphasis added).

The only other articles during this period involving Muslims, though not categorized as such, were about 'curry houses' being incorporated into popular British culture and about cases of discrimination that were anti-Asian. Although the discourse relating to Muslims reflected that of other papers, it was more closed around an Orientalist perspective and delivered through humour. Despite the lack of coverage, the uniformity in the treatment of Muslims resulted in a consistently clear message based on an exclusive agenda that denied Muslims any rights, excluded their voices and perspectives, and championed the rights of the white majority. Given the size of the *Sun*'s readership, more people received this message than any other.

To summarize the main arguments of this chapter:

- Event-led updates allowed the original formulation of the story to be retold, solidifying the discursive interpretation of the newspaper, and adding to its 'regime of truth' (Hall 1992a). For stories in a solely British context, an issue of equity for Muslims was invariably interpreted as Muslims having a politically subversive agenda. Their desire for cultural autonomy was interpreted as separatist and disloyal.
- From an ethnocentric perspective, Muslims were considered to be problematic, their presence and behaviour creating difficulties for the majority population.
- Coverage encoded a view of the world in which Muslims were either passive, subject to the action of others or the proponents of negative actions. Their categorization and construction, for example the criminalizing of Musa Komeagac as a sex offender, dissidents as fundamentalists, and Mohammed Sarwar for fraud and corruption allowed these participants and therefore other Muslims to be subject to state intervention. The high propensity of government action implied that Muslims needed to be managed, either as victims or

troublemakers, allowing for the continuation of prejudicial practices. It therefore delineates, reproduces and concretizes a natural
hierarchy of power relations in society.

- Due to a context in which racism was unacceptable, the press found
  other semantic strategies to discredit Muslims on the basis of flawed
  characteristics.
- In the relational structure of articles (both local and global), Muslim
  behaviour was inextricably linked to their religious identity and thus
  naturalized. This reduced Muslim behaviour to reliance on custom.
  By detailing ritual but not explaining it, Muslims were seen to
  depend on irrational beliefs rather than intellect. The association of
  religiosity with criminality made what was constructed as religious
  absolutism appear fraudulent and therefore manipulative.
- The association between European culture, with its Enlightenment
  history, with modernity, rationality and progression constructed
  Muslims as irrational and primitive.
- Although generally presented as homogenous, particularly within
  the context of one story, certain stereotypical features were highlighted depending on perceived ethnic origins. In the representation
  of Muslims, cultural racism was intertwined with colour racism but
  had its own specificities as identified in the discursive construction
  described here.
- There was greater ideological consensus in coverage the further it
  was removed from the British context.
- The struggle for legitimacy by British Muslims was visible in the
  press as 'the struggle around the image' (Hall 1997a: 257) but
  currently the dominant hegemony was being maintained. Struggles
  existed between elite conservative and liberal groups but there was a
  convergence in the formulations of Muslims. Although the volume
  of coverage was greater in the liberal press, the readership of the
  conservative press was higher. Alternative perspectives rarely went
  unchallenged, were expressed irregularly, in the margins of the
  papers and especially in the unofficial form of letters. Commentary
  was generally used to promote a more populist perspective rather
  than criticism.
- Positive representation was limited to the admiration of values
  important in British culture.
- Muslims were denied the space to represent themselves. Although
  Muslim actors were quoted in the interest of balance, it was less

often and white actors often discredited them. This illustrated the lack of power Muslims had to oppose dominant images.

- The *Guardian* had a greater interest in Muslim issues, was more likely to run stories first and displayed an openness that gave voice to alternative representations. However, its anti-religious and human rights stance meant that Islam (as it understood it) was offensive to its liberal norms. It was therefore more critical of Muslims than other minorities, having a similar framework of interpretation to the other papers.

- The tabloids granted less space to minority issues in general and offered closure in this coverage. Coverage reflected their populist appeal, for example in the focus on relationships. However, while the *Sun* deployed anger or ridicule to highlight the exotic, odd practices of Muslims in order to construct them as outsiders, the *Mail* adopted a more sinister approach to support its anti-immigration discourse.

- *The Times*, while having greater parity with the *Guardian* in terms of the extent of coverage and news values and having more balance than the tabloids, had more discursive equivalence with the *Mail* but with a greater emphasis on the preservation of Christianity.

- Representation also depended on the complex interaction of the political affiliations and interests of papers as well as news production processes. The mobilization of religious identity, therefore, had particular political, ideological intentions that evoked specific discourses and outcomes. However, this was also situated within the 'multilayered construction of social relations' (linked to power) whereby variation and consensus in presentation also occurred because of 'the theorization of difference across a range of levels such as gender, generation and class (Silverman and Yuval-Davis 1998: 13).

Conclusion

Clearly, coverage of British Islam had greater diversity than its international counterpart. Slippages, ambivalences and contradictions existed in a way that prevented a totalizing, homogeneous Islam. The discourse had multitudinal purposes depending on the variety of issues, priorities and loyalties of different sectors of the press, which varied according to events. While there was evidence of aversion towards

Islam, and overall it was possible to say that coverage was negative, this was just as likely to be a result of journalistic practices and uncritical or conservative modes of thought rather than the malicious intention to discredit Muslims. If the (conscious) defamation of Muslims was the primary objective, coverage, even of these topics, might have been a lot more damning. Negative stories in the local press were not generally picked up on (see BMMS for the wealth of stories published in the local press), with the *Mail* mitigating for Sarwar resulting in some positive coverage; there were other factors at play then. Coverage reproduced social and cultural prejudices based on a political, historical conjuncture, which its news values both reflected and helped to construct by reproducing them. Previous research has shown how oppressed minorities tend to focus on their own representation and may sometimes overestimate how Establishment groups are intent on working against them, even to conspiracy level (Sreberny-Mohammadi and Ross 1995). However, it is also recognized that practices of representation take place within a set of (unequal) power relations and even if poor representation is due to subconscious or 'naturalized ideologies', common usage normalizes negative conceptualizations, resulting in the same, significant damaging effects on minority groups (Halloran et al. 1995).

The conceptualization of Islam reported here (as with the quantitative findings) is consistent enough to have a significant impact in creating ignorance with regard to Muslims living in the UK. Societal changes, and the increasing cultural diversity of the UK, are threatening certainties in 'British' perceptions of nation and national identity. To overcome these insecurities, the press emphasizes inherent cultural differences and conflict in order to create symbolic boundaries, which function to keep (illusory) categories of people stable and maintain power relations through the polarization of groups. Press coverage of British Islam represents a project intent on 'cultural closure' (Kristeva 1982 in Hall 1997b).[54] By attempting to establish a common culture, such discourse, in perpetuating the belief that Muslims are wholly different, excludes Muslims from this constructed 'Britishness'. It further attempts to limit Muslim power in the public sphere by presenting problematic issues as resolved.

The lack of publicly responsible discourse has made recourse to law necessary for Muslims, yet this action was interpreted as intolerance of British majority values, which renders Muslims unsympathetic with other readers. For those who have gained access to public life, the negative and controversial are highlighted (Sarwar). The hijacking of these Muslim initiated events and redefinition of their meaning and therefore history, represented a desire, whether conscious or sub-conscious, to reassert control in a period of substantial upheaval. However, the force of change, the need to appear democratic and egalitarian, opened up spaces for the participation of Muslims. Muslim groups are increasingly becoming a substantial lobbying force along the channels expected by liberal society although this does not yet represent a dialogue among equals. Press reaction to these specifically British issues illustrated their difficulty with pluralism or, in the *Guardian*'s case, with incorporating Muslims within it. Some Muslims, then, who voiced cynicism about the motivations for positive policy and presen-tation, which they saw as community appeasement, had good reason to do so. However, these spaces of positive representation offer insights into what may come as societal tensions and struggles in public life increasingly challenge the dominance of hegemonic interpretations.

At present, Muslims appear out of all groups to be the current target for the projection of the 'bad self' in society (Gilman 1985), responsible for its corrupting elements.[55] This emerged in a political context in which the perceived separatism of Muslims constituted them as both a symbolic and a socioeconomic threat. However, the argument cannot be that there is one real Islam against which press coverage is misrepre-sented. Rather, the point is that press coverage reduces the rich variety of Muslim people's lives in all their complexities to a few 'reductive categories' (Said 1978) that have come to represent a fairly homo-genous Islam to the British public. This identity appears to override other demographic factors in association with stereotypical topics (having a specific ideological function). According to Trew (1979: 142), once 'an image and set of terms is established ... [it] provides a basic model which can be deployed again and again as the organizing theme in a cumulative shaping of social perception.'

Although this analysis does not provide the full repertoire of imagery on British Islam (incorporating only a section of the press and therefore media), the evidence suggests there is considerable consistency in terms of the discourse routinely employed to represent British Muslims.

4. Interpreting Islam

I n this chapter I examine how social meanings are produced in the interaction between text and audience. By involving audiences in this study of the meanings of Islam and Muslims, we are able to discover how far audiences share the discourse of the press and the variety of socio-cultural factors important in the decoding of mediated information. If it is assumed that the images people have of Islam and Muslims 'stem from the interplay of beliefs, desires and dispositions with both media and non-media experiences and these "mixes" and the influences will vary' (Halloran and Nightingale 1982: 62), what are the factors involved that result in differential decodings? The main focus of interest here is cultural proximity, based on the hypothesis that knowledge, first-hand experience or familiarity with Muslims undermines negative stereotypes and results in a struggle over meaning.

Approach

Hall's (1980) encoding/decoding model of reception, which will be used here, assumed that while there may be 'preferred meanings' embedded within a text, namely a dominant message or messages, the reading of the message(s) will be dependent on a number of variables.[1] This theory shifted audience studies away from the traditional behaviourist 'effects' model to argue that meaning is produced in the meeting and interaction between text and audience. According to Hall's semiotic model, if different moments in the communication chain in which encoding and decoding take place are asymmetrical, a 'lack of equivalence' ensues, resulting in differential understandings of the text. Hence, the focus is on what audiences bring to texts, their 'interpretative frameworks', rather than what the media do to the audience.

Hall's (1980) model has been criticized for its limited range and 'overtly political' decoding positions, and the 'premature closure of the text' with its 'preferred reading' (Cruz and Lewis 1994; Wren-Lewis

1983: 187). Debate continues to abound over the level of openness or closure of texts. Fiske (1986) has been particularly influential in his work on television, which suggests that texts are polysemous, open to variant readings. However, I would support Hall's conception of 'structured polysemy', that 'all meanings do not exist equally in the message, it has been structured in dominance' (Morley 1980: 10). Texts, as discursive formations embedded in the social structure, limit our understanding and knowledge of the social world. While ideology does then attempt to fix meaning in order to maintain hegemony, meaning is never finally fixed, even after the meeting of text and audience.

The usefulness of the model is in its advocacy of textual analysis, which allows for an examination of the extent to which the determinants of meaning are inscribed within or are external to the text, and which variables are important to our understanding of Muslims, paying particular attention, in this case, to cultural proximity on which the hypothesis is based. It is also a useful starting point from which a range of variant interpretations can be examined. However, the criticisms outlined above have been taken account of in the implementation of the research.

Sample

If direct experience of Muslims is the main factor of interest for interpreting newspaper messages (about Muslims), an in-depth and flexible approach is necessary. Focus groups were therefore selected as an appropriate method because of the importance of examining the social context of public understandings; focus groups are a socially orientated research procedure. The participants were selected on the basis of purposive sampling with the aim of constructing groups that were as internally homogeneous as was feasible (although this is never entirely possible) to limit the number of variables at play and to focus on cultural proximity. As the central comparative aspect was familiarity with and knowledge and experience of Muslims, the groups (two in each category) consisted of:

- Muslims; non-Muslims who mixed frequently with Muslims (contact group); and non-Muslims who had no frequent contact with Muslims (non-contact group);
- the same age group (16–18) recruited through local sixth form

colleges. Youth groups were chosen because of recent arguments surrounding the revival of religious identities and political activism in young Muslims (see Conclusion for a full discussion of this). I also considered that these young people are the adults of tomorrow, the future for British Muslims.[2] Their views were therefore the most relevant for anticipating future attitudes to and the place of these groups in society;

- mixed gender in the non-Muslim groups held in their 'natural' state, namely classroom-based. The Muslim groups were single sex, one group each of women and men, following discussions with Muslim women who insisted on this condition because of the cultural norms monitoring mixing between genders. The Muslim groups, therefore, were amalgamated from existing networks. The nature of these groups therefore reflected the social networks in which they moved. It was hoped that this would result in an atmosphere in which individuals felt happy about disclosing their opinions, that is with like-minded people. However, this resulted in participants with varying ethnic backgrounds assembled together in the non-Muslim (contact) groups, having some restraining effects on discussing cultural and racial issues; and

- participants from in and around the area of Leicester in the East Midlands, although with different socioeconomic positionings. The Muslim participants were mainly from an economically disadvantaged inner city area of Leicester, although they were well educated. Most of the contact group were from an urban middle-class area, also well educated and they expressed liberal views. The non-contact group were from an economically wealthy rural area and they expressed conservative values.

Leicester is known to have a particularly harmonious model of race relations. Although there were no statistics on its Muslim population, the last census (1991) showed that the Asian population accounted for 23.7 per cent of its total population (270,493) and that 78 per cent of the Asians were Indian (60,297). In 1991 there were 2644 Pakistanis and 1053 Bangladeshis, a total of 3697, 1.4 per cent of the total population. This is likely to have grown considerably in the last ten years. The Asian population appeared to have a high level of participation in both the community and economy.[3] However, these statistics did not reveal the level of occupation held by these groups or differentiate the Muslim experience. Because of the local level and small scale of this research, I would not wish to apply a 'falsely universalizing theory' that obscures the diversity of Muslim groups (Harding 1986). Rather than attempting to generalize, this research offers 'a glimpse of culture' that could then be 'set in systematic relationship to other glimpses' (Fiske 1994: 195).

The groups were asked to participate on the basis that the research was about finding out opinions and reactions to newspaper articles. I thought that to reveal the full research purpose would affect the results, although this became somewhat clearer to the participants, particularly to the Muslim groups, when the texts were exposed and discussion commenced.

Each group was presented with a newspaper text. The texts selected were:

- Relationships: The end of the marriage: Sarah Cook: *Mail*, 11 August 1997, p. 17 (analysed qualitatively in Chapter 3: 109–16, Figure 4.1).
- Rushdie/blasphemy: proposals for the introduction of laws on religious discrimination: *Mail*, 30 July 1997, p. 13 (analysed in Chapter 3: 135–6, Figure 4.2).
- Education: funding for two Muslim schools is granted: *Guardian*, 10 January 1998, p. 7 (Chapter 3: 126–7, Figure 4.3).
- Fundamentalism: Egypt accuses Britain of protecting Islamic militants following the attacks at the temple of Hatshepsut, Luxor: *The Times*, 24 November 1997, p. 12 (Chapter 3: 145–6, 149, Figure 4.4).

It was thought that these would provide a range of the discourses circulating in press coverage of these topics, both positive and negative, from a variety of newspapers. While a text was chosen for each of these topics, time limited the amount presented to each group (see Table 4.1).

The participants were first asked to recount the subject matter of the story and give their reactions to it, initially individually in written form, followed by a group discussion. This allowed for an examination of restraining effects and consensus building within the group. Conforming to the group norm can be a particular problem with teenagers (Smith 1977) and some minority groups in which there is a high expectation of conformity among peers. Subjects such as race where

Figure 4.1 **Sarah Cook in the *Mail*, © 11 August 1997 (I thank the *Daily Mail* for permission to use this material)**

Figure 4.2 **Blasphemy, *Mail*, © 30 July 1997 (I thank the *Daily Mail* for permission to use this material)**

Figure 4.3 Education, *Guardian*, © 10 January 1998 (I thank the *Guardian* and Gary Weaser for permission to use this material)

Britain 'protecting Egyptian militants'

By CHRISTOPHER WALKER, MIDDLE EAST CORRESPONDENT

Mubarak views a Nubian statue at the new Nubia Museum in Aswan yesterday

THE GREAT CHRISTMAS AIRFARE SALE

London is not terror haven, say ministers

Figure 4.4 **Fundamentalism, *The Times*, 24 November 1997, ©
Times Newspapers Limited (I thank *The Times* for permission to
use this material)**

Table 4.1   Implementation of focus groups

Group category	Muslim (men)	Muslim (women)	Non-Muslim groups with contact		Non-Muslim groups, non contact	
			A	B	A	B
Number of sessions	2	3	2	2	1	1
Length of sessions (hrs)	1½	1	1	1	2	2
Topics covered (see above)	1 & 2	All 4	2 & 3	1 & 2	1 & 2	3
Number in each group	6	6	12	9	9	7
Total number of participants in category		12		21		16

there is significant approval/public consensus for a particular discourse (anti-racism) often constrains people in exposing private views. However, using pre-existing groups does enable participants to offer each other mutual support in expressing feelings that deviate from mainstream culture, a 'safety in numbers' effect, particularly important for marginal groups.

Further background information, including political/religious affiliation and media usage, was also gathered in the form of a questionnaire (see Appendix C for tabulated data). This allowed the self-designation of ethnic origin and other aspects of identity such as linguistic. This information was gathered in recognition of the heterogeneity of Muslims and self-designation was thought the best method for allowing for the expression of diverse conceptions of complex ethnicity.

This information provided an idea of how the groups were socially situated in terms of the variables considered to be of interest to this research. Attending to these variables allowed for an examination of the interconnections between these forms of differentiation and the meanings generated here through the interaction of text and audience. What, then, were the implications of press coverage for non-Muslims, particularly for those who had little contact with Muslims? What were the implications for Muslims who might have been drawn into a dialectical negotiation of identity? What were the consequences of this limited framework of representation? Did they matter? In this chapter I attempt to address these questions.

Perceptions of Islam: prevalent discourse

Before analysing the different reading positions of the groups, in this section I briefly examine the discourse generated in the groups' discussions about Islam and Muslims, both in response to the texts and their more general knowledge. Specialized computer software that provided information about the number of positive and negative sentences spoken on each topic by each group allowed for the identification of the focus and tone of discussions (Table 4.2).[4] This should not solely be

Table 4.2   Discourse generated in relation to Islam and Muslims (figures represent number of sentences spoken about each topic)

Perceptions	Total Pos	Total Neg	Muslims Pos	Muslims Neg	Contact Pos	Contact Neg	No-contact Pos	No-contact Neg	Total text units
Women	6	87	5	51	1	24	0	12	93
Islamophobia	5	36	3	20	2	16	0	0	41
Segregation	10	59	3	6	2	29	5	24	69
Restrictive	5	115	3	60	2	37	0	18	120
Homogeneity	31	109	22	80	0	17	9	12	140
Conversion	28	63	19	42	0	18	9	3	91
Aggression	3	113	3	55	0	51	0	7	116
Cultural diffs	5	160	1	59	2	52	2	49	165
Westernized	22	4	11	2	6	2	5	0	26
Foreign	2	61	0	34	0	7	2	20	63
Threat	10	43	10	22	0	20	0	1	53
Primitive/tradition	90	102	90	29	0	62	0	11	192
The Other	2	40	0	0	0	0	2	40	42
Wealth	0	15	0	0	0	0	0	15	15
Poor	0	9	0	0	0	0	0	9	9
Acceptance	6	0	0	0	6	0	0	0	6
Illegality	0	25	0	7	0	8	0	10	25
Other	0	13	0	0	0	13	0	0	13
Total	223	1054	87	445	21	321	34	228	1277

relied upon as evidence, for the sentences may differ in size. However, what it did provide was an indication of the time spent on and hence the importance of the topic to a group. It could therefore be used in combination with qualitative analysis to illustrate and confirm findings.

It is evident that the amount of negative discourse clearly outweighed the positive. The negative statements Muslims made dealt with how they thought they were perceived by majority groups and in the media, particularly in relation to restrictive and aggressive images, Muslim women and the Rushdie affair. They were concerned about the media failing to explain their values properly and about the effects this might have on both the faithful and majority population. This negative perception had been found in previous research with minority groups and, as I have found here, their fears were realized in the perceptions of the majority (Gunter and Viney 1993).

Although Muslims were similarly positioned by the texts in terms of the topics discussed, they were more likely to reject these images and transcode their meanings into positive ones. They felt proud of Islam's growth, values and tradition. Conversion and Islam's unified nature were awarded positive attributes while non-Muslims discussed these subjects in negative terms. This constituted a defensive reaction to accusations directed towards Islam, an attempt to educate the non-Muslim researcher and a means of justifying opinions. It was evident that most reactions to texts were based on the value of preserving their own tradition. To these Muslims, upholding the values of Islam was more important than any of the values the Western press espoused, such as mixing in school, romantic love, freedom of speech and other tokens of Western identity like their clothes. It should be noted that the Muslim interpretations were not based on a 'real Islam' but were subjective interpretations in a specific historical context.

From these data, it appears that non-Muslims who have no contact with Muslims are more likely to discuss Muslims positively than those with contact. This was partly due to their attempts to offer alternative solutions to actions in the texts with which they disagreed, for example separate schooling, or was based on their interpretation of the text on another level of difference such as age. Some, for example, felt that Sarah Cook's conversion was 'up to her' because they disliked the imposition of authority. They also perceived the Westernization of minorities as positive.

Non-Muslims who had contact with Muslims tended to make more negative statements mainly because they had more knowledge available to them on which to comment and because of their liberal positions. This was evidence that knowledge does not always produce positive values. They articulated concerns about Muslim aggression, the threat of Islam and its backwardness. The Rushdie affair to them was a poignant example of the threat to freedom of speech, which was continuing through attempts to introduce what they perceived as primitive laws (blasphemy). They were also more aware of Islamophobia. The non-contact group showed little awareness of these issues. Having little knowledge of Muslims, and being largely unable to differentiate between minority groups, their discourse was dominated by cultural differences and the alien character of the Other, as well as by the impact their presence had on the UK economy, which they discussed in wider terms.

In particular, these texts provoked widespread concern about the treatment of women, segregation, the restrictive nature of Islam (which was slightly more for those with contact, again relating to the more conservative outlook of the non-contact group) and cultural conflict. What was beginning to emerge here, in the non-Muslim groups, was not only patterns of understanding that reflected dominant meanings of Islam but also discourse that had currency in different newspapers and among the social groups that consumed them, strongly illustrating the reproduction and circulation of discourse in society.[5] Not only this, but these were collective perceptions, which constituted the groups as 'interpretive communities'. These patterns of interpretation are illustrated strongly in relation to the texts in the following section.

Readings

How did the participants make meaning from these media texts and what interpretive strategies, scripts and frameworks of understanding were used for sense making? Not all these texts, however, contained dominant meanings; in this case it will be read that the texts chosen were oppositional or negotiated with dominant meanings, and the subject position a person then took in relation to the text might, for example, have been oppositional to its preferred meanings while reflecting the dominant meanings in society.

Table 4.3 provides clear evidence of the variant readings by different groups with Muslims mainly occupying oppositional positions and the non-contact groups accepting the preferred readings (the figures represent the number of statements made by each group within each subject position). The qualitative data support this evidence.

The *Guardian* text on education, with its more positive position towards Muslims, was in the main responsible for the more surprising results. For example, 46 of the 49 oppositional statements the non-contact group made were in response to this article. Muslims made only five oppositional statements in relation to this text. Most of these were made in relation to the other more negative texts, while the non-contact group made only three oppositional responses to these.

Table 4.3   Subject position of audience groups in relation to texts

Status	Preferred	Negotiates	Oppositional
Muslims	68	70	182
Contact	150	61	33
Non-contact	203	41	49

Muslim men

Muslim men fitted more neatly into an oppositional position than their female counterparts. They were more likely to have a political conscience, were media literate and read texts as ideological, rejecting them on this basis. However, there were still slight differences between them, reflected in the papers they read, which indicated a more critical perspective. The broadsheet readers were less likely to be positioned by the text in any way. Due to their specific identities as *British* Muslims, these groups did not automatically or always remain in oppositional mode. When the values in the text matched their own (marrying age), they were more likely to accept dominant meanings.

It is fair to say that with the blasphemy article this group took almost an entirely oppositional position. However, the text's macro-structural organization worked to position the subjects into discussing blasphemy rather than religious discrimination. It had an agenda setting effect then, even with this group, who rejected the dominant meanings. The men were much more vocal and emotionally opposed to Rushdie, and they focused their discussion on this aspect of the article. They resisted the text's meanings, arguing that he committed the ultimate sin in betraying his religion, that the book should have been banned, and that Christians were hypocritical in allowing him to criticize Islam and would not allow the same treatment of their religion. They also felt that Islamophobia did exist, that the laws should exist as a point of equality, and that minorities had a right to their religion and other rights despite being a minority. They rejected the representation of Muslims and their reaction to Rushdie's book. However, although they expressed their disapproval of the way the protest against the book was handled, they felt that recourse to these methods was inevitable because Muslims had no other way of voicing their objections in this country. They also objected to the sole focus on Islam in relation to blasphemy and argued that there should be limits to freedom of speech when it was offensive to others.

An initial response to the article as being fairly balanced by some of the less media literate of the group was based on the presence of positive quotes. They were positioned by the text to identify government support for the laws but responded positively in opposition to the intended response. They accepted arguments regarding the unworkability of the law but this was based more on their experiences of the race laws than on textual references, although Northern Ireland was selected as an example from the text. However, because of their opposition to the text, they were more likely to use experience as a resource for resistance.

With the Cook article, however, they accepted more elements of the message (due to cultural distance from Turkey and symmetrical values with the paper). Here they were positioned by the article's representation of the parents' irresponsibility (in taking money for the story) and by the framing of the relationship as a holiday romance:

> *Akbar*: 'Oh come on, if a 12-year-old girl goes on holiday and falls in love with the waiter, it is just a crush if you think about it at the end of the day, a 12-year-old girl and her parents taking her seriously about wanting to marry him and with there being such a distance.'

However, they remained cynical about the article, believing it to be culturally biased, and concentrated on discussing this, attending to the specifics of the article for a much shorter time than any other group. In opposition to the text, they placed more emphasis on the Cooks being at fault rather than the Turk and reacted positively to their conversions:

> *Interviewer*: 'It does say that she still is a Muslim and her parents have converted.'

Iqbal: 'That shows something about Islam, about someone else becoming Muslim in the household yeah and people saying something about Islam in the household and thinking, there's something about this religion.'

Mohsin: 'And she's turned two people to become a Muslim and his family have become Muslim.'

Akbar: 'And this guy Mr Cook, he's turned into a Muslim as well.'

However, they recognized the preferred meaning in the texts and how conversion was usually portrayed. This was mainly concerning elites or as a result of force, resulting in cultural oppression and featured as a means of selling more papers as a point of curiosity by non-Muslims:

Ahmed: 'When Jemima Goldsmith married Imran Khan that was in the papers as well.'

Iqbal: 'Yeah, they were saying that she had to wear a scarf.'

Ahmed: 'Saying how she had to stay in the house.'

Iqbal: 'It's oppression like, just because people wear scarves in this country or people abide by Islam.'

They were also able to show quite easily how the structure revealed its ideological bias. Their awareness of and experience of cultural bias provided them with situation models that made them much more dismissive of both articles. The men, then, focused much more on discussing dominant images of Islam in the form of fanaticism, misogyny, cultural incompatibility, and the perceived threat of Islam in order to reject them:

Akbar: 'At present all I see in the media about Muslims is some geezer getting blown up in a bus or some geezer shouting at somebody else or some women crying.'

Interviewer: 'So why do you think the press are particularly hostile towards Muslims?'

Akbar: 'It's like the fastest growing religion in the world yeah and the colonies are gone, everything's gone and this is like a danger for them now, innit? That's what it is. But if you really think about Islam, it is not about danger, it is not about …'

Mohammed: 'Islam gives you a choice.'

Akbar: 'It is not about to take over the world.'

Mohammed: 'They don't say to people you become a Muslim, they give the choice to people, that's what it is based on.'

Muslim women

The women were much more conformist than their male counterparts. They therefore focused more on responding to questions than pursuing their own agenda. Their desire to portray a reasonable face of Islam was reflected in cautious answers to questions, careful wording and showing awareness of alternative perspectives. They also showed less awareness of news and political issues in general and less media literacy, so were therefore more likely to accept messages within the texts than the men.

Although mainly positioned oppositionally to texts due to their awareness of bias towards Muslims and Muslim identification, they did, however, slip in and out of preferred, oppositional and negotiated positions on the basis of similarly held values or cultural proximity.

In particular, their gender positioned them in opposition to the Cook article. It was its representation of Islam's treatment of women to which they most fervently objected:

Sadia: 'And they basically emphasize that Islam is oppressive and it oppresses women and they keep them in the house, nothing but housewife, no freedom, no freewill. So horrible.'

Shabana: 'The only reason why Islam says that it is not OK, it's OK for them to work but Islam gives women protection and the Western people and the media don't seem to understand that and it projects a very bad image of Islam.'

They also resisted the preferred meanings by attributing the responsibility to Sarah, responding positively to conversion, suggesting that Musa's point of view was excluded and objecting to the use of the term 'Moslem' throughout.

Like the men, they articulated oppositional responses to the blasphemy article. However, their reading of this article illustrated their weaker political identities. They interpreted the article as positive (that is supporting the laws) in response to the event, even though they disagreed with views expressed in it. They were much more cautious in their responses, presenting both sides, speaking in neutral tones and in the third party to avoid controversy. They did not linger on political issues for long, preferring to focus on faith:

> *Amina*: 'All I know is that he (Rushdie), that a lot of people hate him but equally right, a lot of people do follow him and he's been in the news quite a lot.'

> *Shabana*: 'Well, if you are looking at it from Western eyes you could say that it was his opinion and that he did have the freedom of speech but if you see it from a religious perspective and that is any religion right, you would probably say like he should not have slandered it writing contradictory things about Islam and that.'

Although their memories of the Rushdie affair on television correlated closely with media images such as marches and book burning, they objected to this representation. Responses illustrated how reality is viewed from one's own perspective. Here, a participant articulated a belief that the majority of people objected to Rushdie's book:

> *Aisha*: 'If 10 per cent of the people don't like it then that's all right but if 90 per cent of the population don't like it then there has got to be something done about it.'

These responses illustrated the importance of religious identification in framing the interpretation of the Muslims. However, differential points of identification resulted in preferred readings. Their symmetrical values (with the text) led them to agree that Sarah Cook was too young to rush into a marriage. Equally, they stressed the importance of parental responsibility. They were positioned by the Cook text into discussing the actors as they were categorized in the article in terms of age, nationality, and vocation (waiter), and by the blasphemy article by interpreting the law as being exclusive to Islam (also possibly due to the focus on their own collectivities).

Cultural distance was also a factor in accepting dominant meanings. Although they rejected the meanings in the text that implicated Islam, in the Cook article their ignorance of Turkish culture meant that they accepted the events but suggested that they resulted from cultural practices, thus making a 'religion–ethnic culture distinction' (Jacobson 1997: 240). This negotiation with the text shows how cultural distance applies to British Muslims and how Islam alone cannot be taken as a means of opposing representations of it. Knowledge is an important factor in resisting meanings.

The importance of cultural proximity was especially apparent in the Muslims' response to *The Times* text on fundamentalism. In this article, the meanings were multifaceted, with the paper's position shifting in response to various aspects of the event. The Muslims too had to negotiate with the awareness they had, objecting to aspects of the text and to being anchored by others because of their 'conflicting points of identity' (Hall 1992b). They voiced dissent in relation to the stereotypes of Islam and violence. They interpreted the funding of Middle Eastern groups as suggesting that the Middle East was poor and they objected to this, as well as to the idea that these groups were a threat to the UK. However, they agreed with the president that 'killers' should not be allowed to reside in Britain, but suggested that these charges were not supported with evidence. They disapproved of the killings but dissociated them from Islam:

> *Aisha*: 'Yes, I think he's right, he shouldn't let, Britain shouldn't let killers live here because it is not right. If somebody has killed someone, they should serve their time for what they've done. In Islam it says that as well. You shouldn't kill no-one for no reason really.'

They associated the behaviour with other factors:

> *Shabana*: 'They just make blunt points that every terrorist is to do with Islam and sometimes it is not. It's just to do with personal views you know or feuds between people,'

and showed caution about criticizing Muslims at all:

Amina: 'I can't really say that they are wrong because I don't know much about it; if we were to say something about our religion, that's not right, 'cos we don't really have the knowledge to say anything about it, I think we'd be saying something wrong.'

This illustrated how Muslims were inclined to oppose dominant meanings because of their knowledge and experience of cultural bias, but often lacked the specific knowledge to do so. However, this lack of knowledge forced them to engage in a different interpretive strategy. They refocused attention in the article away from the Islamic militants to the theme of *Western interference* in foreign affairs:

Farzana: 'It's like every time there's something goes wrong in a different country, other countries always get involved with what's going on there; they don't leave it to that country to sort it out so it's like too many people get involved in what's going on and then they start accusing people of doing this and doing that so it's not really right.'

This is evidence that people, no matter what material they are given, will at least attempt to formulate meanings that are symmetrical to their own ideologies, even if these appear unsatisfactory and unstable. They used the textual information provided to construct their own meanings, as with attempts to shift the blame for funding to non-Muslim groups. Where a lack of knowledge (of the foreign situation) prevented a rejection of the dominant discourse, British Muslims were exonerated:

Aisha: 'They (the media) just think about what's going on outside of, they don't think about the Muslims here because the Muslims here are really nice and nobody really causes no trouble here, so they just think about what's going on in the Middle East but that's not got nothing to do with Britain 'cos we're not causing nothing over here; we're just living here and doing what we are told to do really.'

Tensions are felt because global mediations of Islam challenge the Muslim reader's experience of Islam in Britain (Ahmed and Donnan 1994). The result is often an anti-local response based on 'kinship' ties that are derived from common experiences of oppression (Gardner and Shukur 1994). According to Jacobson (1997: 254), this 'universalism' provides a 'means of dealing with the ambiguities and contradictions contained within their social environment'.

A further illustration of the complexity of meaning production was in the responses to the *Guardian* text on the funding of Muslim schools. This text negotiated with dominant meanings by supporting the schools and equality for Muslims but introduced an element of doubt through the idea of segregation in accordance with its liberal ideology. Texts then, as well as audiences, are sites of contradictions and tension. The group viewed the text as balanced or positive but not ideological. For them, ideology or bias was associated only with negative representations of Islam. Thus, their responses were oppositional in relation to dominant meanings but in this case correlated with the preferred meanings of the text, supporting funded Muslim schools. The responses to this text illustrated the activity of cultural proximity to the full. Representation was based solely on British Muslims and this allowed a straightforward interpretation based on first-hand knowledge and experience. The point of view represented in the article was naturalized to the Muslims as it represented their own commonsensical perspective. The presence of this article in the groups showed how ideology only becomes apparent when it is in opposition to the readers' ideologies. This was further illustrated by the Muslims' selection of Ray Honeyford's quote in relation to segregation, which *was* seen as biased:

> '*Ray Honeyford*: "I think it is highly unlikely that these schools will attract non-Muslim children and that means separating children not only by religion but by race".'

The inclusion of references to the national curriculum to avert fears about teaching standards were interpreted as a concern by the Muslims who suggested that this might lead to the compromising of Islamic values, illustrating their more extreme position in relation to dominant values compared with that of the paper.

Non-Muslims: contact group

The variable of cultural proximity appeared also to be applicable here because these groups, living in a multicultural environment, displayed a liberal tolerant attitude towards other ethnic groups.[6] They therefore found themselves in a position of negotiation with these texts, for they held strong beliefs on equality and anti-discrimination. However, their liberal ideologies were in direct opposition to how they perceived Islam: as an antiquated religion. This appeared to be based mainly on media representations, for they had failed to become familiar with the complex identities of their ethnic friends. The struggle to reconcile these beliefs was apparent throughout. They were therefore positioned mainly in line with preferred and dominant meanings, which in this context were appropriate to their liberalism.

These groups had both a high political and cultural awareness and a high degree of media literacy. This allowed them to recognize the ideology in the texts, including to some extent the cultural bias. However, their knowledge (in this area) lacked the depth and understanding that would allow them to counter consistent and stereotypical images that had taken such a hold on meanings of Islam. This was particularly apparent with the Cook article where both groups accepted all aspects of the preferred meaning. There was a slight variation in the groups between those who read the article completely symmetrically and those who showed more critical ability. The former were more likely to read tabloid papers, use TV as a source of news and have right of centre views, and the latter were more likely to be regular readers of broadsheets, show an interest in the news and have liberal left of centre political views. Although these participants tried to examine reasons for actions other than those offered by the text, the group dynamic and lack of alternative information secured their positioning.

These groups' political awareness was particularly apparent in the discussion on blasphemy. They were able to discuss things at a high level, introducing related ideas from outside the text, showing evidence of having discussed such topics before, yet their liberal ideologies secured their positioning within the freedom of speech, non-censorship perspective:

> *Mike*: 'I think the first problem is defining religion, which seems to me impossible ... well I'd say religion was impossible to define. You could say militant atheism is a religion and if militant atheism is a religion then clearly it's (the law) nonsense.'

Their interest in and knowledge of politics led them to interpret the article as more about a political battle than faith (and argue that it was politically biased in support of Labour). Again, the text positioned the group to focus almost solely on blasphemy, associating only Muslims with the new laws:

> *Jody*: 'The article is about a law brought about because somebody wrote a book criticizing the Muslims' religion.'

The group supported and proposed anti-discrimination laws as an alternative, but that this was what the article was based on was obscured to them:

> *Harry*: 'I think that's completely ridiculous because now what you are saying is that Christianity is superior to other religions. You are saying Christianity is right but other multicultural religions are less so you have to get rid of all the blasphemy laws altogether.'

> *Mike*: 'Why can't you have just a discrimination law?' (agreement).

They were positioned by virtually every aspect of the text — that the law was outmoded, unworkable (providing the textual example of Northern Ireland), and that freedom of speech was of the utmost importance. While it should be remembered, however, that these views were consistent with their own ideologies, an examination of their written answers showed that an initially positive response was then rejected in the light of the text's feasible arguments:

> *Jack*: 'Initially, it appears a good idea — multicultural society. Quenches freedom of speech.'

> *Fiona*: 'You've got some silly, really old law, thousands of years old that bears no relation whatsoever to present society, the blasphemy laws.'

> *Sarah*: 'It's like in Ireland, it says here that they've had the law or something in here and it hasn't made much of a difference at the end of the day.'

However, the influence of the Rushdie affair on this group, given the age of its members at the time it occurred (ten), illustrated the strength of the hegemonic interpretation on this issue. Their idea of the event totally correlated with media representations of it, in believing that Muslims overreacted, and focusing on the death threat. They had, therefore, a 'culturally shared model of the situation' (van Dijk 1988a):

> *Chrishi*: 'It's just scared people, you know. They are not willing to see change and it's like these Muslims, they saw someone with an idea, with an opinion and because it wasn't stuck to their ideas, they didn't want him. It was like, chuck him out and kill him.'

> *Tom*: 'You know, you don't order someone dead just because they express an opinion.'

For these non-Muslims equality was important but secondary to freedom of speech. They lacked the ability to understand the importance of religion to Muslims and were 'religion-blind' in their identification of group disadvantage. Their perceptions of Islam then were not based on hostility but on a misunderstanding due to limited information and difficulty reconciling what Islam appeared to represent with their own liberal values. Their views conformed to the *Guardian*'s editorial ideologies, which advocated fairness and equality, but found Islam in conflict with these ideologies. It was this that caused them to concentrate on race rather than religious identities:

> *Harry*: 'There's a difference between the religion and people who believe in it, you shouldn't take the piss out of people who believe in it but there is nothing wrong criticizing the religion itself.'

Despite their cultural and political knowledge then, these groups' detailed models of the Rushdie affair (based on press coverage) resulted in a perception of Muslims as uncompromising and a threat. This was apparent even in the most critically aware members of the group:

> *Tom*: 'I mean the Salman Rushdie thing. It's quite ridiculous some of the attitudes people took when he wrote this book. They

just wanted him dead. There were just scores of people wanting him dead, to just burn him alive.'

Phil: 'Did anyone [Muslims] mention any of the things he said?'

Jane: 'Well I've met two and they said that they think Salman Rushdie should be killed.'

These articles worked to confirm and reinforce ideas about Islam as a restrictive religion, views held most strongly by these groups due to their liberal outlook. The groups frequently accused Islam of being 'dictating', 'consuming', 'over-the-top', 'over-protective' and most of all 'strict'. While they were willing to admit the existence of 'Islamophobia', there was a feeling that it might be justified, a view that appeared to be informed by media coverage:

Simon: 'I think it is caused by things like the Salman Rushdie affair, also the massacre in Egypt and Muslims are supposed to be involved, it makes you think, you know, why are they attacking non-Muslims?'

Interviewer: 'Do you think people have got a reason to be Islamophobic then?'

Harry: 'Not exactly Islamapohobic but if you speak out openly against it, I mean look at the Salman Rushdie case.'

Ethnic identification appeared in participants from other ethnic groups who were more sympathetic to the Muslim perspective. They suggested that the laws were probably a good idea because of the discrimination Muslims suffered, but *in this context* they supported their peers' arguments on freedom of speech, while showing caution about judging others:

Meera: 'It's kind of mixed feelings, I mean to me it seems silly to have like, going to jail because you happen to criticize a religion, everyone has a right for an opinion. OK, what you might say might not be right but at the end of the day you should have a right to your opinion, but actually putting it in to the anti-racial law, the discrimination law sorry, that seemed like a good idea in the sense that if you've got racial and sex discrimination you might as well have religious as well.'

Vivek: 'I have two sides to it, it's like I have the science side and I've been brought up to be religious and so I can see both sides.'

This empathy seemed to be based on experiences of discrimination rather than religious empathy. That context was important was illustrated by separate exchanges between Sikhs and Muslims in which the Sikhs were more defensive of their religion in the face of criticism from Muslim participants. However, in a situation that allowed beliefs to be revealed as they were challenged and defended, positions were strongly argued and no false agreement was reached.

The only practising Christian participants argued that religious believers should be able to withstand criticism of their religion and oppose the laws (equally in the non-contact groups). This protected the privileged position of Christianity while appearing to be tolerant, in contrast to Muslims:

Phil: 'I mean some people might mean harm by it, by slandering the Church of England or whatever but I'm not really in favour of religion all the time but [laughs], it doesn't really bother me that much at all.'

The conflict of ideologies this group experienced was all too apparent in its responses to the article on funded Muslim schools. The participants were initially positioned to support this in accordance with their views on equality, particularly on reading about the provision available to other minorities. They picked up on textual factors that suggested a need, waiting lists and religious holidays. However, they also singled out Ray Honeyford's quote on segregation, which was also consistent with their way of thinking. The group was therefore able to justify its views on integration as the preferable method of schooling on the basis of racial harmony, thus resolving its awkward position. Conforming to their liberal principles then, they suggested that religion was a private matter but that religious *education* was necessary to promote understanding. On this basis, they responded negatively to the photograph showing only girls, implying that the sexes would be segregated in these schools. Other textual information was also responded to in this way, for example references to the Islamic curriculum studied at the school provoked remarks about its 'narrow' provision, even though the article also referred to the national curriculum. The more right of centre members (in terms of newspaper readership) introduced other objections, such as the cost to the taxpayer:

Underlined in text: 'to gain grant-maintained status with full public funding' (Chris).

However, in an attempt to reconcile their conflicting positions, the reasons for preferring integration were consistently reinforced:

Chris: 'I think it should be in state schools as well because, I think you should have schools where you have all the religions involved because keeping them segregated is going to make it worse not better.'

Harry: 'I think you should be able to knock down barriers, social barriers in the country, make it multicultural rather than, you know, pointing directly to them, building up the barriers more. We should be striving to make people equal.'

According to van Dijk (1991: 39), liberal society has developed 'norms of an ethical nature', which now 'provide the consensus boundaries of systems of ethnic dominance' and have resulted in 'moderate racism'. This was apparent in the responses of these groups, which were not consistent in their expression of an anti-discriminatory ideology but legitimated it through a 'discourse of tolerance'. However, Shohat and Stam (1994) argue that people can be anti-racist while engaging in Eurocentric thinking (the normalizing of history from a Eurocentric perspective). This could provide one explanation for these groups' responses.

Non-Muslims: non-contact group

These groups generally showed much less awareness and were much less informed about current affairs and political and cultural issues generally. Firmly rooted in dominant right-wing ideologies, living in a rural, monocultural environment, they were nevertheless aware that to be outwardly racist was no longer politically correct. Reactions to the texts were, therefore, as one might expect, positioned by both *Mail* stories by the dominant meanings and showing oppositional positioning to the *Guardian*'s text (also then articulating dominant meanings).

However, these groups showed a higher degree of ambivalence towards the texts, the issues of debate having less salience for them as they were not perceived as having personal consequences.

Their lack of political awareness of and terminology associated with the subject meant that, with the text on blasphemy, the group was forced to accept it at face value. Although they were positioned in every way by the text and perceived it to be relatively balanced (in the representation of two sides), they suggested that it was biased in favour of Labour, to which they responded negatively, suggesting that it was an example of political correctness by the government. Only one participant showed any previous knowledge of Rushdie and these memories correlated with media representations, with the death threat at the forefront. The group, which was situated by its own immediate environment, initially interpreted the text almost solely in relation to Christianity:

> *Gemima*: 'Not really because you don't walk down the street and say you are C of E so I'm going to discriminate against you but you're Catholic so you're OK.'

As a mainly secular group they rejected the laws on the grounds of an absence of need and focused on the rights of the non-religious. They, too, were strongly positioned into discussing the issue of blasphemy rather than discrimination. The selection of a quote by Carmel Bedford of the anti-censorship group by many of the group, about making conversations in the living room illegal, illustrated their identification with this perspective. Freedom of speech discourse prevailed:

> *Lucy*: 'People should be able to speak about such things with others when they are in private, such as their own homes.'

> *John*: 'People should be allowed the right to say what they believe [denied their freedom of speech]. An atheist wouldn't be allowed their rights because they'd be talking against every religion.'

While textual references to equality partly forced them to admit that discrimination was wrong, as in the texts they followed these statements with disclaimers. Although all groups were positioned to deal with the issue of equality raised by the texts, the expressions of the non-contact groups amounted to 'pseudo-equality' (Shohat and Stam 1994) because they were employed in an attempt to justify their conflicting positions.

This group showed less tolerance of minorities, the problems they caused to the majority being of more concern. Muslims were therefore blamed for the introduction of the laws and perceived as over-reacting. One participant suggested that Christians might object to a change in the laws, but was challenged by another who argued otherwise; in her questionnaire, the objector was shown to be a practising Christian. Participants in this group, who were more able to negotiate with the Cook text, were incorporated by the preferred meanings here, having few points of identification. Knowledge and identification with the topic were clearly important then in being able to resist the dominant meanings.

As with the previous text, the Cook article was not recognized as ideological, and cultural bias was barely reflected upon, but in this case it was perceived as sensationalist. This, however, did not prevent preferred readings. Three of the more astute members of the group felt that it was biased in favour of Sarah. These group members articulated a more sensitive and liberal attitude throughout while still remaining anchored by dominant meanings. This could not be accounted for in terms of the variables examined here, such as newspaper readership.

However, while occupying a similar subject position to that of the contact group, this group negotiated with the text on another point of difference. Being more able to speculate generally than with the previous text, knowing something about marriage and relationships, for them age was the point of identification with Sarah, which led to dissenting voices regarding the control that others took in her life (perhaps based on their own experiences with authority):

> *Kath*: 'She changed her religion *but* it was her decision.' (The syntactics indicated an otherwise negative attitude to this action.)

However, the dominant message in the text for them was a warning to young people not to grow up too soon. In this way they accepted the text's message, relating strongly as teenagers and responded with feelings from their own specific cultural perspective that she was missing out on having fun and restricting her life. As with the contact group, the liberation of Western women was juxtaposed against a more primitive, backward society that resulted in an objectionable way of thinking that permitted such cultural abuse:

> *John*: 'He wanted her to stay in the house all day and not go out anywhere, that's what you said: second class, well done Marie' (giggles).
>
> *Interviewer*: What do you mean by second class?
>
> *Marie*: 'Just really that they are not treated as equals, which is a bit different from this culture here because it's starting to change a bit now. Em, women are actually having the right to go out to work and it isn't really that case over there is it?'
>
> *Ellie*: 'Yeah, she was only 14 and she was just like used to going out and having fun and everything, not being like a wife.'

Dismissive of the relationship, they were positioned by the psychological reasons for her conversion and marriage, the bullying. One participant in particular related to these feelings, which resulted in sympathy for Sarah rather than ridicule (feelings I later found out were based on experience):

> *Natalie*: 'It says she was teased at school and everyone hated her and stuff so she probably thought "Oh, somebody loves me or something silly like that.'
>
> *Jo*: 'I feel sorry for her. She craved attention, he showed it, and she grabbed it. She felt fat and ugly when people called her it. He showed her she wasn't and she didn't want to let that feeling go.'

These varying degrees of empathy generated by the text were evidence that the 'scripts' people brought to a text produced differential readings. It was clear that meaning was produced through a range of salient identifications (based on social subject positions).

The group was particularly puzzled by the parents' conversion. This was a result of the textual strategy of withholding explanations that left the reader feeling that such actions were nonsensical. This group's schemas on Muslims were virtually non-existent in relation to other ethnic groups. They therefore relied heavily on the text for information on this subject (despite claiming that it was biased). Their perception of religion as being a series of rituals rather than a way of life, as in the Muslim faith, meant that they found it difficult to identify aspects of religion in the article, apart from the marriage ceremony, although they were subconsciously forming perceptions and making assumptions identifiable in their discussions. The photographs, however, worked as a reminder to some of them of representations they had seen before of girls in headscarves.

These patterns of interpretation were also prevalent in responses to the *Guardian* article on the funding of Muslim schools, to which the group took an oppositional (and therefore dominant) position to its preferred meanings. They identified the text as ideological, supporting Muslims. Initially reminded by the text of the necessity for equality, rather than outwardly opposing any change to the system, they supported integration (as promoting good race relations) because they disagreed with the state funding of separate religious schools from a position of self-interest (and were therefore more engaged in this discussion). Minorities were clearly excluded from Britishness and constructed as foreign. This foreignness was constructed through language, the implication being that Muslims should go to 'normal schools' with 'normal kids'. They were perceived as creating problems for the majority because the schools gave special treatment to Muslims to the detriment of 'British' children and were costly to the taxpayer:

> *Jacky*: 'It's like, I don't know, if the state's putting money in to run these special schools for Muslims, I mean, they are not even conforming to the British way of life, they are like speaking their language and doing all that, which I don't think is right when they are going to be getting a really good standard of education when most schools in Britain need funding.'

Information in the text was selected and used to support their ideologies, for example, the point the article made about funding other religions' schools found a negative response because it was seen as a signal to all sorts of religions being funded at the taxpayers expense. Religion was deemed to be private and unimportant, so those who believed strongly, because they were in the minority, should pay for themselves. While both contact and non-contact groups perceived

Muslims as responsible for their own isolation, the non-contact group reiterated right-wing discourse that suggested that British children (excluding Muslims) were being disadvantaged by moves to aid minority groups. Their avocation of integration for racial harmony, here, appeared to be just an acceptable excuse for their anti-race stance:

> *Anna*: 'By doing this, the gap between Muslims and the British will be widening bad race relations, which leads to racism. And the Muslim children will be receiving a better education than British children.'

When presented with an alternative text, these groups worked harder to justify their ideology. They 'rationalized' their racism, which Cohen (1988: 82) argued is a strategy that emphasizes their own tolerance while negativizing the Other, therefore protecting white privilege, and it 'covers over deeper forms of racism'.

Their ideas about religion were limited by the type of RE they had experienced at school and by local media coverage based on rituals. They therefore had difficulty understanding the importance it could hold for others:

> *Rachel*: 'I mean we come here and don't get any RE or anything like that. Everyone's got the right to their own religion. I just don't think they should have special schools for it.'

When asked how much religion was covered in the news then, the responses were limited by these conceptions:

> *Michelle*: 'Not a lot, unless they are mentioning it to make a point about religion, then they don't really mention it.'

> *Anna*: 'I think if a festival like Diwali, they mention that and they have photos and stuff like that and they put descriptions of what happened like the Caribbean carnival and stuff like that, they always have like reports about that.'

Their awareness of the controversial nature of race, while wanting to express their opinions, saw these couched in careful language:

> *Jacky*: 'I don't know but it's just a dodgy situation isn't it, it's

just the fact that Muslims didn't originate here so you think why should we be paying for extra schools for them, that's the whole issue, it's nothing about racism or anything like that.'

Rachel: 'Oh dear, I mean I've just had loads of experiences, I'm not racist to any other culture apart from Pakistan I suppose, which is really awful but the experiences that I've had like you're in town and there is a whole group of them pushing past you [agreement] they're really ignorant pushing past you.'

The 'Oh dear' here illustrated how the speaker was aware of the difficulty of expressing her feelings without appearing too racist and tried to depoliticize the racism by denying it. The apparent consensus was evidence that these attitudes had been normalized among this group; these adaptations were therefore probably for the benefit of the outsider. One participant was especially keen to try and articulate another side, not wanting to appear overtly racist, but ultimately agreed with the group. Another showed a more sympathetic stance towards Muslims, identifying and recognizing their discrimination. His discourse revealed that cultural proximity was a factor, living in the city centre, mixing with some Muslims. His parents were also *Guardian* readers and it is likely that some of these values were transferred.

In the following sections I examine those variables important in the development of frameworks of understanding and the interpretive strategies that these participants used in their comprehension and decoding of media messages that resulted in the formulation of shared interpretations.[7]

Cultural proximity

It was evident that religious identification (or a form of it) rather than cultural proximity was an important variable in enabling Muslims to resist texts about Muslims even when they were culturally unaware. It was also clear that the 'contact thesis', so often celebrated by previous research as a means of resisting dominant meanings, could be questioned in relation to non-Muslim interpretations of Muslim minorities. While it clearly had an impact on the contact group on the grounds of racial tolerance, these participants lacked interest in or knowledge of their peers' religious identities, some claiming not to know any Muslims, even when Muslims were part of their subject groups:

Interviewer: 'Does anybody know any Muslims?'

Gemma: 'I wouldn't know.'

Sharon: 'I don't know.'

Interviewer: 'you don't know?'

Sharon: 'No, I'm not religious at all so I don't talk about anything like that' (laughs).

Ignorance was clearly a key factor in sustaining dominant ideologies about Muslims and Islam. Unfortunately, these participants lacked any depth of knowledge about Islam that would allow them to reject these meanings, but their multicultural backgrounds encouraged them to be more critical. The media compounded the situation by limiting knowledge that might have improved relations and by causing people to be suspicious of Islam, thus contributing to boundary making. The consequences of this were that the issue of religious identity was not open for discussion; *in fact it was consciously avoided* as a point of dissent and awkwardness in the relationships and for the sake of maintaining harmony. This is consistent with previous research that found that local situations are filtered through the images derived from the media (Hartmann et al. 1974). Troyna (1981) argued that even in areas where people live and work close to one another, interaction can be limited and therefore the media remain the major source of information.

However, as with Troyna's findings, these non-Muslims believed it was their experience rather than media images that informed them about minorities. While the contact groups believed this 'experience' has made them more tolerant and anti-racist, the non-contact groups argued that their 'experiences' (living alongside Muslims but at a distance) had given them a negative outlook. Hartmann et al. (1974) also found that those living around 'immigrant' areas but who had little contact with them were often more hostile than those who did not. However, while 'relative deprivation' was not a factor for resentment in this case, with the non-contact groups being economically secure, resentment of the 'special privileges' minorities were perceived to receive and that left them (the majority) feeling disadvantaged was a key factor in their responses:

Harry: 'Definitely from speaking to people because living in Leicester, it's quite a multicultural place, you are bound to be around this sort of thing, but speak to people I know in Newcastle or somewhere like that where there is hardly any different cultures, they are different in how they act towards them, you know multicultural people' (contact group).

Michelle: 'It's because we see too much of them.'

Caroline: 'It's like we don't have Muslim kids here (at the school) but it's like a bloomin' weekly thing, if you go into Leicester or anything then you just see them, it's what we've grown up with, *them around us*' (non-contact).

The few positive experiences the non-contact group had had were treated as unusual and one-off experiences in which individuals were separated from their racial group:

Kate: 'They were sound, I mean *it was obvious like an Indian house* with all the stuff up and everything *but it just weren't a problem* at all, 'cos *they could all speak English*, we were eating their food and having a laugh with them, playing football with the daughters and stuff like that. I mean it was sound that was. It was a right laugh, it was *unbelievable*' (emphasis added).

According to Cohen (1988), the reference to experience, rather than external modes of influence, authenticates the racism by making it appear a spontaneous and natural response to the Other who is somehow responsible.

Ignorance was clearly an issue for the non-contact group. These participants showed very little knowledge of Islam. Their schemas on religious groups were based on the little information they remembered from school, which included only superficial details and things they found unusual and controversial such as Sikhs carrying swords. This often resulted in the confusion of aspects of different religions and homogenization of minority groups. They were therefore highly reliant on the articles for information about Muslims:

Interviewer: 'What is your perception of Islam and Muslims?'

John: 'From the article, it wouldn't be that good for us.'

Interviewer: 'What do you mean?'

John: 'Well nobody, when you have had the kind of life you have had here, wants to go to some foreign country and [be] treated like a slave, do you?'

Lucy: 'And having to walk round with that thing around her face, a thingy' (laughing).

Interviewer: 'Does anyone know anything else about Muslims?'

Ellie: 'Are they the ones that wear turbans or is that Hindu?'

Interviewer: 'Sikhs.'

Ellie: 'OK' [lots of laughing]. You tend not to take much notice of any other religion than the one you are supposed to be or if you are just not religious you don't really take much notice of any religion.'

Lucy: 'They all seem the same to me, Sikh, Muslim, Hindu people whatever, but they are probably not, I don't know so' ... laughs.'

Interviewer: 'What do you know about Islam?'

All: 'nothing' (laughter).

Interviewer: 'Does anybody know anything?'

Jacky: 'Err ... most of the stuff you see is about war in those countries you don't see anything else, other stories.'

This (in addition to their newspaper readership) worked to dispel specific images of certain groups, for example the fundamentalist. This was demonstrated by the way the different groups articulated about Muslims and aggression (Table 4.4). Incidences of aggression to which the groups referred included mainly wars, fundamentalism, terrorism, extremism, atrocities against human rights, killing and violence, yet this was only a marginal image for the non-contact group. Rather, Muslims were grouped together with other minorities as a threat in terms of cultural and population invasion, with similarly negative implications.

Table 4.4   Text units retrieved from the aggression code

Aggression	Muslims	Contact Group	Non-Contact
Representation of Muslims as aggressive	39	7	1
Perception of Muslims as aggressive	8	22	6

Religion, ethnicity, language groupings

The importance of religious identification among the Muslims in these groups appeared to have overridden differing ethnic and language groups, holding, as they did, virtually a singular perspective in relation to these texts. Because of the intention to encourage homogeneity, however, only a small number outside the majority ethnic grouping participated and one could argue that, in that they were all 'British Muslims' of the same age and level of education (see Appendix C), they had similar reference points. This was not the result of a consensus effect but was clearly illustrated by their strongly held views. Even those Muslims whose first language was given as English argued just as strongly in defence of Islam (in contrast with previous research findings, although again only a small number here). Religious identification was not a particularly important variable for other religious groups. The opinions expressed by a Gujarati-speaking Hindu of Indian extraction were very different from those of a Gujarati-speaking Muslim of Indian extraction. In relation to these articles, it was the 'Muslim' identification that was most important in resisting the preferred meaning.

Attitude to religion/other religions

Examining the participants' attitudes to religion in general and to other religions provided an insight into the frameworks of knowledge of the groups that might have affected their interpretations and provided a point of comparison for their positions on Islam. As might be expected, the non-Muslims' attitude to religion was one of secular privatization, a position held most strongly (as an ideology) by the contact group. The non-contact group, in general, was less tolerant and perceived religion as 'unimportant'. However, while the contact group espoused a 'live and let live' philosophy, this appeared to be only if it had no personal consequences for them:

Tom: 'It doesn't bother me in any way providing everyone stays to themselves and don't try and infringe on your liberty, you know, do what you want, it doesn't bother me' (contact group).

Natalie: 'Yeah, it's like one religion has to pray about six times a day or something towards Mecca and you don't really want that if you are working on a production line or something because you can't stop the production line for them to pray' (non-contact group).

By contrast, religion was considered to be of some importance to all the Muslims. An illustration of this was the initial reaction of the Muslim men to participating in the research, treating it with triviality. However, they became very serious when we began to discuss Islam. These Muslims believed that although society was becoming more multicultural, it was dominated by Christian norms. However, they believed that the average Briton did not take his or her religion seriously and that this was at the heart of many problems in society. To them, it was the strength and growth of Islam that was perceived to be a threat. Increasingly, researchers are finding that religion is a more significant source of identity than ethnicity for young Muslims (Jacobson 1997; Modood et al. 1997), a point that is explained more fully in the conclusion to this chapter.

This contrasted with the other religious groups for which religion appeared to have little significance. Despite this, they showed some empathy with Muslims based on an ethnic identification but, *in this context*, they identified more with the values of their non-Muslim peers. The lack of empathy with religion by non-Muslims clearly contributed to their interpretation of the texts, which was exacerbated by the way Islam was presented within them.

The participants lacked knowledge about the representation of other religions in the media, partly through lack of interest and possibly because of an absence of coverage. Generally, and consistent with previous research on minority groups (Sreberny-Mohammadi and Ross 1995), Muslims felt that their religion was the most poorly represented, but it is likely that all religions are badly portrayed (due to a secular press):

Abdullah: 'Yes that's true as well, like when Rushdie wrote about the Muslims and Islam, like it took centre stage again; all the press were covering it. Recently he wrote about Hindus and his book was banned in India but nobody heard about that.'

However, while other ethnic groups lacked knowledge about coverage of their own religions, they felt that they were unlikely to receive much coverage:

Kirpal: 'I haven't seen any other religions in the paper to be truthful, I haven't seen any Hindus in the paper and our religion's definitely never in the paper.'

Local coverage of minority religions was considered to be positive:

Meera: 'If you look in the local papers it has got quite a lot of a mix of religions, I mean because in this community there are quite a lot of Asians, you do see a lot of stuff in the local newspaper.'

Non-Muslims felt that the media were probably biased against all religions, though less against Christianity (due to societal norms), but that there was also an absence of coverage in the national press. However, the non-contact group did not question this (poor) representation as a false one. Generally, non-Muslims showed indifference to other religions, in contrast with their severe criticism of Islam. Several Muslims, however, expressed some antagonistic attitudes to other religions, although they were reticent to do so in this context. They were, therefore, generally evasive but more willing to criticize Christianity because to them it represented the central starting point of their persecution in the West and was seen as hypocritical in its judgements against them:

Farzana: 'Yes, there has always been a kind of a feud between Muslims and Jews but I don't think he should just talk about killing just like that' (words stilted).

Ahmed: 'The article would make me think about … how many leaders of great religions [Christianity] are backing certain people and allow discrimination against other religions.'

Mohammed: 'I don't think they would allow a Muslim guy to write about Christianity in the way he [Rushdie] wrote about Islam anyway.'

This provided insight into the frameworks of understanding of particular groups, the importance of religion to Muslims and lack of importance to non-Muslims, which affected their interpretations. It is clear from these data that Islam has more salience (for negative reasons) in the press and that this is apparent in the public's (critical) discourses.

Familiarity with media coverage

By identifying the participants' familiarity with media coverage of Islam outside the texts used in the research, an indication of what other factors were informing the participants could be gained. Despite some contradictory spaces in press discourse, the content analyses had found the existence of dominant meanings in relation to Islam and at the time of the group research this was particularly apparent in the coverage of the Saudi nurses. The saturation level of this coverage, and the fact that it was recent, meant that it was known by most of the participants, although their differing interpretations were revealing:

> *Sadia*: 'It's like, if somebody goes to another country, they have to abide by their laws and if they don't, they have to pay the consequences and they knew, nobody knows whether they were guilty or not guilty, but if they knew that the Saudi government was like this and if they done something the punishment was really fierce so you have to consider everything' (Muslim).

> *Chris*: 'Yeah, but the fact that the issue is that these women were, you know, there seems to be little if any evidence against them which matters and they were tortured for their confessions and that was part of their society and that has been highlighted by this case' (contact group).

> *Kate*: 'Now that gives you a negative opinion of Muslims full stop, about them like keeping them in jail, doing this and that to them, you know, I don't know. The thing is though, you don't take into account that it is a totally different culture, that's normal for them to do stuff like that' (non-contact group).

The subjects were positioned according to their social/cultural identification with a particular 'side'. All subjects were positioned to attend to the issue of Saudi punishments but while the non-Muslim groups'

discourse reflected dominant press discourse, the Muslims tried to mitigate for the Saudi authorities.[8]

Actual familiarity with the news stories encountered (through the
texts) in these groups was poor, even among the Muslims who, in
common with previous research on minorities and their perceptions of
media representation, despite having clear theories on the hostility of
the media, could only provide general examples of this (Halloran et al.
1995). The Rushdie affair was, however, of salience for the Muslim and
contact groups, an indication of the notoriety of the story in the UK.[9]
Table 4.5 shows the total recall of news stories on Islam.

Table 4.5   News stories recalled by different groups

Associated topics	Muslims	Contact group	Non-contact group
Fundamentalism	Oklahoma World Cup threat Pakistan hostages	Nation of Islam Luxor Israel/'Arabia'	Oklahoma
Conflict	Middle East Afghanistan Bosnia	Saddam Hussein	Vague notion of foreign wars/ conflict
Conversion	Jemima Khan Mike Tyson Mohammed Ali Cat Stevens		
UK	Pigs in the window Schools Prince Charles	Schools (local)	Pigs in the window
Primitive Ethnicity	Saudi nurses	Saudi nurses Norman Tebbit (multiculturalism debate)	Saudi nurses Sikhs and sword carrying Animal sacrifices

Knowledge of particular events reflected the groups' general levels
of cultural and political awareness in this area, with the Muslims having
greater knowledge. Research on news recall suggests that people have
difficulty remembering news items but are likely to remember what is
salient to their own views and interests (Dahlgren 1988a). People are
also more likely to recall stories given particular prominence by the
media, whose meanings then gain currency in society. The non-

Muslims not only had a patchy knowledge but also remembered events that were negatively framed in the press and were dominated by conflict, aggression and irrationality. Although most events recalled were fairly recent, the results illustrated how events such as the Oklahoma bombing remained in the collective memory even if an unjustified association was made (because it fits with preconceptions). It is this culture of ignorance that fuels negative perceptions of Islam.

It is also of note that the level of interest in a particular news story did not appear to correlate with the familiarity of that story. Those who claimed to be disinterested were just as likely to be familiar with events as those who were interested. However, this variable was measured only by self-identification. Both contexts therefore, overestimation and underestimation, were influential factors. Also measured were statements of interest and disinterest towards the stories discussed in the groups. The level of disinterest evident (Table 4.6) was not only a reflection of age but also of relevance, which would account for the level of recall. However, I would argue that levels of recall are not an accurate reflection of the way media discourse enters and circulates in society. While actual events are easily forgotten, meanings are continually produced and reproduced across stories.

Table 4.6 Statements of interest made by participants in relation to texts examined

	Muslims	*Contact*	*Non-contact*	*Total*
Interest	29	3	2	34
Disinterest	39	36	95	170

The attitude of this participant was reiterated by many non-Muslims:

> *Jack*: 'Not particularly concerned with this issue, as it is not something that personally affects me, neither will it really affect me to any major degree' (contact group).

It is an indication that even those who mix regularly with ethnic groups perceive ethnic issues as something separate to the lives of the majority, as 'minority issues'.[10]

The lack of engagement by the Muslim participants, despite their interest in their representation, was partly based on their age and distaste for these stories but also on the lack of relevance in the foreign element of the stories. The articles solely about British Muslims were therefore considered to be the most interesting, though the women stated a preference for the article on schools because of their interest in 'faith' issues, while the men stated a preference for the section on Rushdie because of its emphasis on politics, although, given the age of the story, they expressed a desire to see it dropped (there appeared to be social/cultural factors at play here in the choice of preferred articles partly in relation to the research context). It was evident that the intentional formatting that caused people to feel distanced from the main actors (Muslims), and therefore unsympathetic towards them, also had some effect on the Muslim groups.

Media bias

The extent to which participants were media literate was also an important factor in being able to resist textual meanings. The difference in the groups' awareness of cultural bias has already been made evident. Most of the participants had a genre schema for news, that generally bias existed in the media, that this was a negative aspect and that journalism should be neutral.

The Muslim groups were not only more concerned about bias than the other groups but they also showed greater awareness of the selectivity, journalistic practices, norms and ignorance that led to such bias. They were generally more cynical about the intentions of the press and were more likely to judge articles as false constructions in their totality. They were especially critical of the misuse of Islamic terminology that promotes ignorance.[11] Similarly, the contact groups showed a sound awareness of the effects of using certain sources, structuration and use of language in articles. Their awareness of news values was also high. The non-contact groups' awareness of these practices was much less sophisticated (see fourth quote below):

> *Humera*: 'I think it's quite biased because they've only got the President's side of the story really, they haven't got nobody else backing it up and there is not much supporting evidence for most of these things they've said as well' (Muslim).

> *Mohammed*: 'It's just a clever editing trick that's what it is. I see

it on television all the time when you see things about Muslims, it was about Salman Rushdie again, it was about some guy asking him, a scholar, a guy asking him what he thought about Salman Rushdie and he was saying about Islam and what should happen and after he finishes talking, he says something like, 'Muslims are living in peace and harmony' and straight after he finished there is a picture of Khomeini and then back to the conversation again so it's like "yes" "yes", "yes", but on the other hand it is like Khomeini wants to kill everyone.' (Muslim)

Will: 'It's got conflict between laws, conflict between countries as well potentially.'

Dave: 'Yeah, it's got a lot of sensationalism in it like, you've got the 18 and 13, you've got the Western and the Islam bit, so it was interesting but this comes a long way after the real story doesn't it?'

Nina: 'I don't think there would have been such a problem with this, with the age gap if the guy hadn't been from Turkey and Muslim' (men and women in contact group).

Interviewer: 'Why do you think newspaper reports portray it like that?'

Peter: 'They are trying to make you feel *sorry* for her as well' (non-contact group).

While most participants, then, were vocal about media bias, this reaction was mainly based on schemas relating to the tabloid press, a type of journalism based on hyperbole, sensationalism and commercialism. This then appeared to be a somewhat standard response to questions about media bias, and not directly related to the articles presented to the groups, evident particularly in the non-contact group. Only a couple of individuals suggested that the broadsheets were biased. All groups stated in some form or another that these types of articles were not news but 'stories', news being perceived as predominantly hard news appearing in broadsheets and on television. This did not stop them applying generalized 'facts', retrieved from the articles to or about Muslims:

Chris: 'What you read in the papers, you can't trust a word of it.'

Mike: 'I think that definitely.'

Chris: 'right the way through the paper to the sports news at the back, it's all rumours and lies' (contact group).

Interviewer: 'Do you think newspapers are biased?

All: 'OH yeah definitely'.

Rachel: 'And if they've got an opinion, they'll put that forward and not really consider the other side.'

Anna: 'Definitely yeah. The tabloids are anyway' (non-contact group).

Despite this belief in bias then, most of the non-Muslims felt that the articles contained the basic facts and that ignoring the sensationalism could make an accurate reading of the event:

Simon: 'You see if you're interested in it, you just have to read through and get your own opinion and just ignore all the phrases and things. You know, because it's obviously going to be hyped up in any paper' (contact group).

Yet there were different responses to the question of media bias against Muslims. For the Muslim participants there was no question that the media was biased against them. This was a negative *expectation* (part of their news schema) that they brought to the texts and that affected their interpretations of the articles:

Farzana: 'I wouldn't read it at all. I would just look at that word 'Moslems' and just think stereotyped Muslims and think it was probably something about war and leave it.'

Although the contact groups conceded that the media were probably biased against Muslims (context effects?), they argued that this was probably unintentional and to some extent justified, in general then suggesting that these were realistic representations. However, the non-contact groups felt that there was not enough coverage of Muslims in the media for it to be biased. This was likely to be an illustration of both their general lack of interest or awareness of other cultures and ethnic issues, and a reflection of the papers they read, mainly the red-top tabloids such as the *Sun*, for which minority interests have less news value. There were even a couple of instances of non-Muslims suggesting that the media were biased in favour of Islam, which was particularly prevalent in the groups during discussions of the more positive article on Muslim schools.

While this provided evidence that groups were predispositioned in different ways to the news and had different expectations of the genre, awareness of media bias did not appear to make a difference in rejecting dominant meanings of Islam within specific articles. The strong consensus that the media are biased may partly result from the group effect, namely general pressure not to appear naive.

Media literacy

Having an awareness of media bias did not seem to make any difference to the participants' readings of Islam. Do greater levels of media literacy result in more oppositional understandings? The media literate (measured in terms of awareness of presentational factors and accurate perceptions of the paper) in these groups were more likely to be regular readers of the broadsheets, particularly the *Guardian*, which claimed to have an interest in the news. The Muslims and the contact group best fitted these categories and were also the most media literate.

The men showed a much higher degree of media literacy than the women, although this was also a reflection of the greater number of men in the contact group and larger number of women in the non-contact group. It is safe to say that in the mixed groups gender was not the crucial variable. Men and women showed an equal awareness in the contact group and an equal lack of awareness in the non-contact group. However, there was a significant difference in awareness between the Muslim groups. Men here certainly showed a much greater awareness of the media and political issues in general. According to van Dijk (1988b), having a news schema aids comprehension of news texts. This may be one factor in the lack of recognition of the preferred meanings in texts by women.

While media literacy appeared to make a difference to the critical ability to deconstruct texts, for these participants were more aware of the papers' structures, formats and political biases (although doing media studies did not seem to be a significant factor), it appeared to make little difference to perceptions of Islam. However, given that it enhances critical ability, when combined with knowledge of Islam media literacy can contribute to countering negative images.

Interpretive strategies

Frameworks of interpretation are based on 'scripts' that include direct experience and knowledge, media and cultural norms. As well as the 'scripts' that readers bring to texts, this research showed that readers pay attention to the macro-structure, headlines, labelling, lexicalization, semantics and visual cues to make sense of the articles.

Table 4.7 Use of textual references (evidence) by different groups

	Muslims	*Contact*	*Non-contact*
To show awareness of bias	56	27	1
To support arguments (in favour of dominant meanings)	2	48	44
Total	58	75	45

Having analysed the surface structure according to their own frameworks of understanding, the participants used aspects of the text both to illustrate textual bias and to provide evidence for their claims. Muslims used textual references mainly as examples of bias towards Islam, which is further evidence of their asymmetrical position in relation to the texts (Table 4.7). Of these references, 43 were attributable to men, which again showed their greater media literacy in comparison with women. The men showed particular distaste for Rushdie by drawing on his face and writing abusive comments by it. Muslims used textual references within the preferred meaning if they were in keeping with their views, for example, quotes that supported the blasphemy laws:

Sadia: 'I mean, the person mentioned in here, Dr Hammed, he thinks it's positive as well and all the evidence given here suggests it is positive.'

Non-Muslims, particularly in the non-contact groups, having views that are more in line with the articles, were more likely to make meaning 'upwards' from the text rather than 'downwards' towards it (Corner 1991). They therefore used textual references as evidence to support their views, investing these with some authority. This showed the greater media/source dependency of these groups for information. It was also evidence of selective perception, that readers select quotes from sources that support their own readings of the text and pay attention to information that fits with group schema (van Dijk 1987). This was particularly evident in the non-Muslims' reading of the *Guardian* text on schools when they used information provided to raise doubts.

When the contact group used references to show awareness of bias, this was largely political bias. However, the less their awareness of bias, the more likely they were to be positioned by an article's sources. Rhetorical devices, syntactical and semantical organization clearly exert constraints on meaning when readers do not have alternative information, in other words they are not socially situated to reject preferred meanings:

> *Rich*: 'She doesn't look that mature in the pictures either. I mean the one with the husband's family, the bottom one, she just looks like a kid and has no idea' (contact group).

> *Chris*: 'I think it [Muslim schools] will be very em, if you read the article it says, you know they are being taught the Koran and stuff and it's going to be very orientated towards that religion and perhaps they are not going to be given a fair idea of what's going on sort of when they get out of the school then they are going to have to live in the real world with other people from other cultures and if they've totally been brought up to that culture then they are going to be shell-shocked when they get out' (contact group).

The evidence here supports other research that shows that semantic processing often takes place on very little contact with the text (van Dijk 1988b). A glance at the headline may be all it takes for people to decide whether it is of interest or relevance to them, which affects a decision to carry on reading. If there is some ambiguity, a glance at the picture or highlighted text qualifies this:

Shabana: 'I'd just usually read the headline and then turn the pages.'

Sadia: 'It's just the title and the way it is set out and the picture, it's like …'

Aisha: 'Oh, it's a Muslim there, I'll read it.'

Humera: 'Yeah, the first thing you see if you see an Asian on the newspaper or the news you always get interested and read it or listen to it, you know' (Muslims)

Marie: 'I'd read the things in big print like "I feel like an old woman not a teenager" and the bits under the photograph but if none of that's interesting, I probably wouldn't have read it' (non-contact group).

Due to the low levels of interest non-Muslims had in these texts, it is likely that only a skim reading would take place, in which case it is also likely that they would be taken at face value. It is in the rereading and studying in a critical context such as this that texts become ideological. However, it was evident that, even in rereading, participants selectively absorbed parts of the text, just enough for it to be meaningful to them:

Dave: 'Well there was the sex abuse. I think that was dragging her back to the honeymoon.'

Will: 'And he did take her to Turkey.'

Dave: 'I thought she just went over there and just stayed there.'

Will: 'I don't know.'

Nina: 'It doesn't really say. It doesn't make the facts very clear does it?' (contact group).

As an example of the cognitive processing of media texts, all groups showed evidence of misreading the article; the participants above, for example, believed that Musa forced Sarah to go back to Turkey. This further indicated that people skim for the information they need for a general impression and then fill in the blanks with what is most appropriate to their view of an event. These details tended to be in line with the preferred meaning of the article and thus did not provoke any challenge but confirmed it all the more.

Having established that the media are biased, what is the perceived influence of the media according to these groups? The Muslim participants overwhelmingly believed that non-Muslims were influenced by negative media coverage of them, that media coverage was partly responsible for negative attitudes towards them and, once formed, that these attitudes were difficult to change. The women also showed concern about the impact of this sort of coverage on believers, leading to a loss of faith. This, they suggested, was due to a lack of understanding of Islam, to the amount of coverage it received and to the size of the tabloid readership, but they also acknowledged the likelihood of a lack of interest among non-Muslims in Islam. None of the participants considered that the media might influence them in any way.

While non-Muslims rejected the idea that they were influenced when asked directly (due to the insignificant amount of coverage and a belief that experiences counted for more), in the discussion they often referred to the influence of particular stories on their attitudes.

Only Muslims, then, awarded any importance to future counter-action. Training to deal with 'ignorance' and ensuring (knowledgeable) Muslims more access to the media so that Islam could be presented 'properly' were offered as possible strategies, although they also expressed some scepticism about their ability to affect change. The contact group, on the other hand, offered proposals for more action on discrimination, for tolerance and equality but no practical ideas for the media. The non-contact groups offered no proposals for change.

Media usage and cultures of understanding

While media usage bore no relation to the ability to resist dominant meanings of Islam, there was a correlation between media usage and how far a person was informed and aware of current events. The participants' views correlated closely with the newspaper they read; readership of alternative newspapers like the *Socialist Worker* was also a good indication of a reader's views. However, the single *Muslim News* reader did not show any more critical awareness than her fellow Muslims.

Media usage, in terms of frequency of use, did not alone provide an indication of who was more likely to be informed. Choice of newspaper was also significant. Those who chose broadsheets were more likely to be critical and aware of current issues. They were more likely to be interested and to seek out the news frequently. This applied in both the Muslim and contact groups, with *Guardian* readers being the most critical (there were no broadsheet readers in the non-contact groups). Participants who reported an interest in the news and read regularly but chose tabloid papers were considerably less informed, with *Mail* and *Express* readers slightly more informed than the red-top tabloid readers. There were exceptions to this, such as individuals who reported having little interest in the news yet appeared to be quite astute about current affairs. There seemed to be other reasons for this awareness: they often listened to the radio or their parents read a more informative paper (indicating the values of the parents). Those participants who reported having little interest in the news, who rarely read newspapers and then only tabloid papers had the lowest political awareness.

These results provided evidence for Lacey and Longman's (1997) cultures of understanding (the concerns, interests and values of a group, or those through which the group understands the world) as interpretative communities shared by newspaper readers. In their own research on environmental coverage and public understandings of it, they found that some newspapers have a strong relationship with their readers through which they are able to build 'cultures of understanding' on particular contemporary issues. 'Cultures of understanding' are particularly useful as they show a newspaper's power to sustain selected cultural items and manipulate differences, given a captive and trusting audience. If our own newspapers are instrumental in defining reality for us, we are then more likely to reject the discourse of others if they disagree with that of our own.[12] I would suggest that the interpretive groups in this study also showed strong 'cultures of understanding' of Islam in relation to readership. The contact group's discourse resonated with the (various but limited) discourses of broadsheet/middle tabloid papers, and the non-contact group's with the red-top tabloids' 'cultures of ignorance'. Not only were the members of the non-contact group limited by their historical and social backgrounds in their capacity to express their understandings of a media text, but also the discourse needed to criticize effectively had not been made available to them (apparent in their ignorance of key terms) and this prevented them from engaging in democracy. The lack of coverage of ethnic minority groups in these papers contributed to their sense of the Other. For example, the 'culture of idiocy' promoted in the *Sun* was reflected in the dynamics of the groups that treated the issues lightly. The non-contact groups also showed a lack of knowledge and understanding of minority issues, which can only increase their marginalization in society.

The range of interpretations, then, is based on different socio-demographic anchorings. These variations made little difference, however, when it came to formulating a negative understanding of Islam among non-Muslims.

The core findings of this chapter based on research *within these focus groups* were as follows:

- The media appear to be an important resource on 'public knowledge' of Islam and Muslims in the UK (Corner 1991). The media limit the framework and discourses within which Islam is 'known' but the success of the discourse is in its 'fit' with preconceptions. People are selective in the textual 'evidence' they choose to support their views. The media help sustain dominant discourses by presenting Muslims within a framework of conflict and by using categorization to mobilize specific identities, which result in essentialized polarized groups. Religious identifications are therefore most important for Muslims in the decoding of these texts. Other points of identification sometimes result in a preferred reading by Muslims.
- Non-Muslims are anchored by textual information through a lack of knowledge of Muslims. Even groups that mix with Muslims lack the depth of knowledge to understand and develop counter ideologies. While non-Muslims argue that their experiences inform their beliefs about Muslims, these experiences are filtered through and ultimately shaped by media information.
- People in a multicultural environment are more aware of issues relating to culture. These participants are sensitive to liberal ideals of equality and fairness and relate to discrimination and race, but they lack an understanding of religious issues and hold a negative perception of Islam as a restrictive and oppressive religion.
- The cultures of ignorance present in the non-contact group, generated by the complex interaction of norms and values and by newspapers that provide a framework for interpreting experience, often work to block out stereotypical ideas of Islam (due to the lack of differentiation between minority groups). However, the Muslims are homogenized into a negative idea of the Other, an economical and cultural threat. Although all the non-Muslims who participated

in this research engaged in 'ethnic blame discourse', this non-contact group was in particular fuelled by racial envy, with their 'racist imagination' hyperbolizing their own disadvantage (Cohen 1988).

- The Cook article showed how multiple points of identification operate in responding to texts. Like most texts, its meanings were multilayered with a range of dominant values to position its audience. This was most effective with the non-contact group, which was caught in the dominant meanings, and least with the Muslims who focused more on the text's cultural bias. When non-Muslims find few points of connection with the text, discussion becomes difficult.

- These groups therefore constituted 'interpretive communities' in their shared frameworks and perspectives. Apart from knowledge and cultural proximity (which also position Muslims in relation to foreign cultures), group norms (social, cultural and political) and media literacy were significant in the reading of these texts, in addition to more traditional demographic variables.

- While media literacy is important to the critical ability to recognize, deconstruct and reject preferred meanings, it alone is not capable of producing alternative readings in relation to Islam. This depends on alternative knowledge.

- In the Muslim groups, the men were generally more aware of and interested in news and current affairs. The women were more restrained and keen to present a reasonable face of Islam. However, all these Muslims strongly believed that the media were culturally biased. For non-Muslims, this awareness extended only to general bias based mainly on sensationalism. This awareness was not a factor in resisting ideology for non-Muslims.

- All groups were aware of the issue of 'political correctness' surrounding race and were careful and guarded with language — often resulting in muted racism — but tested the limits of what was acceptable in their own environment.

- Our impressions of the world and our interpretations of the perceptions of others appear to be informed largely by our own immediate environment. For example, most participants in the contact group thought that the majority of people in Britain were secular and 'not racist'.

Conclusion

This research provides evidence to suggest that British Muslims are 'known' to non-Muslims in the UK mostly through the media. It is the media that define the meaning of the Muslim presence in Britain, as found in previous research on the ethnic Other (Hartmann et al. 1974), and provide us with our 'ways of seeing' (Dahlgren and Chakrapani 1982). There is evidence of an ideological reproduction of dominant discourses in relation to Islam in terms of gender, primitivism, separatism, restriction and cultural difference. These discourses have been naturalized and allow the perpetrators to take on a superior stance. However, their presence does not automatically imply a passive audience; rather this process of reproduction is active, working through the social factors that audiences bring to texts (Corner 1991). The media influence our ideas about Islam by interpreting events to 'fit' with the majority view or beliefs, concerns and values of the target audience, which in this case was already predispositioned to an Orientalist discourse (Lacey and Longman 1997). Where they do not 'fit', negotiation or a conflict of interests takes place, which results in rejection, yet contested spaces appear to be rare (among non-Muslims) in the production of meaning in relation to British Islam.

This news framework has been found to limit knowledge of Islam. It structures the terms in which debate is seen and restricts the discourses available to people, thus making the construction of alternative images difficult. Texts inform people of what is currently acceptable thinking (apparent in the contact group's unwillingness to criticize the ethnic Other but not Islam). The desire to show understanding and tolerance that was evident among non-Muslims (particularly in the contact group) is an illustration of how insensitive and limited media coverage can 'block' people's ability to do so (Lacey and Longman 1997).

These texts allowed a limited scope for differential decodings among non-Muslims. The marginal differentiation appeared to reflect the contradictions in newspaper discourses, which, as has been apparent, are extremely limited. According to van Dijk (1991), it is difficult for white groups to develop counter-ideologies on ethnic discourse, for they do not encounter racism on a regular basis.

The participants who were most able to reject negative representations in texts were those who had more knowledge of the subject area, and the level of this knowledge was affected by various factors such as parental influence, political knowledge and sympathies. Zaller (1992) contends that knowledge is important in being critical as it provides a basis for independent thought. However, according to Fan (1998), most people need some interpretation of events (and are dependent on this) because of the speed with which issues appear and disappear off the agenda and the lack of alternative information.

These findings show that cultural or religious proximity is important for decoding culturally encoded texts. But rather than simply knowing others, it is crucial that the contact includes *knowing about* and understanding complex identities and being able to recognize and deconstruct one's own cultural values in relation to others. The participants who had contact with Muslims were able to separate Muslims they knew as friends from what 'real Islam', which is in fact a media construction, represented to them. That most of their perceptions of Islam were derived from the media was an illustration of the power of the media to have such an impact even when contrary evidence existed in the realm of personal experience. The fact that members of other ethnic groups shared these ideas about Islam despite their own experiences of prejudice made the point particularly clear. It was starkly illustrated by the contributions of a Sikh, whose understandings of Islam, despite being best friends with a Muslim, reflected dominant meanings. She, as others, used the texts to give meaning to experience. It was in this way that the texts helped shape meaning, adding to the groups' models of the situation. They reminded Muslims of their exclusivity position in society and non-Muslims of the threat to their own interests, which for the contact groups was largely their values and for the non-contact groups economical disadvantage. While cultural proximity has proved to be important in identifying with the ethnic Other, it is clearly not enough to know and mix with Muslims. To override dominant media representations, the contact must include dialogue that encourages an understanding of Islamic beliefs and practices, and a sense of how these are interpreted through one's own cultural frameworks.

In addition to cultural proximity, religious identification is an important variable for Muslims when decoding media texts about Islam. While this research provides some evidence of the hybrid identities so celebrated in contemporary theory on the diasporic experience, it also supports arguments about the reassertion of local identities (particularism) in resisting dominant narratives (Ahmed 1992; Bhabha 1994; Hall 1992b; Robins 1991; Thompson 1995). It is argued that processes of globalization, including the migration and displacement of peoples across borders, have permitted the formulation and reformulation of new identities (with multiple subject positions) through the interaction of differences as traditions and boundaries are destabilized in the post-modern world (Cohen 1997; Gilroy 1997; Hall 1988). This is sometimes seen as a solution to the problems of an uncertain existence (Hall 1992b). This syncretic (fusion of) identification (Cohen 1997) appears to be at work here, in particular for the non-Muslim ethnic subjects of the research. *In this context*, the Muslims' real lived experience of an intercultural existence, disadvantage and marginalization alongside cultural rejection, which the texts elicited, resulted in a disaffection for which the solution was a reassertion of religious identity. Processes of media globalization increase the religious identification as the inequalities Muslims suffer internationally are recognized (Ahmed and Donnan 1994). This 'mediated consciousness' (Gilroy 1997) results in 'imagined communities' in which at specific moments global religious identifications override local national interests (Anderson 1983; Gilroy 1988; Werbner 1994).

Alongside these processes, the uncertainties of the global village in which Muslims are 'an ever-present ubiquitous reality' (Ahmed and Donnan 1994) have resulted in a defensive construction of nationality, a discursive strategy to exclude Muslims by host countries (Hall 1992b; Woodward 1997). In this historical trajectory, fixed, essentialist, pure identities are manufactured to provide ethnic certainties (Gilroy 1997). While these are imposed on the Other, nationality has become the main source of identity for the majority (Gellner 1983). The negative expectations and meanings projected onto texts by Muslims, which result in resistance, are a consequence of exclusion and the reality of their position in Britain in their encounters with discrimination. They pay less attention to textual content, being immediately dismissive (particularly the men), as they experience 'cognitive dissonance' over what it means to be a Muslim (Höijer 1998: 178). The women achieve harmony through selectivity and by paying attention to discourses that decrease dissonance. This 'discursive discomfiture' (Dahlgren 1988b: 297) has led to a counter-identification with religion, which has restored self-confidence and strength to young Muslim communities (Jacobson 1997; Werbner 1994). Although it is evident that they are not totally at one with their global counterparts, the identification based on recognition of inequalities across the world further reduces alienation and anxieties.

While it is recognized that all identities are multilayered, particularly through processes of translation, identity shifts according to the way in which subjects are addressed (Hall 1992b). News stories contribute to how we understand our relations with others, and the power of the media is in their ability to define and locate people into certain subject positions, mobilizing identities and excluding or including groups of people. The emphasis on differences, constructed within a framework of conflict and a 'culture clash', while invoking 'Muslim' as a discursive, social category, practised in these articles, encourages the subjects to respond as groups, exacerbating predispositions (Turner 1985). Newspapers manufacture and then exploit bounded impermeable differences, which make the polarization normative; 'identities are produced, consumed and regulated within culture — creating meanings through symbolic systems of representation about the identity positions we might adopt' (Woodward 1997: 2).

The unfortunate consequences of these reductive processes are evident from this audience research. Issues are presented in black and white rather than allowing identification and resolution. By concentrating attention on conflicts that seem unsolvable, genuine issues are hidden and hence less likely to be acted upon. This was evident in the macro-structural organization of the blasphemy article. Its attention to the Rushdie affair raised accusations of provocation by the Muslims (for employing these examples when others could have been used). They did, however, rise to this provocation.

Social distance was increased as the groups took oppositional sides in line with the identities that were mobilized. The Muslims' commitment to their religious identities was reinforced and expressed through social practices and markers of difference that confirmed the media images to the non-Muslims through experience (Jacobson 1997). Furthermore, this increased antagonism between different disadvantaged groups, further consolidating and naturalizing both the differences and the boundaries. Hence, we witness the circularity of power, 'this cycle between reality and representations makes the ideological fictions of racism empirically "True"' (Mercer and Julien 1994: 137–8). Such media coverage therefore invokes social solidarity, accounting for the ethnic consensus apparent here. This works to maintain power relations and cultural hegemony. The 'myth of confrontation' is sustained (Halliday 1996).

This research provided further evidence that in decoding news 'macrostructures, schemata, detailed models, general world knowledge, scripts, attitudes and perspectives and news values are the major determinants that account for variance' (van Dijk 1988b: 159). However, these readings provided evidence that decodings are socially patterned, for these groups shared the same frameworks of interpretation *on this issue*, based on identities mobilized in discourse. Interactions are always social as they are 'embedded in a wider system of social and symbolic relations erected on the basis of systematic inequalities' (Murdock 1998: 205). Within the groups, the responses were not entirely homogenous and there was some evidence of diverse subject positions based on a multiplicity of identity sources, for example the Muslim women identified with Sarah Cook in both her conversion to Islam and as women, which resulted in a different reading from the men. The extent to which these identifications were activated, particularly among the non-Muslim participants, was a sign of the media's effectiveness in defining the situation. While these socially shared meanings appeared to be clear-cut, they were in fact never static and were always being refined through the interaction of textual understandings, socio-demographic factors and personal interaction.

The findings, therefore, were significant in identifying some of the limitations of the method used. As expected, the production of meaning was more complex than the encoding/decoding model allowed, for various reasons including the 'overtly political' nature of the decoding positions (Wren-Lewis 1983) that force readers into pre-existing categories. This research confirmed that not only do people move between these 'ideal typical positions' (Hall, cited in Cruz and Lewis 1994: 256) when reading a text but also that there are different levels of reading. Not all resistant readings could be described as consciously political. The Muslim women, in particular, reconstructed their own meanings (rather than recognizing the ideology and rejecting it). In several cases the participants responded to the event being portrayed rather than to the paper's construction of it. This occurred when the Muslim women responded positively to the proposed blasphemy laws and so, too, to the article. According to the encoding/decoding model, they were positioned oppositionally to the preferred meaning in the text but did not recognize their oppositional position; rather they saw themselves agreeing with the text. The non-Muslims reading this article also believed it to be positive (the contact group ideological) in supporting the law and Labour. They therefore claimed to disagree with the article when in actual fact they were in agreement with its preferred meaning. Are these examples of Eco's (1972: 110) aberrant decoding or 'mis-readings'? He suggested that this was the norm for mass media messages because of the contradictions in the ideologies of text and reader. Or did the readings identified here constitute the 'preferred readings' to each group involved, as Wren-Lewis (1983) might have suggested? Corner and Richardson (1986) would argue that responses such as these to the event were indicative of a 'transparent' reading of the text while those that recognized the text's preferred meaning as explicitly ideological were 'mediated'. Sometimes, a recognition of the mediation process in producing meaning was based on whether the ideology was 'revealed' to the reader because it was at odds with his or her own positions (non-contact group and education article). At other times it depended on the ability of critical individuals to deconstruct texts (media literacy) combined with high levels of media interest and knowledge of relevant information. However, recognizing that a text was ideological did not necessarily mean that its message was resisted.

These results provided an indication of the range of possibilities available to readers when interpreting texts. They were not statically placed in a position of oppositional or dominant reading, since meaning is multilayered, having contradictory spaces, and relates to a multiplicity of identifications and interests. How useful then is the model? Well, using and identifying these decoding positions has allowed the scope for possible readings to be established, locating shared communities of meaning. Perhaps what I have provided approximates the 'set of rules' (proposed by Morley 1981) for decoding texts on Islam: cultural proximity, knowledge and media literacy. It is these factors, then, that are also key to challenging negative images.

It is clear that the instability and complexity of meaning and its continual reinterpretation cannot easily be mapped and fixed. It will continue to be a challenge to identify how these meanings then circulate in society and the ways in which participants act on this information. However, this research has sought to capture a moment of meaning at a given historical conjuncture. It showed what people were willing to say publicly about Islam; these therefore were the meanings circulating in society that had and have real consequences for Muslims and herein lies their importance. While a case can be made for the interpretive production of meaning from this research it appeared to make little difference in terms of social practice. The differential interpretations of non-Muslims resulted in the same consequences for Muslims — alienation and disadvantage. For Muslims, a cycle of empowerment and frustration ensued. Yet the responses of the contact group (to the ethnic Other) also showed that with responsible information and contact progress could be made. Countering this 'cycle of truth' and its negative effects will require media literacy education to promote the critical skills necessary to enable textual deconstruction, although this alone is not enough. I have shown here that people need not only close contact with people from different religious and ethnic groups but also a greater range of information and space within which this can be used to interpret and deconstruct experiences resulting in a deeper under-standing of their own and others values, beliefs and cultures. Inevitably, the media have a significant role to play here.

Conclusion

T his book has addressed questions about the social meanings of British Islam circulating in British society. Through examining representations of British Muslims in sections of the British press and the ways Muslims are known within different audience groups, it has made visible convergences and divergences within press coverage and the frames of expectations of the audiences, and illustrated the strong consensual interpretive frameworks that exist with regard to Muslims in mainstream British society.

Examining press material quantitatively revealed limited frameworks and themes associated with British Islam. However, these emerged as more detailed than their global counterparts, uncovering frameworks of interpretation that incorporated discourses relating to the representation of minority groups in Britain generally. This suggests that within a national context, salient issues relating to national identity and inclusivity take precedence in the representation of minority groups and are equally prominent in the representation of British Muslims.

However, although coverage of British Islam appeared to be increasing, it still constituted only a small proportion of total coverage of Islam. This suggested that 'Islam' continued to be interpreted as predominantly a foreign phenomenon. While coverage of Islam accounted for only a small proportion of news coverage as a whole, Islam had a greater salience than any other religions traditionally associated with the East.

Although British Islam was covered more widely in the liberal press, this constituted only a small proportion of the sector and, given the much larger readership of the conservative press, was likely to be less significant in the dissemination of ideas about Islam. Despite greater attention by the *Guardian* to minority issues, the convergence between the broadsheets in terms of their agenda on what aspects of Islam were considered 'newsworthy' appeared to outweigh the differences between them. In addition, the gap in the volume of coverage between the liberal and conservative broadsheets chosen for this study was closing. This suggested that spaces for oppositional interpretations were severely marginalized and dominated by conservative coverage in the reporting of British Islam.

The qualitative analysis aimed to explore further these initial and tentative theories and to develop the repertoires of representation of British Islam. The findings demonstrated not only the extent of diversity in the discourses available but also the consistency of these across the range of topics (and stories) found in the quantitative analysis. The discursive variance (apart from the expected political criterion) depended on whether a topic contained enough of a foreign element, including information on its nature and origins, to apply national/ethnic stereotypes. The greater the distance of the event from the UK, the greater the essentialist construction based on ideas about Islam and the specifics of Islam within a given country, and the greater the ideological consensus in and between papers. These stories were relatively consistent in their application of relevant aspects of the Orientalist discourse in its original sense. The more an article focused on British issues, the greater its divergence from this global narrative. However, there were also certain common themes in the treatment of these stories. Discourses of inclusivity, economy, separatism and loyalty were prominent. Based mainly on official formulations, these articles represented the strategic discursive construction of the nation, its identity and culture, in a bid to protect this construction from deterioration in the interests of the in-group, and by marginalizing the out-group.

Although these variations represented the core images to be found on Islam in the newspapers examined here, they did not represent total coverage. Coverage is not homogenous. Differential representations reflect not only the variety of values held by different elites in British society but also the news values/conventions of the newspaper forms. Hence, the *Guardian*, as champion of the racialized Other in British society, contested widely held views most frequently. However, this research has shown how its exclusive form of liberalism did not always extend to Muslims because its secular approach, derived from the Enlightenment's separation of public and private spheres, marginalizes religion to the private realm. Its liberal approach to human rights further rendered 'Islamic' practices irrational and barbaric. Voices of dissent therefore appeared mainly in the margins of the paper while the bulk of coverage shared the news values, constructions and categorizations of its conservative counterparts.

The *Sun*, on the other hand, demonstrated different news values. Its populist discourse resulted in Islam being 'not covered' (Said 1981). It clearly engaged in Orientalism with regard to its foreign coverage, but its Orientalist construction of the internal Other was more dominant than in any other paper. The Other was at all times clearly delineated as 'foreign' and subject to ridicule, contributing to a culture of idiocy and avoidance in the public domain. The strategic closure around this representation, which covered over any other differences in British society, has clear implications for the exclusion of Muslims from 'Britishness'.

The increasing tabloidization of the press does not bode well for Muslims. Current variations between papers belie a similar purpose, tending to reveal more about the state of the British nation than they do about Islam. The consistency of the discourse across stories within the papers naturalizes this set of interpretations, giving them their 'truth'. In this way the discourse is essential to the maintenance of power relations, acting as a form of social control.

Does such a regime of representation actually matter? What are the implications for coverage for those who have little contact with Muslims and for Muslims themselves? Do media themes dominate audience understandings? Audience research suggests that non-Muslims share the interpretive frameworks of the press and its variations, expressing a predominantly conservative ideology with regard to Muslims. For the non-contact groups in the research this was expressed within a culture of ignorance, while the contact groups adopted an exclusive liberalism, similar to that of the liberal press. Cultural proximity is only partially successful as a factor in rejecting dominant ideologies, for Muslims in terms of religious identification and for the contact group in terms of anti-racism. Knowledge, group norms and media literacy are other factors important in the decoding of media texts on Muslims, the consistency of which, within the groups, constituted them as 'interpretive communities' in their shared perspectives.

The Muslims adhered to a notion of 'conspiracy theory', partly as a response to experiences of cultural racism, causing them predominantly to reject the ideologies presented to them in the texts. However, it appears that the media does have a role in setting the agenda for issues that are open for discussion. How far this is practised outside a research group that specifically introduces these issues is a matter for further investigation. These findings also contribute to an expanding body of research that shows that religious identification is of growing importance to young Muslims. The media appear to play a role in this by disseminating representations that constitute cultural identity.

While not necessarily suggesting a cause and effect between press representations and audience 'opinion' (reception analysis has enabled researchers to avoid dealing with 'effects'), the results demonstrate a strong correlation between the two. Given the lack of alternative information available to these non-Muslims, this would suggest that the media contribute to the perpetuation and maintenance of a range of dominant ideologies on this issue. These ideas will continue to be promoted through the groups they inform. While there is evidence of some negotiation within the groups, this bears little challenge to dominant meanings and occurs mainly from a desire to present 'the best self' or stems from the multiple points of identification offered by texts.

Do these findings then fit with theories of a Western Orientalist media discourse that constructs Islam as an undifferentiated global aggressor? This project supports the claim that the global image is relatively standardized. Coverage seems to fall into an international relations perspective heavily coloured, it appears, by Western/US foreign policy dictates. Britain's relationship with America in relation to foreign policy would therefore account for these 'stable ideological formations' (Trew 1979: 141). It also appears that there are some persistent ideas that have found their expression in coverage of British Islam: that Islam is static and that Muslims are resistant to progress, engage in antiquated and repressive practices that abuse human rights, and often use their religion to manipulative ends. The use of specific terminology and extreme individuals to reveal the hierarchy of access in which Muslims are unable to represent themselves is also apparent. That Islam is deemed an alien culture with the allegiances of its people held elsewhere is equally evident. Islam is given consistently as the prime motive for (anti-social) behaviour, which renders social causation with a group of people for this aspect of their identity (Muslimness) and then prefers a solution based on control. The resulting picture of the more rational, humane, democratic and superior host country or culture is inevitable. Equally, this representation is considered unproblematic in all but a few articles in the *Guardian*.

However, this theory neither embodies the diversity of representation within specific national contexts nor takes into account the distinctions made between Muslims based on national/ethnic stereotypes, which results in a more diverse, though still limited and reductive range. This wider diversity in the frameworks of interpretation is due to local factors that impinge on dominant representations. Britain's relationship with its minorities, for example, its established religion and ideas of what constitutes a multicultural society, is very different from that of America. The organization and composition of the press also varies from country to country. In the UK, different groups have differing conceptualizations of the inclusivity of British society. The result is not only a departure from the US driven global image but also diversity within the national context. In addition, Eurocentric thinking not only accounts for a lack of understanding of religion and its importance to certain groups, but also leads to sympathy towards notions of equality. The tensions between these opposing views result in expressions amounting to 'pseudo-equality' (Shohat and Stam 1994: 48).

In Chapter 1, I addressed the question of the continuing relevance of Orientalism. This research shows how the discourse of Orientalism has been transcoded and transferred to the internal Other. Its central elements were used to exoticize and render the internal Other as inherently different if not ultimately 'foreign'. It is functional in that it allows the Other to be managed and promotes an agreed sense of national identity at the Other's expense in order to protect and maintain social systems and structures. By representing Muslims in such a way, it absolves responsibility for including them and thus necessitating this change. The hegemony is maintained. Rather than rendering Orientalism outdated (due to the demise of national distinctions), processes of globalization have increased the need for such constructions in creating stable boundaries as anxieties increase. In limiting the frameworks of interpretations to containing ethnocentric ideological assumptions with strategic interests, the Orientalist discourse continues to be a contemporary force.

While Orientalism persists in the way Islam is understood, in a British context it incorporates a wider range of discourses relating to minority groups and religion. If what is being played out in the press is a negotiation around national cultural identity, are all minorities in Britain treated in a similar way to Muslims? And, given the secular nature of the press, are all religions treated in the same way? Clearly not: although minority groups continue to be problematized, explicit hostility has shifted to Muslims in the current political epoch.[1] Ethnic minorities continue to be represented in a race relations paradigm, which excludes Muslims or the identification of Muslims. The media have closed the concept of Islam. When the frameworks of meanings associated with Muslims are not to be signified, racial terms rather than the category 'Muslim' are used.[2] Equally, although not dealt with systematically by this thesis, religious groups are treated with different political, social and cultural criteria from Islam.

In some criticisms of media representation, for example those of Esposito (1992), Halliday (1992) and Hassan (1997), examples are offered of 'real' Muslims, egalitarian and observant or victimized to counter the 'misrepresentations'. Often, groups look to the specifics of their own identity, their 'experienced reality' to invalidate the representations of themselves and groups to which they belong in the media (Eldridge 1991: 348). This presupposes that there is some neutral image that could replace the 'distorted', an issue that was raised in Chapter 1 in relation to 'the real Orient' and cross-cultural representation. The replacement of those images identified here with another unified image would be equally unsatisfactory. What has been emphasized throughout this thesis is that there is no one correct image. Cultural descriptions should therefore represent the variety of *interpretations* of Muslim life, including that of the non-observant Muslim, not to mention the numerous interpretations of Islam across countries, sects and races. News does not 'misrepresent' Muslims as such, but it reduces the rich variety of life to a simplified limited framework informed by 'Occidental cultural legacies' that are transmuted within contemporary political conditions (Caldwell 1977: 30). The intention of this research has been to show what this framework looks like. Islam should not be constructed as the sole explanation for the behaviour of a multitude of different people unified into a collectivity through external definition.

The news genre clearly has effects on Islam's representation. For example, general news values are applied in terms of elitism, negativity and personification. However, while it is the tendency of news to limit the public sphere, the reductive and limited news frame that has developed around Islam has an additional selective emphasis based on cultural prejudice, which feeds into news processes and journalistic practices. Therefore, as has been found in the coverage of other ethnic minorities in Britain, Muslims have a higher news value when they are a source of problems for the dominant majority. Galtung and Ruge's

(1965) notion of cultural proximity is significant. The more culturally distant an event is from people's experience the more it has to resonate within accepted categories; in other words an event has to be one that captures attention particularly easily, has already entered the public imagination and fits in with a pattern of expectation. The lower the perceived rank of the culture, the more unusual and yet stereotyped the event has to be. It must be unambiguous. These events acquire presentation in terms of 'ideal types', giving the impression of uniformity and homogeneity. A continuity effect then develops so that once a channel or chain of news becomes open, an event acquires a news value that can be artificial. This demonstrates the importance of examining the context of mediated issues in order to provide a valid analysis. In attending to the conventions of news, it would appear that this research provides some insight into the possible representations of Muslims in other news forms.

The competing discourses found in the press and between the Muslim and non-Muslim audience groups in this research represent a struggle for power in Britain that is both real and symbolic. As Muslim groups grow more and more disenchanted with media representations and their marginalizing effects, a struggle around the image is taking place. Increasingly, Muslims are becoming a more powerful lobbying force and they have made efforts to create a representative body with which the government can negotiate and which the media can use as a credible source to limit the exposure of extremist groups. This has led to the formation of the Muslim Council of Britain,[3] which appears to have been effective in lobbying New Labour. Part of this success is due to New Labour's official ideological approach to minority groups. In its 1995 submission to the United Nations Committee on the Elimination of Racial Discrimination (CERD), it stated that its objective was to enable minorities 'to participate freely and fully in the economic, social and public life of the nation, with all the benefits and responsibilities that entails, while still being able to maintain their own culture, traditions, language and values' (Runnymede Trust 1997: 1). While engaging in a rhetoric of inclusivity and a celebration of the success of blacks and Asians, Jacques (*Observer*, 28 December 1997: 14–15) argues that New Labour has been selective in its incorporation of groups into its idea of a new 'national renaissance'. Jacques suggests that while black and Asian youth culture is celebrated for providing role models, Muslims are marginalized as having no contribution to make.

On this basis, I would suggest that while New Labour appears to have provided some space for Muslim participation in its vision of a plural society, this has amounted to little more than courting the community. Action such as funding two Muslim schools is, I believe, a way of placating Muslims. Providing small gestures of appeasement that have little impact on the status quo quietens protest from Muslims but causes little dissent among the majority community, so therefore has little effect on the social structure. However, despite this, these small steps are an improvement on previous relations. Has this shift in the political landscape altered representations? Or has it, as Jacques suggested, led to new and encouraging attitudes existing alongside continuing old patterns of discrimination? Jacques's article in the *Observer*, for example, provided a positive illustration of a new inclusive representation, celebrating commonalties and contributions but it was followed, over the page, by an article on the Middle East that discussed conspiracy theories in relation to the death of the Princess of Wales. This engaged in a traditional Orientalist discourse, signifying the inherent irrationality of Muslims and homogenized Muslims by referring to a number of events to illustrate this: Rushdie, the Luxor massacre, Iran, and Yasser Arafat.[4] However, this was also an example of the distinctions made in the press between foreign and British Muslims. Are the more positive examples of representation equally false constructions, gestures of appeasement? Will the increasing visibility of Muslims, as they struggle for recognition, lead to a more defensive approach by those who oppose this, attempting to fix identities in the continual process of society's redefinition? Ros Coward (*Guardian*, 11 May 1999: 15) argues that there is 'unparalleled disaffection' among the majority population to 'the rhetoric of minority rights' that was employed in the wake of the London nail bomb attacks of 1999. She suggests that there is a growing resentment among 'ordinary people' who, despite adhering to the politics of equality and anti-discrimination, feel disadvantaged in relation to 'privileged' minorities. Majority groups are feeling increasingly threatened by this exemption to consensual order, especially at a time of considerable ethnic, cultural and demographic change.[5] There was certainly evidence for this, particularly among the non-contact groups.

While there is some evidence for improvements in the *Guardian* in the form of positive features, conscious use of lexical items such as 'Islamists' and the employment of two Muslim journalists, Faisal Bodi and Faisal Islam, the latter to comment on non-Muslim affairs, many of the activities in which Muslim groups are involved are still ignored by the media as they continue to adopt traditional frameworks in relation to Islam. For example, a meeting between the Muslim Council of Britain and the Labour Party on 6 May 1999 to celebrate the contribution of Muslims to Britain was followed the next day with coverage about Mohammad al Fayed, who attended the meeting, having again been refused British citizenship. Despite some ability to set the agenda then, Muslims continue to be interpreted predominantly within an ethnocentric framework. These frameworks have become the organizing factor for representing Islam and continue to be routinely applied, as coverage in 1999 confirmed (see Appendix D, which can be compared with earlier quantitative data in Chapters 2 and 3). A similar volume of coverage on similar topics ensued in that year. More ominously, coverage of fundamentalism grew to 20 per cent of reporting on British Islam. Outside the dominant framework that had been established (politics, relationships, crime, and Rushdie and related concerns), which covered 72 per cent of articles in 1999, two topics increased in prominence. These were immigration and the Nation of Islam. Immigration has been revived as a hot political issue in recent years because of the increase in refugees from Eastern Europe. The Nation of Islam overtook both the Muslim Parliament and al-Muhajiroun as a prominent example of an extremist group for the press, partly because of its appearance at the Stephen Lawrence inquiry, which it was accused of hijacking for political gain. Islam's relationship with Christianity also featured highly in articles because of a debate about the contents of the faith zone in the Millennium Dome.

The issue of racism was also significant in 1999, evidence of the continual struggle for representation by Muslims. Its presence in the *Mail*, however, was functional, to illustrate the lunacy of 'political correctness' in education policies, the police and the military. Other main stories included a series of reports on disputes over circumcision, often between Muslim and non-Muslim parents, and the trial of a mother and brother for the honour killing of a Muslim woman who fled from an arranged marriage and which resulted in a government inquiry into 'forced marriages'. Reflection on Princess Diana's relationships and on Jemima and Imran Khan continued, further adding to the negativization found in this narrowing and persistent framework.

Early indications from the data available from coverage in 2000 show a continued focus on asylum and, linked to it, fundamentalism, forced marriages and human rights legislation, which allows Muslims to challenge British law on such issues as polygamy. The *Mail* continued to focus heavily on 'political correctness', but ironically the government's efforts to withdraw Clause 28 forbidding the promotion of homosexuality in schools, by far the predominant story in 2000, saw Muslims constructed positively in allegiance with groups opposing the change in law. However, domestic coverage appeared to drop in the year 2000 as coverage of Islam was dominated by global events. Given the Orientalist construction of these events in all papers, this is not a positive occurrence and demonstrates the importance of continued scrutiny of coverage.

Despite Muslim lobbying, there is as yet no clause in the NUJ's code of practice about religious discrimination, only one relating to racism. The relatively ineffective Press Commission's code refers only to the disapproval of 'prejudicial or pejorative' references to a person's race or religion within a framework that prioritizes freedom of speech (Runnymede Trust 1997: 25) Yet, given that representation takes place within an unequal set of social relations, would such changes, if they came about, have any impact?[6] White, middle-class males dominate the media, particular in the upper echelons, and it is probable that they believe the ideology they reproduce to be natural and common-sensical. While some academics have spoken of the need for more people from ethnic minorities to work in the media, others believe it would simply lead to their incorporation into the system through learnt professionalism. For all groups to be represented fairly in the media on a democratic basis, would an overhaul of both the democratic system in society and therefore other structures within this society be required, along the lines of Husband's (1996) 'multi-ethnic public sphere'?[7]

Because of the way in which they have been categorized in the media, Muslims have found it necessary to adopt a Muslim collectivity in which Muslim identity is central to try to present news organizations with alternative information about them. Their identity is therefore both projected and imagined. Muslims are attributed with characteristics that have ideological significance within a collective construction. Trew (1979: 118) suggests that news frameworks work 'cumulatively to link events of various kinds under the same stereotypes and headings and to express the perceptions as those of specific social forces or groupings'. The group categorization is continually applied and constructed in

opposition to other groups. According to Cohen (1988: 72), it constitutes a 'totalizing strategy' with which an individual is constructed as a
Muslim whatever other characteristics or commonalties he or she may
share with other groups.[8] It turns issues of importance to the nation into
specifically minority issues and promotes disinterest among the
majority population. And it limits democratic participation not only
among non-Muslims over these issues but also among Muslims because
their feelings of alienation prevent action and resolution. The conflictual framework within which different groups are constructed
(which focuses on essential differences rather than commonalties) per-
petuates the 'myth of confrontation', 'the clash of civilizations', which
suggests that Western cultures and Islam can never get on and therefore
Muslims cannot integrate, further marginalizing their place in society.
The media play a significant role in promoting the making of such
boundaries by locating, naturalizing and closing identities. While I have
argued that identities have fluidity, the audience groups in the research
illustrated how people can be mobilized on the basis of common and
oppositional identities as the media attempt to fix them. Addressed as
groups, the Muslims, for example, made religious identifications above
other levels of differentiation because the textual categorization focused
on and attacked their religion. The cultural relativism newspapers practise and express through the idea of a cultural clash leads to misunderstanding and antagonism, and exacerbates tension, resulting in the
polarization of groups and hence in sustaining social relations. Social
action then contributes to the 'social construction of reality' (Eldridge
1991: 335). The narrowing of issues to binary oppositions, for example
to issues of freedom of speech versus racism, occurs from both the left
and the right of the political spectrum. Neither of these perspectives
allow for any real debate on issues such as 'how to resolve the tensions
between the preservation of the distinct cultural identity of minority
communities on the one hand and the encouragement of social integration on the other' (Halstead 1988: 64).

Theories on the representation of Islam have drawn attention to a
radical and explicit anti-Islamic presence in the media. The overall
picture of Islam that is produced in the media over a period of time
creates this effect. However, this research shows the gradations of
difference in such representations. Binary forms of representation are
more often utilized in foreign news, while the representation of British
Islam is more complex, with discourse sometimes attempting to

formulate a pluralist version of the country. Much of this global anti-Islamic discourse enters the framework of reporting on British Muslims, but the process is subtler. It has to be. Not only is there a lack of conflict for the media to focus on in Britain, but also issues and events are closer to people's knowledge and experiences.[9] The underlying discourses and the way in which articles on British Muslims are framed (constructed around conflict) subtly transmit ideologies that over a period of time and coverage reinforce the ideologies disseminated through coverage of global Islam. It should be remembered that while it is possible to separate the coverage of Islam into news abroad and at home for the purpose of analysis, given that Muslims are largely presented as undifferentiated, the picture of them created in the media is the same for both types of coverage, which the audience studies demonstrated. The limited coverage of British Muslims is outweighed by the vast amounts of global coverage with which it must compete. A recent article introducing the Muslim Council of Great Britain in the *Guardian* (19 November 1997), while fairly positive and highlighting Muslim sources, was embedded with scepticism about factionalism and divisions in the Muslim community. This article was located among seven other stories in which global Islam was represented as extreme, including stories on the Egyptian fundamentalists (after Luxor), fighting in Algeria and Afghanistan, the Iraqi crisis, Islamists in Turkey, a letter on Rushdie and freedom of speech, and a special report on Jordan. The presence of these articles brings into question the statement from 'many prominent Muslims' in the article on British Islam that the very images embedded in the stories are unrepresentative.

It is clear then that there are problems in constructing a dualism between the existence of either a global or a local narrative. As Sardar (1999) suggests, diversity across the spectrum of representation does exist but does not preclude a general negativization. Such diversity still exists within a meta-narrative. Contemporary coverage is increasingly the outcome of translocal processes that have made it difficult to disentangle the local and global. Both coverage and, in particular, Muslims responses to it illustrate processes of 'glocalization' at work (Robertson 1992: 175); the concept of *glocalization* takes account of the mutually constituting forces at work, 'the global production of the local in the global and the localization of the global' (Barker 1999: 42).

The outcome of these processes is a representational paradigm that is 'Islam', which has some strength and on this basis appears to have a considerable collective effect. This research shows that press coverage matters. In defining the social reality through which Muslims are known, definitions that are 'pervasive and authoritarian' (Murdock 1998: 211), coverage helps us make sense of the social meanings of Islam and therefore has a significant role in contributing to and sustaining these meanings. The patterns of representation that have been explicated through this research, despite their differences, have similar effects. They legitimize current social relations of dominance, power structures and therefore continuing patterns of discrimination. Muslims are predominantly excluded from Britishness. The sense of mistrust, alienation and disempowerment this causes, can only contribute to hindering positive social relations.

There is, however, some room for optimism. This research has revealed the spaces of opposition that already exist and that could be expanded. The audience research illustrates the desire of non-Muslims (contact group) to learn about and be sensitive to other cultures, but media information is limiting their knowledge and understanding of Islam. This suggests that if exposed to a greater diversity of information, relations could be improved.

These data are insufficient for making conclusive remarks about the complex process of the production of meanings. Their multiplicity and fluidity mean that the category 'Islam' will be subject to continuous historical and social change and its media representation will undergo similar transformations. These conclusions are therefore tentative and are put forward to provide an insight into the social meanings produced about Islam at a given time and place and at a specific historical and political conjuncture. However, they provide a context in which further research can be undertaken, and therefore constitute a vital part of a process through which we can build a picture of a social phenomenon under study.

Appendix A: Topical clusters: themes and meanings of British Islam

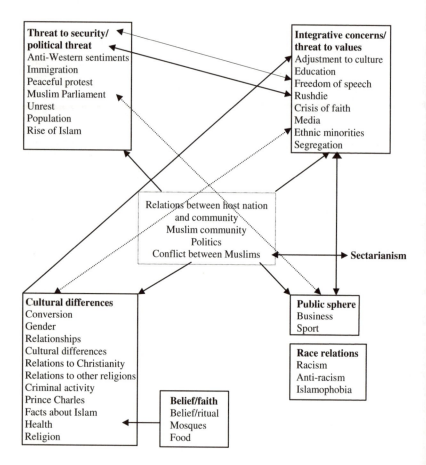

Appendix B: Glossary of terms used in discourse analysis*

Detraction: where a disjuncture occurs between the headline and report (van Dijk 1991).

Global coherence: relations between facts (between articles) (van Dijk 1988b: 61–65).

Local coherence: relationships between facts (in sentences) (van Dijk 1988b: 61).

Macrosemantics: global (overall) meanings (van Dijk 1988b: 26).

Macrostructure: the hierarchical organization of the text (van Dijk 1988b: 32).

Metonymia: a figure of speech in which one word or phrase is substituted for another with which it is closely associated (see van Dijk 1991: 222).

Modality: 'comment' or 'attitude' ascribable to the source of a text, for example giving permission or expressing desirability (Fowler 1991: 85).

Nominalizations: sentences without full clauses with active verbs, often used to conceal responsible agency (van Dijk 1991: 63).

Participants: the entities involved in the process (Trew 1979: 123).

Process: term used by Halliday as 'covering all phenomena to which a

---

* Most of these linguistic tools are described in any of the books utilized here, but I have, however, provided a reference for easy referral.

specification of time attaches whether events, relations or states' (Trew 1979: 123).

Propositions: single sentence clauses (van Dijk 1988b: 31).

Register (linguistic): 'a set of meanings that is appropriate to a particular function of language, together with the words or structures which express these meanings' (Halliday, quoted in Fowler 1991: 37).

Schemata/superstructure: overall organizational patterns (van Dijk 1988b: 26).

Semantics: meanings of words, sentences and discourse (van Dijk 1988b: 25).

Speech acts: social acts by the use of words, for example promise, accuse, congratulate (van Dijk 1988b: 26).

Transactive clause: a process with two participants, one the active clause, one acted upon (Trew 1979: 124).

Appendix C:
Tabulated demographic details (audience)

Table C1   Gender of participants: focus groups

	Female	Male	Total	%
Muslim	6	6	12	24
Contact	8	13	21	43
Non-contact	13	3	16	33
Total	27	22	49	
%	55	45		

Table C2   Religious affiliation by (reported) origin

	Indian	African	Philippine	Malawi	Mixed race*	Punjabi	Total
Hindu	1				2		3
Catholic			1				1
Muslim	7	3		1	1		12
Sikh						2	2
Total	8	3	1	1	3	2	18

*   African/Indian.

Table C3 Importance of religion by religious groupings

	Not important	Sometimes important	Important	Very important	Total	%
None	11				11	22
Christian	14	3		1	18	37
Sikh		1	1		2	4
Hindu	1	2			3	6
Muslim			5	7	12	24
Atheist	3				3	6
Total	29	6	6	8	49	
%	59	12	12	16		

Table C4 First language (reported) of ethnic minority group members

	Gujarati	English	Punjabi	Katchi	Total
Hindu	3				3
Muslim	10 (83%)	1		1	12
Sikh			2		2
Total	13	1	2	1	17

Table C5 Interest in news

	Interested		Sometimes		No interest	
Muslim	7	58%	1	8.0%	2	16%
Contact	15	71%	2	9.5	3	14%
Non contact	9	56%	6	37.5	1	6%
Total	31	63	9	18	6	12

Unreported cases = 2 Muslims, 1 contact group.

Table C6   Newspaper usage

	Everyday	Regularly	Occasionally	Rarely	Unreported
Muslim	4	4	0	2	2
Contact	7	5	4	4	1
Non contact	5	4	4	3	0
Total	16	13	8	9	3
%	32	26.5	16	18	6

Table C7   Main source of news

	TV		Newspaper		Radio		Teletext		Personal contacts		Satellite	
Muslim	7	58%	2	17%	1	8%					1	
Contact	14	66%	6	28.5	1	5%	2	9.5	1		1	
Non-contact	15	94%	5	31%	3	19%						
Total	36	73%	13	26.5	5	10%	2	4%	1	2%	2	4%

Note: some students chose more than one type of medium.

Table C8   Newspaper readership

	Muslim	Contact	Non-contact	Total	Parents' paper N	%
Local	5	6	8	19	14	74
The Times	2	3		5	5	100
Guardian		6		6	4	67
Sun	2	3	5	10	5	50
Mirror	1	4	1	6	3	50
Express	1	1	2	4	2	50
Mail		1	3	4	3	75
Independent		1		1	1	100
Socialist Worker		2		2		
Church Times		1		1		
Muslim News	1			1		
Total	12	28	19	59	37	63
More than one paper		11*	3*			28

*   The breakdown is included in the above.

Appendix D:
Significant topics in 1999

Newspaper topic	Guardian	The Times	Mail	Total
Fundamentalism	55	42	10	107
Politics	12	19	26	57
Relations to Christianity	13	11	8	32
Relationships	10	12	9	31
Crime	6	14	11	31
Education	15	6	3	24
Immigration	11	8	4	23
Racism	9	6	4	19
Nation of Islam	7	3	4	14
Belief	3	7	1	11
Freedom of speech	3	4	2	9
Rushdie	3	2	2	7
Religious discrimination	6	0	0	6
Royalty	0	1	4	5
Total	153	135	88	376
% Total articles in 1999	69.8	70.6	79.2	72.1
Total articles in 1999	219	191	111	521

Notes

Preface: after 11 September 2001

1. Evidence is already emerging of the extent to which the British media are minimizing the reporting of public dissent to the war (Miller, D. *World opinion opposes the attack on Afghanistan*, 21 November 2001. http:// staff.stir.ac.uk/david.miller)
2. Had newspapers been more critical of this, the allies might have felt the need to explore other possibilities. This was evident from the US government's initially cautious approach to avoid accusations of 'knee-jerk reactions'.
3. Part of the legislation package rushed through as a consequence of the attacks.
4. This culminated in the self-aggrandizing stance it assumed on 24 November when it revealed its own role in investigating 'terrorist cells'.
5. It confirmed its own fears by producing a poll that 'finds' that four out of ten British Muslims 'believe Osama bin Laden was right to mount war on America' (4 November).

Introduction

1. This constitutes a massive construct but is used frequently in the literature to describe a geopolitical region, a set of societies seen to be sharing similar economic, social and cultural characteristics. Given its origins, where it has been used ideologically to signify modernity (Hall 1992b), it is increasingly displaced by the use of 'North' and 'South' (though not unproblematically).
2. These theories are developed further in Chapter 1.
3. 'Ideology' is defined here as 'the mental frameworks — the languages, the concepts, categories, imagery of thought and systems of representation which different classes and social groups deploy in order to make sense of, define and figure out and render intelligible the way society works' (Hall 1986: 29).
4. 'Stereotypes' as meaning 'reduced to a few essentials, fixed in nature by a few, simplified characteristics' (Hall 1997b: 249).
5. I use the term 'minority' here in its political sense, to signify marginalized groups rather than just numbers of people.

6. Halliday 1992; Silverman and Yuval-Davis 1998.

7. It is not entirely correct to set apart the religious reference 'Muslim' with 'white'. However, it does enable some point of comparison given the ethnic make-up of Muslim communities in the UK.

8. Obscuring 'white' Muslims. The method of compiling statistics on the Muslim population varies with each research project and results in the concealing of some groups (Knott and Noon 1982). However, the inclusion of a question on religious affiliation in the 2001 census will rectify some of these inadequacies and provide much needed up-to-date information.

9. Given that the highest proportion of Muslims in Great Britain are South Asian (65–75 per cent) (Runnymede Trust 1997), it is likely that this is the most common representation of British Muslims in the British press.

10. Defined as 'an outlook or world-view involving an unfounded dread and dislike of Muslims which results in practices of exclusion and discrimination' (Runnymede Trust 1997: 1).

11. Although they did not coin the term, arguing that it already had a presence in the British Muslim community due to experiences of discrimination. It was first used, however, in the USA in relation to Russia and its activities in Afghanistan, *Insight*, 4 February 1991, p. 37 (Runnymede Trust 1997: 1).

12. It is not my intention to homogenize British society here. This interpretation of events is what has been found through analysis (of press articles and the literature).

13. Silverman and Yuval-Davis (1998: 13) use the concept of 'racialization' as 'a definition of the essentialist construction of groups produced through a discourse of cultural absolutism/relativism'. They argue that cultural racism is not a new phenomenon and has always been central to understanding the Other, but has gained in significance as biological constructions are no longer viable.

14. Meaning is understood as 'the process of making sense of the world around us' (Dahlgren 1988b: 287).

15. Though it is not my intention to detail and justify the methodologies used in this project, further details can be obtained from the author.

16. Sampling decisions are discussed further in Chapter 4.

Chapter 1: Representing Islam: in theory and practice

1. This tendency to differentiation, Ahmad (1992) also suggests, is presented as a given feature of humanity rather than as a social construct.

2. To call these movements 'Islamic' is to offend the majority of Muslims. I use Sayyid's terminology 'Islamism', which he defines as 'a discourse that attempts to centre Islam within the political order' (Sayyid 1997: 17).

He equates it with other political discourses such as socialism and liberalism in all their diverse forms. These groups may be 'committed to the rule of law as well as terrorists and oppressive regimes which maintain they are motivated by Islamic principles' (Runnymede Trust 1997: 8).

3. Resulting in the disenchantment of the petty bourgeoisie, disillusioned at not entering power after post-colonial mobilization. Gilsenan (1990) suggests that this accounts for the educated and professional nature of many Islamic groups.

4. Sayyid (1997) highlights how the restriction of public space led to the politicization of the mosque, providing a discursive space and leading to a politicized religious vocabulary.

5. This is an example of writers referring to a 'real Orient' to counter the 'distorted' image of Islam. Although I am giving expression to these here, I will not continue with this practice while presenting my own findings due to my own ideas about representation and reality.

6. See Shohat and Stam 1994, for their critique of Eurocentrism within popular culture.

7. Having emerged in the context of globalization and the demise of biological definitions of race and resulting in exclusion from cultural conceptions of nation (Giroux 1994; Gordon and Klug 1986; Hall 1992b).

8. This global hostility (of Muslims) is also transferred via the media to the non-Muslim community resulting in further antagonism.

9. In other words, they are being recognized by researchers who are asking more questions about ethnic identity.

10. Elite here refers to members of higher socioeconomic groups, but it has in studies sometimes referred to other groups with a superior position in society, such as men and the white majority.

Chapter 2: Framing Islam: a quantitative analysis

1. Over a period of three years, 1994 to 1996.

2. The commercialization of news is making this increasingly questionable. However, this conception of the broadsheets still circulates among news-makers and the general public, particularly in comparison with tabloid journalism.

3. *Guardian*, 13 November 2000; *Media Guardian*, p.6; Peak and Fisher (1997).

4. Due to a combination of operating in an increasingly commercial market and the shift of the political centre to the right.

5. Currently at 460,427 daily sales compared with its 1965 circulation of 829,000 (*Guardian*, 13 November 2000, *Media Guardian*, p.6; Peak and Fisher 1997).

6. Incorporating Golding and Elliot's (1979: 156) 'home news abroad' and 'foreign news at home' categories.

7. It could be argued that the amount of material generated on global Islam is a reflection of the numerous countries that constitute Islam internationally. However, given the home news focus of the British press, this indicates a perception of Muslims as having little to do with daily activity in Britain.

8. Numbers for global include the British coverage, namely global = total coverage.

9. Unless identified separately, reference to the *Guardian* also includes the *Observer*. The same applies for *The Times*/*Sunday Times*.

10. The *Observer* and *Sunday Times* reflect the fluctuation of their sister papers with the *Sunday Times* also showing an increase in each year. However, both papers have similar averages of coverage: the *Observer* has about 33 articles a year, accounting for 20 per cent of all articles in the *Guardian*/*Observer*, the *Sunday Times* has 34 articles a year, 31 per cent of *The Times*/*Sunday Times* coverage.

11. These patterns prevail in terms of total news coverage (all articles included in the papers annually regardless of subject). Both papers show an increase in total annual reportage from 1994 to 1999 with a greater increase in *The Times* (from 89,985 to 113,946). The *Guardian*'s total coverage remains fairly steady, rising from 71,548 to 77,405 articles in 1999. So, although *The Times* included a similar quantity of articles on British Islam as the *Guardian* by 1999, these accounted for a lower percentage of its total annual copy, 0.16 per cent compared with the *Guardian*'s 0.28 per cent. The reporting of Islam globally accounts for 0.7 per cent of *The Times*' total coverage and 1.7 per cent of the *Guardian*'s, being further evidence of the *Guardian*'s greater interest in minority/foreign news (but also evidence of the limited attention to Islam in general).

12. All totals include the Sunday papers unless they are identified separately.

13. From this point on, the data are based on the three-year period under analysis only, 1994–96.

14. This difference in news values is also illustrated by a different criterion for the inclusion of obituaries. Although the total amount of obituaries is the same for each paper over the three years, on closer examination, the amount for each paper differs widely in each year despite a similarity in news-gathering techniques for obituaries.

15. Only global coverage due to the laborious task of separating international from local news that requires an examination of every article.

16. Over the three-year period there were 10,577 articles on Judaism (35.3 per cent); 10,548 on Christianity (35.2 per cent); 6507 on Islam (21.7 per cent); 1070 on Buddhism (3.5 per cent); 978 on Hinduism (3.2 per cent) and 260

on Sikhism (0.86 per cent). Coverage was relatively consistent in each year (Figure 2.4).

17. Focusing on events that fit with the news values of a particular culture for which news-gathering mechanisms are organized to maximize the retrieval of these events.

18. Although, as Downs argues, minority issues receive much less interest generally than majority concerns.

19. However, articles are also widely dispersed among subject areas. This is partly due to methodology. Certain topics, for example, might have been subsumed under others, for example Islamophobia into discrimination, thus providing more substantial percentages, but this would also have been reductive.

20. To clarify the difference between topics and themes. The topic is the main subject of the article analysed. Themes are broader issues or discourses that run across topics. These will become more apparent through the qualitative analysis.

21. For definitions of code categories please contact the author.

22. Normal news stories are defined as a news story in which a Muslim has been involved and is identified as such but in which their 'being a Muslim' is a subsidiary factor to the central interest of the story, for example a car crash.

23. This did reflect policy decisions in allocating services in terms of racial groups, but the disadvantage this caused and the protests Muslims made regarding this policy were not attended to in the press coverage.

24. Realistic group conflict theory postulates the argument that ethnic groups are more likely to be involved in crime due to their real deprivation and disadvantage, which creates intergroup conflict which the media then reflects (Levine and Campbell 1972).

25. Articles focusing mainly on facts about Islam were more likely to be applied generally than to Muslims within a particular location, so would have been removed on initial analysis, thus explaining their low occurrence.

26. It is also a consequence of this coding frame, which only identifies articles in which the word 'Muslim' is mentioned. It is a matter for further analysis to establish in what type of stories about Muslims their religion is not specified.

27. One problem with content analysis is its artificial fragmentary nature, forcing discrete categories when many of the topics have elements of more than one or all of the themes running through their depiction.

28. By actor I mean the central character discussed in the article.

29. Actors from other religions occupy similar non-Establishment roles as community members and spokespeople.

30. Not all social roles are shown in this graph. Others included academics, business figures, committee members, and reports with different types of

actors, police officers, and athletes. There were fewer women in all these positions.

31. These were the articles in which women appeared most frequently, but not necessarily more often than men. However, women were mentioned more frequently than men in articles on conversion, gender and relationships.

32. This could reflect the low participation of Muslim women in employment for socio-cultural reasons (Anwar 1993).

33. *British Muslims Monthly Survey*, Centre for the Study of Islam and Christian–Muslim Relations, Selly Oak Colleges, Birmingham.

34. For example, the topic of conversion is almost exclusively covered in relation to Islam. Cultural differences are reified in terms of the problematization of the Other and the meanings established are based on age-old practices of alienating the religion, preventing further conversions and the spread of Islam.

Chapter 3: British Islam: a discursive construction

1. The *Guardian*, 13 November 2000, Media Guardian, p. 6; Peak and Fisher, 1997.

2. In terms of international reportage, the *Mail* covered Luxor and the fate of the Saudi nurses in detail. Other coverage included items on suicide bombers, idiosyncratic articles such as the production of 'appropriate' dolls in Iran and only transient attention to other global conflicts. This clearly established the paper as parochial, interested only in events affecting Britain. Other articles appeared only to construct an image of fanaticism and difference.

3. These extra articles were necessary because, at the time of analysis (1997), there appeared to be little substantial coverage in this area. Later in this year, more coverage of education emerged, increasing the numbers. These provided further evidence of the prevalent discourses. However, including articles from 1996 was only possible with the broadsheets as a result of the availability of electronic searching.

4. As coined by John Arlidge in the *Observer*, 25 May 1997.

5. See Appendix B for glossary of discourse terms.

6. Other depictions symbolize her status before the event. Dressed in school uniform and exhibiting displeasure, they represent her insecurity, reinforced by textual references to her ugliness and having suffered from bullying. This has the effect of reproducing assumptions that women embrace Islam out of fear and vulnerability (Holt 1996).

7. All articles in this chapter are from 1997 unless stated otherwise.

8. 'Global' and 'local' take on different meanings in discourse analysis (see Appendix B). In this chapter global coherence is the general coherence of

the story across articles and local coherence the coherence of facts within a specific article.

9. I do not wish to suggest that this issue is of equal importance to all Muslims, according Muslims a lack of divergence of which the press is guilty on this issue. The tendency here to represent Muslims as 'aggregates of people' reads unsympathetically and weakens their case for reform (Fowler 1991).

10. But the nature of multiculturalism and its substance in the UK are not debated. 'Multicultural' here is being used strategically.

11. There is an element here in the liberal press that conceives of minorities as having problems and therefore needing assistance, as well as the common conception of causing problems, as in the right-wing press.

12. 'The counter strategy of taking an existing (negative) meaning and reappropriating it with a new (positive) meaning'.

13. The absence of foreign references (prevalent in the quantitative analysis) was due to the lack of coverage on Islamic fundamentalism in education in 1997. An analysis of this coverage may find less variation in its presentation between papers.

14. It is my contention that the national press prefer to use girls wearing as near to the full black *chador* as possible, other than in circumstances previously alluded to, in contrast with the Muslim press, which show women in a wider variety of dress. However, the material analysed here did not provide sufficient evidence for this and requires further investigation.

15. Equality in education had more widespread acceptance (if only on the surface) than other areas, which was borne out in the quantitative findings.

16. www.mcb.org.uk, 22 June 2001.

17. Rebecca Smithers, *Guardian*, 17 April 2000.

18. For many Muslims, it was this event that led to the demonization of Muslims in the UK. According to Dr Zaki Badawi, 'The truth of the matter is that when Rushdie was incarcerated, so was the Muslim community' (quoted in *The Tablet*, 3 October 1998).

19. According to Silverman and Yuval-Davis (1998), the Rushdie affair exposed Britain's 'multicultural' project as a compensatory model based on a conception of immigrants as a problem and was therefore a way of containing the potential threat. For proposed alternative systems of multiculturalism, see Modood and Werbner (1997), and Shohat and Stam (1994).

20. Continued attention, therefore, focused on ongoing restrictions, the effects of the *fatwa* on Rushdie's life and censorship.

21. These two significant articles were written by academics (referred to subsequently by their name), 'The law should let sleeping dogmas lie' by Paul Bar, Senior Fellow, Institute of Community Studies' (*The Times*), and

in the *Guardian* 'Time to get rid of the crime of blasphemy' by John Gray, Professor of Politics at Oxford University. This added authority and credibility to the papers' stance.

22. A subtle reference to the reaction of Muslims to *The Satanic Verses*?

23. It should be noted that the further away from 'news' we get, the more editorial controls loosen, allowing populist views to be expressed, apparent in this article.

24. Coverage of discrimination towards Muslims was low because it was perceived in racial terms. Many Muslims were therefore not recognized in this area so their disadvantage was overlooked. Structurally, Muslims cannot complain about discrimination on religious grounds, the lack of evidence for discrimination is then used as an excuse for not implementing legislation (Unsworth 1995).

25. The space the *Guardian* gave to 'Islamophobia' was evidence that this had provided Muslims with a 'political language, images and cultural symbols' with which to make political progress in the face of a discredited anti-racist movement and the limitations of racial classification (Gilroy 1988: 50). However, Gilroy argues that the dangers of this are that it causes a convergence of culturally opposed groups' view of race purely in terms of culture and identity, which creates the cultural clash conception prevalent here, resulting in 'the circularity of power'.

26. It was evident that the requirement by the broadsheets to 'appear' to be objective meant that more explicit ideology was formulated through commentary.

27. However, the actions that were included were negative and represented both the restrictions minorities placed on the majority and the actions to which minorities were subject, 'Ban, Shelves, get rid of, cursed'. See Appendix B for a definition of terms.

28. Stories about Rushdie tend to be placed in a highly international context, raising fears about Islam's global power and possible disloyalty.

29. Including Article 9 of the European Convention of Human Rights on the grounds that Muslims' ability to practise their religion freely in Britain was being curtailed in many areas of social and economic activity; the UN declaration on the elimination of all forms of intolerance and discrimination based on religion or belief (1991); the Universal Declaration on Human Rights, Article 18 and the International Covenant on Civil and Political Rights, Article 18 (UKACIA 1993).

30. Coverage of this issue represented, therefore, another example of press 'shelving' of issues without proper discussion and resolution (Lacey and Longman 1997).

31. Although the threat in the UK was dismissed through Muslims being described as 'tinpot' (25 September 1998), a recurrent practice in the *Guardian*.

32. The lexical use of 'deal' also raises questions about the strength of a conviction that is discarded for economic gain.
33. Thought to be a product of the early part of the twentieth century, though this is debatable (Caplan 1987).
34. This interpretation of fundamentalism is Western and does not take account of the various interpretations in the Islamic world (see Modood 1990). It also rarely applied to other forms of religious fundamentalism, Jewish or Christian.
35. Although Modood (1990) argues that Britain's Asian community was constructed as such during the Rushdie affair. I would agree that by presenting Muslims as extreme, connections to fundamentalism can be implied and the global coherence of coverage may have this effect but generally and explicitly the application of this term is limited to foreigners.
36. The global (overall) meanings (van Dijk 1988b: 26).
37. Corresponding with other coverage of British Muslim women, she wore a simple headscarf, which allowed readers to sympathize rather than feel alienated from her, as a full *hijab* might have done.
38. Although, to some extent, this is due to the reactive nature of news when little other information is available.
39. At this point in the coverage, the *Mail* focused on the nurses' innocence, reporting on the discrepancies in the evidence, evidence that cleared them, and the inadequacies of the Saudi justice system.
40. The term 'regime' is used by the press to describe a totalitarian, undemocratic government and only applied in a negative context. Mullan shows how it has evolved from the 1950s when it was a neutral word meaning a system of government ('When is a terrorist a freedom fighter?' *Guardian*, 29 August 1998).
41. Which is within the law so provided a further contrast between Britain's lawful behaviour and the fundamentalist's unlawfulness.
42. Research showed that public opinion was overwhelmingly opposed to organizations defined in the media as 'terrorist' (Hewitt 1992).
43. This 'translocation' of the news event by reporting British Muslims' reactions to it made assumptions about their connection with it (Golding and Elliot 1979: 156). These connections had not similarly been made between British Muslims and Muslims in Kosova, despite their many fund- and awareness-raising activities in the UK.
44. The speed with which this was introduced and lack of attention to definitions of terrorism contrasted sharply with the stalling on religious discrimination legislation (see *Q News*, 1 September 1998; *Muslim News*, 25 September 1998).
45. Following this event, for example, bin Laden was implicated (in 1999) in providing the financial backing for the Luxor attack. It is important to

remember that these events and the reporting of them took place before 11 September 2001. I am not commenting here on bin Laden's innocence or guilt but a process of selective representation and association by which *all* Muslims become implicated in the global terrorist networks.

46. In contrast with how it was reported in the Muslim paper *Q-News*, as the 'minor charges' of 'exceeding electoral expenses and back-dating voters onto the electoral role' (February 1998 (285, p. 9).

47. Linton (1995) argued that 1995 saw a huge swing to Labour by traditionally Conservative papers while still supporting conservatism. The *Sun* made this explicit, whereas *The Times* tended to remain faithful to its readership. However, Labour was coming under increasing criticism from these papers because of its perceived pro-Euro sympathies.

48. Modality was defined by Fowler (1991: 85) as 'comment' or 'attitude' ascribable to the source of a text, for example; giving permission or expressing desirability.

49. Whereas journalists assume that minority groups are too sensitive to discrimination, research shows that they try to ignore it as much as possible (Essed 1991).

50. It has been argued elsewhere that the concept of sleaze has allowed the media to set boundaries on the activities of public officials (van Dijk 1988b).

51. The focal agent of the headline attributed by its syntactic structure.

52. A change in the Scottish correspondent in *The Times* may have been one of the reasons for this new approach. It should also be noted that only the articles appearing in *The Times* and *Guardian* on 26 March drew any significant attention to these positive strands of discourse (other coverage regarding his acquittal was marginal and understated). This was significant in comparison with the huge quantity of negative coverage that preceded his trial. Although coverage closed on this more positive presentation, the discourse previously disseminated (equally in the wider context of Muslim representation) may already have had its effect.

53. Revealed by 'Tonight with Trevor McDonald', ITV, 27 May 1999, 10.00 p.m.

54. Again, I do not wish to take an individualist approach, implicating individual journalists, but argue that the reproduction of particular discourses occurs as a result of wider institutional practices and interests. These operate on a number of levels and are subject to organizational constraints. This, combined with cultural norms, often means that they are reproduced at a subconscious level — hence the tension that exists in arguing that the negativization of Islam occurs as a result of particular interests while these representations are not always maliciously intended.

55. For example, recent coverage of the Stephen Lawrence case, which introduced the phenomenon of 'institutionalized racism' to the media through

the *Guardian*, has been overwhelmingly supportive. A three-page analysis
(23 February 1999), however, saw the reporting of 'Islamic activist guilty
of attack on constable' adjacent to it, reinforcing stereotypes of violent
'mob' behaviour (of Muslims).

Chapter 4: Interpreting Islam

1. By 'reading', I mean 'the capacity to identify and decode a number of
   signs' and 'to put them into a creative relation between themselves and
   with other signs' (Hall 1980: 135, quoting Terni). Hall argues that this
   capacity is socially constructed rather than, as Terni suggested,
   subjective.
2. It is estimated that around 70 per cent of British Muslims are under the age
   of 25 (Runnymede Trust 1997).
3. Data from 'Leicester, *key facts:* ethnic minorities, 1991 census',
   Environment and Development Department, Leicester City Council,
   1995.
4. All the material gathered from these groups was coded to variables of
   interest along with codes that had emerged out of the process of analysis,
   for example expressions of Islamophobia. These data were inputted and
   analysed using the computer programme NUD.IST 4 (Non-Numerical
   Unstructured Data Indexing Search and Theorising), which allowed for
   more complex cross-reference searching. For example, by searching the
   parent node 'Gender' by 'Reading' it was possible to examine any differences between sexes in their adoption of the preferred meaning (and
   between groups, for text was automatically organized in this way). The
   programme also allows one to examine data quantitatively. The retrieval of
   data coded at specific nodes showed the quantity of text units coded there
   (in this case sentences) and therefore allowed one to identify the frequency
   with which the different groups discussed a subject.
5. Although the discourses of the press and the audiences here appeared to be
   matched I am not suggesting a cause and effect relationship but a correlation between the two.
6. This attitude varied from being very positive to grudgingly accepting the
   situation among some members of the group. However, this diversity was
   absent in attitudes to Islam.
7. Some of these were measured by the questionnaire and others through the
   focus groups' discussions.
8. At the time coverage was fairly consensual, only after the nurses sold their
   story to one paper did coverage diversify.
9. Some Muslims *had* seen coverage of the funding of Muslim schools and
   some of the non-Muslims the Cook story. This was likely to be based on the
   salience of the stories for the groups.

10. Although this probably reflects the general trend that people tend to be interested only in issues that directly affect them, it is also a reflection of how these issues are presented to the public. In fact minority issues do directly affect these groups but they are encouraged to consider them as somewhat distant from their immediate concerns.

11. Yet they too showed a degree of ignorance about other cultures, religions and appropriate terminology, one Muslim referring to '*Christianism*' in society.

12. Shared socioeconomic factors result in the choice of certain newspapers. These newspapers then defend and maintain the myths of particular groups and deride the myths of others, enticing other people into readership by making the news available within a 'cultural idiom' acceptable to them (Bailey 1977). Lacey and Longman (1997) argue that it is not a question of whether papers print what readers want to hear or shape public opinion, but they do both by building on existing prejudices and exacerbating them.

Conclusion

1. Although research continues to find the presence of racism in various British media forms, it is generally thought that this has shifted to a form of 'new racism' due to the illegitimacy of outright extreme opinion, which appears, as this research has found, apparently legitimate when applied to Muslims (Barker 1981).

2. I use the term racial here as ethnic would incorporate religious belief. Often in these cases, however, the press uses ethnic categories such as 'Asian', which connote a number of elements of ethnicity including religious beliefs without referring to them. This works to exoticize and delineate 'the Other'. However, religion is not referred to explicitly unless specific meanings are to be signified.

3. This group was conceived in early 1994, arising from the National Interim Committee on Muslim Affairs. It held its first General Assembly in March 1998. A brief history can be found in *The Newsletter of the Muslim Council of Britain: The Common Good*, 1, issue 1, p. 2.

4. Equally, external events such as recent attempts by Iran to reform and liberalize somewhat under the leadership of moderate Mohammed Khatami have not softened Islam's media image.

5. This is yet another example of negative discourse in the liberal press.

6. Muslim groups argue that the commitment to the protection of Muslims by official bodies has symbolic significance so is worthwhile.

7. However, I hope that my own research findings can contribute to a growing body of evidence that can be used by Muslim groups to lobby the government and media institutions for policy change, ultimately promoting public awareness.

8. I have argued that this is a selective process in that Muslims are chosen to represent the group based on the purpose of the signification but once categorized as Muslim, this dominates any other identity construction that may be possible.

9. This 'lack of conflict' is one reason why British Islam is less interesting to the British news media.

References

Abelman, R. (1991) 'Influence of news coverage of the 'scandal' on PTL viewers', *Journalism Quarterly*, 68 (1/2) 101–10

Abu-Rabi, I. (1997) 'Facing modernity: ideological origins of Islamic revivalism', *Harvard International Review: In the Name of God: Islam in politics and power*, 19 (2) 12–15

Ahmad, A. (1992) *In theory: classes, nations, literatures* (London: Verso)

Ahmed, A. (1992) *Postmodernism and Islam: predicament and promise* (London: Routledge)

— (1993) *Living Islam: from Samarkind to Stornaway* (London: BBC Books)

Ahmed, A. and H. Donnan (1994) 'Islam in the age of postmodernity', in A. Ahmed and H. Donnan (eds) *Islam, globalisation and postmodernity* (London: Routledge) 1–12

Anderson, B. (1983) *Imagined communities* (London: Verso)

Anderson, E. W. and K. H. Rashidian (1991) *Iraq and the continuing Middle East crisis* (London: Pinter)

Anthias, F. and N. Yuval-Davis (1992) *Racialized boundaries: race, nation, gender, colour and class and the anti-racist struggle* (London: Routledge)

Anwar, M. (1993) 'Muslims in Britain: 1991 census and other statistical sources' (*CSIC Papers Europe 9*) Birmingham, University of Birmingham, Centre for the Study of Islam and Christian–Muslim Relations

— (1996) 'Pakistanis in Britain and Birmingham', in J. Akhtar (ed.) *Pakistanis in Britain in the 1990s and beyond* (Birmingham: Pakistan Forum) 8–34

Asad, T. (1990) 'Ethnography, literature and politics: some readings and uses of Salman Rushdie's *The Satanic Verses*', *Cultural Anthropology*, 5 (3) 239–69

Ashcroft, B. (1995) *The post-colonial studies reader* (London: Routledge)

Bailey, F. G. (1977) *Morality and expediency* (Oxford: Blackwell)

Barker, C. (1999) *Television, globalisation and cultural identities* (Buckingham: Open University)

Barker, M. (1981) *The new racism* (London: Junction)

Bell, A. (1991) *The language of news media* (Oxford: Blackwell)

Bhabha, H. (1994) *The location of culture* (London: Routledge)

Bhatnagar, R. (1986) 'Uses and limits of Foucault: a study of the theme of origins in Edward Said's "Orientalism" ', *Social Scientist*, 158, 3–22

Bishara, A. (1995) 'Islam and politics in the Middle East', in J. Hippler and A.

Lueg (eds) *The next threat: Western perceptions of Islam* (London: Pluto Press) 82–115

Bresheeth, H. and N. Yuval-Davis (1991) *The Gulf War and the New World Order* (London: Zed Books)

Brown, M. (2000) 'Religion and economic activity in the South Asian population', *Ethnic and Racial Studies*, 23 (6) 1035–61

Bruck, P. (1989) 'Strategies for peace, strategies for news research', *Journal of Communication*, 39 (1) 108–29

Bulliet, R. W. (1997) 'Day after tomorrow: the future of Islamic movements', *Harvard International Review: In the Name of God: Islam in Politics and Power*, 19 (2) 34–37, 66

Bunyan, T. (1991) 'Toward an authoritarian Europe state', *Race and Class*, 32, 19–27

Caldwell, M. (1977) 'Orientalism in perspective', *Bulletin of the British Association of Orientalists, New Series*, 9, 30–8

Caplan, L. (1987) *Studies in religious fundamentalism* (London: Macmillan)

Chibnall, S. (1977) *Law-and-order news* (London: Tavistock)

— (1981) 'The production of knowledge by crime reporters', in S. Cohen and J. Young (eds) *The manufacture of news: deviance, social problems and the mass media* (London: Constable) 75–97

Cohen, P. (1988) '"It's racism what dunnit": hidden narratives in theories of racism', in J. Donald and A. Rattansi (eds) *Race, culture and difference* (London: Sage) 62–103

Cohen, R. (1997) *Global diasporas: an introduction* (London: UCL Press Limited)

Corner, J. (1991) 'Meaning, genre and context: the problematics of "public knowledge" in the new audience studies', in J. Curran and M. Gurevitch (eds) *Mass media and society* (London: Edward Arnold) 267–84

Corner, J. and K. Richardson (1986) 'Documentary meanings and the discourse of interpretation', in J. Corner (ed.) *Documentary and the mass media* (London: Edward Arnold) 141–60

Corner, M. (1986) 'How journalists should handle race stories: and why they often fail', *New Equals*, 25 (4) London: CRE

Cottle, S. (1991) 'Reporting the Rushdie affair: a case study in the orchestration of public opinion', *Race and Class*, 32 (4) 45–64

— (1992) '"Race", racialisation and the media: a review and update of research', *Sage Race Relations Abstracts*, 17 (2) 3–57

— (1993) '"Race" and regional television news: multiculturalism and the production of popular TV', *New Community*, 19 (4) 581–92

Cruz, J. and J. Lewis (1994) 'Reflections upon the encoding/decoding model: an interview with Stuart Hall', in J. Cruz and J. Lewis (eds) *Viewing, reading, listening: audiences and cultural reception* (Oxford: Westview Press) 253–74

Curran, J. and J. Seaton (1992) *Power without responsibility* (London: Routledge)

Dahlgren, P. (1988a) 'What's the meaning of this? Viewers' plural sense-making of TV news', *Media, Culture and Society*, 10 (3) 285–301

—— (1988b) 'Critique: elusive audiences', in R. Dickinson, R. Harindranath and O. Linné (eds) *Approaches to audience: a reader* (London: Arnold) 298–311

Dahlgren, P. and S. Chakrapani (1982) 'The Third World on TV news: Western ways of seeing the "Other"', in W. C. Adams (ed.) *TV coverage of international affairs* (New Jersey: Ablex Publishing) 45–63

Daniel, N. (1993) *Islam and the West: the making of an image* (Oxford: One World)

Dennis, D. (2001) 'The World Trade Center and the rise of the security state', *Ctheory: Theory, Technology and Culture*, 24 (3)

Djerejian, E. P. (1997) 'The arc of crisis: the challenge to US foreign policy', *Harvard International Review: In the Name of God: Islam in Politics and Power*, 19 (2) 32–3, 65–6

Downs, A. (1972) 'Up and down with ecology: the "issue attention cycle"', *Public Interest*, 28, 38–50

Eco, U. (1972) *Towards a semiotic inquiry into the television message*, CCCS Working Papers in Cultural Studies, 3, Birmingham: University of Birmingham

Eldridge, J. (1991) 'Whose illusion? Whose reality? Some problems of theory and method in mass media research', in K. B. Jensen and N. W. Jankowski (eds) *A handbook of qualitative methodologies for mass communication research* (London: Routledge) 331–50

Entman, R. E. (1990) 'Modern racism and the image of blacks in local television news', *Critical Studies in Mass Communication*, 7 (4) 332–45

—— (1992) 'Blacks in the news', *Journalism Quarterly*, 69 (2) 341–61

Epstein, E. (1973) *News from nowhere: television and the news* (New York: Random House)

Esposito, J. L. (1992) *The Islamic threat: myth or reality?* (Oxford: Oxford University Press)

Essed, P. J. M. (1991) *Understanding everyday racism* (Newbury Park, CA: Sage)

Fairclough, N. (1995) *Critical discourse analysis: the critical study of language* (Harlow: Longman Group Ltd)

Fan, D. P. (1998) *Predictions of public opinion from the mass media: computer content analysis and mathematical modelling* (London: Greenwood Press)

Fiske, J. (1986) 'Television: polysemy and popularity', *Critical Studies in Mass Communications*, 3 (4) 391–408 (Annandale, VA: Speech Communication Association)

—— (1994) 'Audiencing: cultural practice and cultural studies', in N. K. Denzin and Y. S. Yvonna (eds) *A handbook of qualitative research* (Thousand Oaks, CA: Sage) 189–98

FitzGerald, M. and C. Hale (1996) *Ethnic minorities, victimization and racial harassment* (London: Home Office Research and Statistics Directorate)

Foucault, M. (1980) *Power/knowledge* (Brighton: Harvester)

— (1982) 'The subject and power', in M. Dreyfus and P. Rabinow (eds) *Michael Foucault: beyond structuralism and hermeneutics* (Brighton: Harvester) 208–26

Fowler, R. (1991) *Language in the news: discourse and ideology in the press* (London: Routledge)

Galtung, J. and B. Ruge (1965) 'The structure of foreign news', *Journal of Peace Research*, 2, 64–91

Gans, H. (1979) *Deciding what's news: a study of CBS evening news, NBC nightly news, Newsweek and Time* (New York: Random House)

Gardner, K. and A. Shukur (1994) '"I'm Bengali, I'm Asian and I'm living here": the changing identity of British Bengalis', in R. Ballard (ed.) *Desh Pardesh: the South Asian presence in Britain* (London: Hurst) 142–64

Gellner, E. (1983) *Nations and nationalism* (Oxford: Blackwell)

Giddens, A. (1990) *The consequences of modernity* (Cambridge: Cambridge Polity Press)

— (1991) *Modernity and self-identity: self and society in the late modern age* (Oxford: Polity Press)

Gill, R. (1996) 'Discourse analysis: practical implementation', in J. T. E Richardson (ed.) *Handbook of qualitative research methods for psychology and the social sciences* (Leicester : British Psychological Society) 141–56

Gilman, S. (1985) 'Introduction: what are the stereotypes and why use texts to study them?', in S. Gilman (ed.) *Difference and pathology: stereotypes of sexuality, race and madness* (London: Cornell University Press) 15–35

Gilroy, P. (1988) 'The end of antiracism', in J. Donald and A. Rattansi (eds) *'Race', culture and difference* (London: Sage) 49–61

— (1997) 'Diaspora and the detours of identity', in K. Woodward (ed.) *Identity and difference* (London: Sage) 301–46

Gilsenan, M. (1990) *Recognizing Islam* (London: I.B.Tauris)

Giroux, H. (1994) 'Living dangerously: identity politics and the new cultural racism', in H. Giroux and P. McLaren (eds) *Between borders: pedagogy and the politics of cultural studies* (New York: Routledge) 29–55

Glasgow University Media Group (1976) *Bad news* (London: Routledge & Kegan Paul)

Goldberg, D. T. (1993) *Racist culture: philosophy and the politics of meaning* (Cambridge, MA: Blackwell)

Golding, P. and P. Elliot (1979) *Making the news* (London: Longman)

Gordon, P. and F. Klug (1986) *New right, new racism* (London: Searchlight Publications)

Green, S. J. D. (1990) 'Beyond *The Satanic Verses*: conservative religion and the liberal society', *Encounter*, 74 (5) 12–20

Gunter, B and R. Viney (1993) *Seeing is believing: religion and television in the 1990s*, ITC Independent Research Monograph (London: John Libbey)

Hafez, K. (2000) *Islam and the West in the mass media: fragmented images in a globalizing world* (Cresskill, NJ: Hampton Press)

Hall, S. (1977) 'Pluralism, race and class in Caribbean society', in S. Hall (ed.) *Race and class in post-colonial society* (Paris: UNESCO) 150–82

— (1980) 'Encoding and decoding', in S. Hall, D. Hobson, A. Lowe and P. Willis (eds) *Culture, media and language* (London: Unwin Hyman) 128–38

— (1986) 'The problem of ideology: Marxism without guarantees', *Journal of Communication Inquiry*, 10 (2) 28–43

— (1988) 'New ethnicities', in J. Donald and A. Rattansi (eds) *'Race', culture and difference* (London: Sage) 252–9

— (1992a) 'The West and the rest: discourse and power', in S. Hall and B. Gieben (eds) *Formations of modernity* (Cambridge: Polity Press and Buckingham: Open University Press) 275–332

— (1992b) 'The question of cultural identity', in S. Hall, D. Held and A. McGrew (eds) *Modernity and its futures* (London: Polity Press and Buckingham: Open University Press) 274–325

— (1997a) 'Representation, meaning and language', in S. Hall (ed.) *Representation, cultural representations and signifying practices* (London: Open University and Sage) 15–74

— (1997b) 'The spectacle of the "Other"', in S. Hall (ed) *Representation, cultural representations and signifying practices* (London: Open University and Sage) 225–90

Hall, S., C. Critcher, T. Jefferson, J. Clarke and B. Roberts (1978) *Policing the crisis: mugging, the state, and law and order* (London: Macmillan)

Halliday, F. (1992) *Arabs in exile: Yemeni migrants in urban Britain* (London: I.B.Tauris)

— (1995) '"Islam is in danger": authority, Rushdie and the struggle for the migrant soul', in J. Hippler and A. Lueg (eds) *The next threat: Western perceptions of Islam* (London: Pluto Press) 71–81

— (1996) *Islam and the myth of confrontation: religion and politics in the Middle East* (London: I.B.Tauris)

Halloran, J. D. and V. Nightingale (1982) *Young TV viewers and their images of foreigners: a summary and interpretation of a four nation study* (Leicester: University of Leicester Centre for Mass Communication Research)

Halloran, J., A. Bhatt, and P. Gray, (1995) *Ethnic minorities and television: a study of use, reactions and preferences* (Leicester: University of Leicester Centre for Mass Communication Research)

Halstead, M. (1988) *Education, justice and cultural diversity: an examination of the Honeyford affair, 1984–85* (London: Falmer Press)

Hamilton, P. (1997) 'Representing the social: France and Frenchness in post-war humanist photography', in S. Hall (ed.) *Representation, cultural repre-*

sentations and signifying practices (London: Open University and Sage) 75–150

Hansen, A. and G. Murdock (1985) 'Constructing the crowd: populist discourse and press presentation', in V. Mosco and J. Wasko (eds) *The Critical Communication Review*, 3 (New Jersey: Ablex) 227–56

Harding, S. (1986) *The science question in feminism* (Ithaca: Cornell University Press)

Hartmann, P., C. Husband and J. Clark (1974) *Race as news: a study in the handling of race in the British press from 1963 to 1970* (Paris: UNESCO)

Hassan, A. (1997) *Invitation to Islam: Islamic stereotypes in Western mass media*, Internet http://psirus.sfsu.edu/IntRel/IRJournal/sp95/ hassan.html

Herbert, D. (1993) 'God and free speech: a Quaker perspective on *The Satanic Verses* controversy', *Islam and Christian–Muslim Relations*, 4 (2) 257–67

Hewitt, C. (1992) 'Public's perspectives', in D. L. Paletz and A. P. Schmid (eds) *Terrorism and the media: how researchers, terrorists, government, press, public, victims view and use the media* (London: Sage) 170–207

Hilgartner, S. and C. I. Bosk (1988) 'The rise and fall of social problems: a public arenas model', *American Journal of Sociology*, 94 (1) 53–78

Hindmarsh, J. (1996) 'Genre and narrative analysis, module 5: unit 29', MA in Mass Communications, Distance Learning (Leicester: University of Leicester Centre for Mass Communication Research)

Hippler, J. (1995) 'The Islamic threat and Western foreign policy', in J. Hippler and A. Lueg (eds) *The next threat: Western perceptions of Islam* (London: Pluto Press) 116–53

Höijer, B. (1998) 'Social psychological perspectives in reception analysis', in R. Dickinson, R. Harindranath and O. Linné (eds) *Approaches to audience: a reader* (London: Arnold) 166–83

Holt, M. (1996) 'A tangle of meanings: women and the contemporary Islamist Movement' (paper presented to the Middle East Society, University of Cambridge) May

Huntington, S. (1996) *The clash of civilizations and the remaking of the world order* (New York: Simon & Schuster)

Husband, C. (1994) 'The multi-ethnic public sphere: a necessary project. Turbulent Europe: conflict, identity and culture' (paper presented at the European Film and Television Studies Conference, London, July)

— (1996) 'The right to be understood: conceiving the multi-ethnic public sphere', *Innovation*, 9 (2) 205–15

Irwin, R. (1981) 'Writing about Islam and the Arabs', *Ideology and Consciousness*, 9, 102–12

Jacobson, J. (1997) 'Religion and ethnicity: dual and alternative sources of identity among young British Pakistanis', *Ethnic and Racial Studies*, 20 (2) 238–56

Jalal al-'Azm, S. (1981) 'Orientalism and Orientalism in reverse', *Khamsin*, 8, 5–27

Joshua, H., T. Wallace and H. Booth (1983) *To ride the storm: the 1980 Bristol "riots" and the state* (London: Heinemann)

Jupp, V. (1996) 'Documents and critical analysis', in R. Sapsford and V. Jupp (eds) *Data collection and analysis* (London: Sage) 298–316

Kappert, P. (1995) 'From Romanticism to colonial dominance: historical changes in the European perception of the Middle East', in J. Hippler and A. Lueg (eds) *The next threat: Western perceptions of Islam* (London: Pluto Press) 32–57

Karim, K. H. (2000) *Islamic peril: media and global violence* (Montreal: Black Rose Books)

Katz, E. (1992) 'The end of journalism? Notes on watching the war', *Journal of Communication*, 42 (3) 5–13

Katz, P. A. and D. A. Taylor (1988) *Eliminating racism* (New York: Plenum Press)

Kellner, D. (1992) *The Persian Gulf TV war* (Boulder, CO: Westview Press)

Kerr, M. (1980) 'Review of "Orientalism"', *International Journal of Middle East Studies*, 12, 544–7

Knott, K. and P. Noon (1982) 'Muslims, Sikhs and Hindus in the UK: problems in the estimations of religious statistics', *Religious Research Paper 7* (Department of Sociology, University of Leeds)

Kramer, M. (1997) 'Ballots and bullets: Islamists and the relentless drive for power', *Harvard International Review: In the Name of God: Islam in Politics and Power*, 19 (2) 16–19, 61–2

Kristeva, J. (1982) *Powers of horror* (New York: Columbia University Press)

Kroker, A. and M. Kroker (2001) 'Terrorism of viral power', *Ctheory: Theory, Technology and Culture*, 24 (3)

Kushnick, L. (1970) '"Black power" and the media', *Race Today*, 2, 439–42

Lacey, C. and D. Longman (1997) *The press as public educator: cultures of understanding, cultures of ignorance* (Luton: University of Luton John Libbey Media)

Levine, R. L. and D. T. Campbell (1972) *Ethnocentrism: theories of conflict, ethnic attitudes and group behaviour* (New York: John Wiley)

Levinson, S. (1983) *Pragmatics* (Cambridge: Cambridge University Press)

Lewis, B. (1982) 'The question of "Orientalism"', *New York Review of Books*, 29, 51

Lewis, P. (1994) *Islamic Britain: religion, politics and identity among British Muslims* (London: I.B.Tauris)

Linden, I. (1995) 'Christianity and European pluralism' (paper presented at the Birmingham Seminar on Islam and the West: Perceptions and Realities of Plural Societies, Centre for the study of Islam and Christian Relations) September

Linton, M. (1995) 'Was it the *Sun* wot won it?' (paper presented at the seventh *Guardian* lecture, Nuffield College)

Livingstone, S. (1990) *Making sense of television: the psychology of audience interpretation* (Oxford: Pergamon)

Lueg, A. (1995) 'The perceptions of Islam in Western debate', in J. Hippler and A. Lueg (eds) *The next threat: Western perceptions of Islam* (London: Pluto Press) 7–32

Lunt, P. (1996) 'Rethinking the focus group in media and communication research', *Journal of Communication*, 46 (2) 79–98

McManus, J. (1994) *Market-driven journalism* (London: Sage)

Mani, L. and R. Frankenberg (1985) 'The challenge of "Orientalism"', *Economy and Society*, 14 (2) 174–92

Männistö, A. (1997) 'Islam in Finnish newspaper photos: making myths visible', in A. Linjakumpu and K. Virtanen (eds) *Under the olive tree: reconsidering Mediterranean politics and culture*, Research Institute Occasional Papers 73 (University of Tampere: Tampere Peace) 148–62

Mercer, K. (1988) 'Recording narratives of race and nation', in K. Mercer (ed.) *Black film, British cinema*, ICA Documents 7 (London: British Film Institute) 4–14

— (1994) *Welcome to the jungle: new positions in black cultural studies* (London: Routledge)

Mercer, K. and I. Julien (1994) 'Black masculinity and the politics of race', in K. Mercer (ed.) *Welcome to the jungle: new positions in black cultural studies* (London: Routledge) 131–70

Merton, R. K. (1957) *Social theory and social structure* (Glencoe, IL: Free Press)

Miller, D. (1994) *Don't mention the war: Northern Ireland, propaganda and the media* (London: Pluto Press)

Mir, S. (1998) *Muslims: within Hollywood and without*, Internet: http://php. indiana edu/~smir/holly.htm, 27 July

Modood, T. (1990) 'British Asian Muslims and the Rushdie affair', *Political Quarterly*, 61 (2) 143–60

— (1993a) 'Establishment, multiculturalism and British citizenship', *Political Quarterly*, 64 (4) 57

— (1993b) 'Muslims, incitement to hatred and the law', in UK Action Committee on Islamic Affairs (UKACIA), *Muslims and the law in multifaith Britain: need for reform*, memorandum submitted by the CRE to The Rt. Hon Michael Howard, MP, Home Secretary for the consideration of the Second Review of the Race Relations Act 1976, 69–81

— (ed.) (1997) *Church, state and religious minorities* (London: Policy Studies Institute)

Modood, T. and P. Werbner (1997) *The politics of multiculturalism in the new Europe: racism, identity and community* (London: Zed Books)

Modood, T., S. Beishon and S. Virdee (1994) *Changing ethnic identities* (London: Policy Studies Institute)

Modood, T., R. Berthoud, J. Lakey, J. Nazroo, P. Smith, S. Virdee and S.

Beishon (1997) *Ethnic minorities in Britain: diversity and disadvantage* (London: Policy Studies Institute)

Morley, D. (1980) *The nationwide audience: structure and decoding*, British Film Institute Television 11 (London: British Film Institute)

— (1981) 'The nationwide audience: a critical postscript', *Screen Education*, 39, 3–14

Morris, C. (1989) 'Disinformation', *The Voice of the Arab World*, 2 (4) (London: Morris International Associates Ltd)

Mowlana, H. (1993) 'The new order and cultural ecology', *Media, Culture and Society*, 15 (1) 9–27

Murdock, G. (1982) 'Large corporations and the control of the communications industries', in M. Gurevitch, T. Bennett, J. Curran and J. Woollacott (eds) *Culture, society and the media* (London: Methuen) 118–50

— (1984) 'Reporting the riots: images and impacts', in J. Benyon (ed.) *Scarman and after* (Oxford: Pergamon) 73–95

— (1990) 'Redrawing the map of the communications industries: concentration and ownership in the era of privatisation', in M. Ferguson (ed.) *Public communication: the new imperatives. Future directions for media research* (London: Sage) 1–15

— (1998) 'Mass communication and the construction of meaning', in R. Dickinson, R. Harindranath and O. Linné (eds) *Approaches to audience: a reader* (London: Arnold) 205–17

Nazlee, S. (1996) *Feminism and Muslim women* (London: Ta-Ha Publishers)

Nielsen, J. (1991a) 'A Muslim agenda for Britain: some reflections', *New Community*, 17 (3) 467–76

— (1991b) *Muslims in Western Europe* (Edinburgh: Edinburgh University Press)

— (1992) *Islam, Muslims and British local and central government*, CSIC Research Papers 6 (Birmingham, Centre for the Study of Islam and Christian–Muslim Relations)

Nonneman, G. (1996) 'Muslim communities in the new Europe: themes and puzzles', in G. Nonneman, T. Niblock and B. Szajkowski (eds) *Muslim communities in the new Europe* (Reading: Ithaca Press) 3–24

One World Broadcasting Trust (1993) *Islam and the media: how broadcasting in Britain approaches the issues of the Muslim world* (a report of the 1993 conference and programme awards presentation, British Academy of Film and TV Arts, London, Monday 22 November)

Parekh, B. (1997) 'Religion and public life', in T. Modood (ed.) *Church, state and religious minorities* (London: Policy Studies Institute) 16–22

Paterson, C. (1997) 'Global television news services', in A. Sreberny-Mohammadi, D. Winseck, J. McKenna and O. Boyd-Barrett (eds) *Media in a global context* (London: Edward Arnold) 145–60

Peach, C. (1990) 'The Muslim population of Great Britain', *Ethnic and Racial Studies*, 13 (3) 414–19

Peak, S. and P. Fisher (1997) *The media guide* (London: A Guardian Book, Fourth Estate)

Potter, J. (1997) 'Discourse analysis as a way of analysing naturally occurring talk', in D. Silverman (ed.) *Qualitative research: theory, method and practice* (London: Sage) 98–114

Richardson, J. E. (2001) 'British Muslims in the broadsheet press: a challenge to cultural hegemony?' *Journalism Studies*, 2 (2)

Roberts, C. L. (1983) 'Attitudes and media use of the moral majority', *Journal of Broadcasting*, 27, 403–10

Robertson, R. (1992) *Globalisation* (London: Sage)

Robins, K. (1991) 'Tradition and translation: national culture in its global context', in J. Corner and S. Harvey (eds) *Enterprise and heritage: crosscurrents of national culture* (London: Granta Books) 21–44

Rodinson, M. (1979) *Marxism and the Muslim world* (London: Zed Press)

Romer, D., K. Jamieson and N. de Coteau (1998) 'The treatment of persons of color in local television news: ethnic blame discourse or realistic group conflict?' *Communication Research*, 25 (3) 286–305

Runnymede Trust (1996) 'Arms, aid and asylum', *The Runnymede Bulletin*, 291 (January) 2

— Commission on British Muslims and Islamophobia (1997) *Islamophobia: a challenge for us all* (London: Runnymede Trust)

Said, E. (1978) *Orientalism* (New York: Vintage)

— (1981) *Covering Islam: how the media and the experts determine how we see the rest of the world* (New York: Pantheon)

Sapsford, R. and P. Abbott (1996) 'Ethics, politics and research', in R. Sapsford and V. Jupp (eds) *Data collection and analysis* (London: Sage) 317–42

Sapsford, R. and V. Jupp (1996) *Data collection and analysis* (London: Sage)

Sardar, Z. (1999) *Orientalism* (Buckingham: Open University Press)

Sayyid, B. S. (1997) *A fundamental fear: Eurocentrism and the emergence of Islam* (London: Zed Books)

Schlesinger, P., G. Murdock and P. Elliot (1983) *Televising 'terrorism': political violence in popular culture* (London: Comedia)

Schulze, R. (1995) 'How medieval is Islam? Muslim intellectuals and modernity', in J. Hippler and A. Lueg (eds) *The next threat: Western perceptions of Islam* (London: Pluto Press) 57–70

Sennett, R. (1971) *The ideas of disorder* (Harmondsworth: Penguin)

Shayon, R. L. and N. Cox (1994) *Religion, television and the information superhighway* (Philadelphia: Waymark Press)

Shohat, E. and R. Stam (1994) *Unthinking Eurocentrism* (London: Routledge)

Silverman, M. and N. Yuval-Davis (1998) 'Jews, Arabs and the theorization of racism in Britain and France', in A. Brah, M. Hickman and M. Mac an Ghail (eds) *Thinking identities: ethnicity, racism and culture* (London: Macmillan)

Smith, K. H. (1977) 'Small group interaction at various ages: simultaneous talking and interruption of others', *Small Group Behaviour*, 8, 65–74

Solomos, J. (1988) *Black youth, racism and the state* (Cambridge: Cambridge University Press)

Sreberny-Mohammadi, A. and K. Ross (1995) *Black minority viewers and television: neglected audiences speak up and out* (Leicester: University of Leicester Centre for Mass Communication Research)

Stamm, K. R and R. Weis (1986) 'The newspaper and community integration: a study of ties to a local church community', *Communication Research*, 13, 125–37

Thompson, J. (1995) *The media and modernity* (Cambridge: Polity Press)

Trew, T. (1979) 'What the papers say: linguistic variation and ideological difference', in R. Fowler, R. Hodge, G. Kress and T. Trew (eds) *Language and control* (London: Routledge & Kegan Paul) 117–56

Troyna, B. (1981) *Public awareness and the media: a study of reporting on race* (London: CRE)

Tuchman, G. (1978) *Making news: a study in the social construction of reality* (New York: Free Press)

Tunstall, J. (1971) *Journalists at work. Specialist correspondents: their news organisations, news sources and competitor colleagues* (London: Constable)

Turner, B. S. (1989) 'From Orientalism to global sociology', *Sociology*, 23 (4) 629–38

Turner, J. C. (1985) 'Social categorization and the self-concept: a social-cognitive theory of group behaviour', in E. J. Lawler (ed.) *Advances in group processes* (Greenwich, CT: JAI Press) 77–122

UKACIA (1993) *Muslims and the law in multifaith Britain: need for reform*, memorandum submitted by the Commission for Racial Equality to The Rt Hon Michael Howard, MP, Home Secretary for the consideration of the Second Review of the Race Relations Act 1976.

Unsworth, C. (1995) 'Blasphemy, cultural divergence and legal relativism', *The Modern Law Review*, 58 (5) 658–77

van Dijk, T. (1983) 'Discourse analysis: its development and application to the structure of news', *Journal of Communication*, 33 (2) 20–43

— (1987) *Communicating racism: ethnic prejudice in thought and talk* (Newbury Park, CA: Sage)

— (1988a) 'How "they" hit the headlines: ethnic minorities in the press', in G. Smitherman-Donaldson and T. A. van Dijk (eds) *From discourse and discrimination* (Detroit: Wayne State University Press) pp. 221–62

— (1988b) *News as discourse* (New Jersey: Lawrence Erlbaum Associates)

— (1991) *Racism and the press* (London: Routledge)

Vertovec, S. (1996) 'Muslims, the state, and the public sphere in Britain', in G. Nonneman, T. Niblock and B. Szajkowski (eds) *Muslim communities in the new Europe* (Reading: Ithaca Press) 169–87

Werbner, P. (1991) 'The fiction of unity in ethnic politics: aspects of representation and the state among British Pakistanis', in P. Werbner and M. Anwar
(eds) *Black and ethnic leaderships in Britain: the cultural dimensions of
political action* (London: Routledge) 113–45

— (1994) 'Diaspora and the millennium: British Pakistani global–local
fabulations of the Gulf War', in A. Ahmed and H. Donnan (eds) *Islam,
globalisation and postmodernity* (London: Routledge) 213–36

Westwood, S. (1991) 'Red Star over Leicester: racism, the politics of identity,
and black youth in Britain', in P. Werbner and M. Anwar (eds) *Black and
ethnic leaderships in Britain: the cultural dimensions of political action*
(London: Routledge) 146–69

Wetherell, M. and J. Potter (1992) *Mapping the language of racism* (New York:
Columbia University)

Wiegand, K. E. (1999) 'Islam as an ethnicity? The media's impact on
misperceptions in the West', in K. Hafez (ed.) *Islam and the West in the mass
media: fragmented images in a globalizing world* (Creskill, NJ: Hampton
Press) 235–52

Winter, T. (1999) 'Islam and Britain: converging and diverging religious and
cultural stands', in *Mutualities: Britain and Islam: conference report*
(London: British Council) 7–9

Woodward, K. (1997) *Identity and difference: culture, media and identities*
(London: Sage Publications in association with the Open University)

Worrall, A. (1990) *Offending women: female lawbreakers and the criminal
justice system* (London: Routledge)

Wren-Lewis, J. (1983) 'The encoding/decoding model: criticisms and redevel-
opments for researching on decoding', *Media, Culture and Society*, 5, 179–97

Yuval-Davis, N. and M. Silverman (1998) *Racialised discourses on Jews and
Arabs in Britain and France* (research report presented at the University of
Greenwich) January

Zaller, J. R. (1992) *The nature and origins of mass opinion* (Cambridge: Cambridge University Press)

Index